How to Build
a Theory in
Cognitive Science

SUNY series in Philosophy and Biology
David Edward Shaner, Editor

HOW TO BUILD
A THEORY IN
COGNITIVE SCIENCE

Valerie Gray Hardcastle

STATE UNIVERSITY OF NEW YORK PRESS

Chapter 5 is based on "Reduction, Explanatory Extension, and the Mind/Brain Sciences," *Philosophy of Science* 59 (1992): 408–428, by permission of *Philosophy of Science*.

Figure 3.1 is reprinted from T. J. Sejnowski and P. S. Churchland (1988) "Brain and Cognition." In M. I. Posner (ed.) *Foundations of Cognitive Science*. Cambridge, MA: MIT Press, pp. 301–356, with permission of the publisher..

Figures 3.4 and 3.5 are reprinted from W. Heilingenberg and G. Rose (1985) "Neural Correlates of the Jamming Avoidance Response (JAR) in the Weakly Electric Fish *Eigenmannia*," *Trends in Neuroscience* 8(10): 442–449, with permission of *TINS* and the authors.

Published by
State University of New York Press, Albany

©1996 State University of New York

For information, address the State University of New York Press,
State University Plaza, Albany, NY 12246

Production by Kay Bolton
Marketing by Nancy Farrell

Library of Congress Cataloging-in-Publication Data

Hardcastle, Valerie Gray.
       How to build a theory in cognitive science / Valerie Gray
   Hardcastle.
           p.   cm. — (SUNY series in philosophy and biology)
       Includes bibliographical references and index.
       ISBN 0–7914–2885–0 (alk. paper). — ISBN 0–7914–2886–9 (pbk. :
   alk. paper)
       1. Philosophy of mind. 2. Philosophy and cognitive science.
   3. Functionalism (Psychology) 4. Reductionism. 5. Cognitive
   science—Philosophy.   I. Title.   II. . Series.
     BD418.3.H37 1996
       128'.2—dc20   95-46981
                                                                         CIP

10 9 8 7 6 5 4 3 2 1

For Gary

CONTENTS

Acknowledgments   ix

Chapter 1   Cognitive Science Is Not Cognitive Psychology   1

Chapter 2   The Dilemma of Mental Causality   13

Mental States as Higher Level Properties / 15
Privileged Regularities and Ceteris Paribus Clauses / 18
Screening off Causes / 24
Ignoring the Realism/Antirealism Debate / 29

Chapter 3   Hierarchies in the Brain   33

The Neuron / 34
The Methodological
   Individualism/Anti-Individualism Debate / 36
Hierarchies in Neuroscience / 41
"Privileged" Causality in Neuroscience / 54
Explanation in Cognitive Science / 60

Chapter 4   Computationalism and Functional Analysis:
            A Pragmatic Approach   63

Formal Accounts of Computationalism / 64
Computational Satisfaction and True Computation / 69
Functionalism and Functional Analysis / 71
Philosophical Functionalism / 73
An Example / 75
The Function/Structure Distinction / 79

Chapter 5   Reductionism in the Cognitive Sciences   85

Reductionism in Philosophy of Mind / 86
Arguments against Reductionism / 88
Cognitive Theories of Emotion: A Test Case / 91
Explanatory Extension / 95

Chapter 6   The Dual Memory Hypothesis and the Structure of
            Interdisciplinary Theories   105

            Developmental Studies for a Dual Processing System / 106
            The Distinction between Implicit and Explicit Memory / 111
            Neural Evidence for the Dual Memory Hypothesis / 121
            The Theoretical Framework / 131
            "Two-Part" Interdisciplinary Theories / 132
            Putting It All Together / 138

Chapter 7   Interdisciplinary Theories and Bridge Sciences:
            The Case of Event Related Potentials   141

            The Challenge / 143
            ERPs / 146
            The Timing of Priming / 150
            Bridge Sciences / 169

Appendix: Cognitive Science and the Semantic View   175

Notes   181

References   205

Index   241

ACKNOWLEDGMENTS

I owe many thanks to many people without whom this book would not have appeared. First and foremost, I am tremendously indebted to my husband Gary, to whom this book is dedicated. He gave me the emotional and intellectual space to do this project, even though his personal cost for doing so was great. I hope this book measures up to the sacrifice.

Bits and pieces of this book in various versions were read by John Bickle, Jerry Doppelt, Michael Dietriech, Marjorie Grene, Gary Hardcastle, Todd Jones, Patricia Kitcher, Philip Kitcher, Jim Klagge, Dan Lloyd, Sandy Mitchell, Lenny Moss, Helen Neville, Peter Pruim, Adina Roskies, and Oron Shagrir. I appreciate all of their comments and worries. The remaining errors are mine.

The empirical research reported in chapter 7 was carried out courtesy of Dr. Helen Neville and her wonderful lab at the Salk Institute. Without her help and the patient instruction of Sharon Corina, Margaret Mitchell, and Chris Weber-Fox, I would not have been able to do such an interesting project. Besides, the Neuropsychology Lab is a terrific place to raise children, as mine were.

A shorter version of chapter 3 was read at the 1993 conference for the International Society of the History, Philosophy, and Social Studies of Biology, and an earlier and much shorter version of chapter 4 was read at the 16th Annual Wittgenstein Symposium in Kirchberg, Austria; a variation on this theme was also presented at the 1994 Philosophy of Science Association Conference in New Orleans. The empirical results were presented at the 1993 meeting of the Southern Society for Philosopohy and Psychology in New Orleans. My thanks to the participants for their suggestions and discussion.

Research for this book was supported in part by a fellowship from the American Association for University Women, two summer stipends from the McDonnell-Pew Foundation for Cognitive Neuroscience, a research assistantship from the Philosophy Department at the University of California, San Diego, a research grant from the College of Arts and Sciences here at Virginia Tech, and a research grant from Virginia Polytechnic Institute and State University.

Finally, I thank Kay Bolton and the editorial staff at the State University of New York Press for their help and patience; David Shaner, the editor of the Philosophy and Biology Series, for his encouragement; and Karen Snyder, our departmental secretary (and much more), for always knowing how to get me out of my difficulties.

Chapter 1

Cognitive Science
Is Not Cognitive Psychology

> Information-processing theories of the cognitive
> mind/brain can explain certain features of cognition
> that cannot be explained by means of lower level neu-
> roscientific accounts.[1]

> Suppose that a neuroscientist has . . . arrived at your
> campus for a lecture. You eagerly ask him, "Tell me,
> Professor X, when your subject Joe images a small pine
> tree at an angle in the center of his imagistic 'field',
> what is going on at the neural level that explains the
> intentionality of Joe's imaging?" Professor X consults
> his table of psychoneural correlations and replies, in
> deep, serious tones: "I'm so glad you asked that. The
> explanation is simple. When Joe exercises his imaging
> capacity in that way his brain is moving form neural
> state N624 to neural state N1009." "Thank you, sir:
> that's very enlightening," you reply, as your mind
> draws a complete blank.[2]

This project opens with a series of biases and reactions. The most immediate and obvious is that the brain is quite important in understanding
cognition. Indeed, I would daresay that the brain sciences are an *essential* component in a mature cognitive science. For those not well
acquainted with the recent history of debates among some philosophers
and psychologists over the nature of cognition, this may seem a pretty
uninteresting and weak claim. How else do we think but with brains?
On the other hand, for those intimately acquainted with recent dia-
logues, dialectics, and diatribes, my "bias" might appear almost hereti-
cal: one should not confuse the hardware with the software, as it were.

And certainly one should not embrace one for the other with full knowledge of forethought.

My second bias, which will turn out to be tied to my first, is that theories in cognitive science are strongly interdisciplinary. Cognitive science is not just cognitive psychology with a few additional bells and whistles. The corollary to this claim is that one should not conflate pedagogical issues in teaching cognitive science to neophytes (e.g., how best to present the material in an orderly manner) with the actual products of research by our scientific communities, who pay little mind to whether their discoveries and conclusion are palatable to those on the outside. I doubt that anyone would claim to find this bias even remotely controversial. Nevertheless, those who deny my first bias are quite often guilty (at least in their actions) of also denying the second. Allow me to explain.

Early writings in the philosophy of mind and the cognitive sciences stress two fundamental notions. First is that species of thought are species of information processing construed as formal symbol manipulations. Allen Newell and Herbert Simon are credited with the insight that the mind can be formally construed as a symbol-manipulating system.[3] They argue that we can describe human behavior by "a well-specified program, defined in terms of elementary information processing." (See table 1.1 for a general description of this sort of information-processing system.) As an instance of a Turing Machine, this general system has only a few primitive capacities but is an extraordinarily powerful machine. It can store (and recall) symbols and create new symbols to stand for those symbol structures. It can compare tokens of symbols and then classify them as the same or different. However, the most important capacity of this machine, and the capacity that gives it its true power, is its ability to act contingently—it can execute different information processes, depending on which symbol structure it encounters. In this way, the machine can respond to context. Using structures built out of symbols, it can designate environmental events and its own processes, on which it then bases its responses. This information-processing system became the dominant model for the human mind in psychology and elsewhere after Neisser's classic (1967) work, *Cognitive Psychology*, which incorporated many of these ideas.

The second defining idea is that formally described systems are multiply instantiable. As far as I know, Putnam (1960) first remarked on this fact in the context of studying the mind. He argued that the formal definitions of processes in the cognitive sciences describe events that we

Table 1.1 Postulates for a General Information Processing System

---

(1) A set of symbolic tokens connected by a set of relations makes up a "symbol structure," which is stored and retained in some memory register or other.

(2) If a symbol's designation is fixed by an elementary information process or by the external environment, then it is "primitive."

(3) These symbol structures then act as either inputs or outputs (or both) for an "information process."

(4) The symbol structures refer to objects if information processes that take the symbol structure as output, either:

    A. affect the object itself, or
    B. produce symbol structures that depend upon the object.

(5) An information processor has three basic components:

    A. a fixed set of elementary information processes;
    B. a short-term memory register that holds the input or output symbol structures of the elementary information processes;
    C. an interpreter which, as a function of the symbol structures in short-term memory, determines the sequence of the elementary information processes to be executed by the information processing system.

(6) The symbol structure is a "program"

    A. if the object a symbol structure designates is an information process and,
    B. if given the proper input, an interpreter can execute the process.

---

can conceive *solely* in terms of input, output, and various functional or causal relations.[4] Minds just are (or can just be conceived as) things that exhibit the appropriate cause relations. Consider a mousetrap for an analogous example. What counts as a mousetrap is something that takes in a live mouse and then turns out a dead one. Mousetraps can be built out of just about any substance. If we ask what unites all legitimate token mousetraps under that type, no answer can be given in terms of underlying physical substances. Mousetraps can be made out of wood, metal springs, poison, plastic, baseball bats, and so on. What unites these objects is not the stuff from which they are made, but the purposes they serve. They all deliver dead mice when given live ones. Hence, we understand mousetraps just in terms of inputs, outputs, and certain relations between them.

These sorts of formal or functional definitions in science contrast with understanding objects or properties in terms of some developmental history. For some things, how they got to be here is important for understanding what they are. These are things that cannot be understood purely formally. For example, the property of being a codependent is not formally defined. In brief, a codependent is someone who supports addictive personalities. But the causal relations that codependents enter into might not differ much from those who are not codependent, or might not be distinguishable from the relations of noncodependents, were it not for the codependent's particular history. Codependents typically engage in solicitous behavior, usually with respect to people in trouble whom they care about, and this behavior helps boost a codependent's self-worth. Insecure kind people act in the same way. What makes codependents codependent is not their behavior per se, but the history of their relationships that leads them to act in this way.

The purely formal approach to mentality tells us that we could conceivably find minds comprised of appropriately connected neurons, or silicon chips, or zinc, or some alien substance. Since these definitions say nothing about the ontological status of mental events, the same type of mental state could be realized in any number of underlying things, and they would all count as tokens of that type as long as they give the correct outputs for specified inputs and maintain appropriate causal connections with other mental states. In other words, the study of mind is analogous to the study of mathematics: neither requires an actual, physical instantiator to get the study underway.

There is a strong methodological advantage in adopting this perspective. If we can define mental states in terms of inputs, outputs, and causal relations, then we have an easy way (relatively speaking) to explore the implications of particular theories: computer simulation. If the underlying stuff does not impact the relations under study, then theoretically at least we could design computer programs to mimic the hypothesized causal relations to test whether our model gives us the outputs we expect for the inputs we choose.

Compare this project with computer simulations of the weather. The variables that figure into determining the weather for any particular day are enormously complex; it is exceedingly difficult for any human to track them all. But we can devise computer programs that calculate the values for all the variables and their interactions for each iteration of time. These programs map the weather with an extraordinary degree of precision, at least for a few days. Something similar should be available for human cognition. In real life there are simply too many contingencies for scientists to be able to test their simple theories. Even in the fairly constrained environment of a laboratory in which subjects are only given a few inputs at a time, interactions with things that scientists cannot control can easily swamp the effects that they are trying to test. But with computer simulations, we can control all the inputs a system receives. Though these systems would then only mimic aspects of cognition, they still present a powerful tool for testing hypotheses in addition to laboratory work.

Moreover, computers can track exceedingly complicated causally interactive algorithms in ways that we cannot. Computers give us one easy and relatively inexpensive path for exploring rough and ready new ideas about how our mental states interact before designing time-consuming and expensive laboratory experiments. Explaining mental states in terms of their causal interactions radically expands the possibilities we have for exploring and testing hypotheses and theories of mental cognition.

These two assumptions taken together, that the mind can be understood as a formal symbol manipulating device and that "mental programs" can be multiply instantiated, led many early on to conclude that the underlying instantiating stuff was simply unimportant.[5] Nowadays, however, even the staunchest "formalists" would agree that the brain sciences can be useful in understanding cognition. Not surprisingly, they concede that studying the brain may tell us something about the program that it is running.

In fact, the rise of neural net modeling[6] in conjunction with concrete results from neuroscience regarding how minds actually work demonstrated three important facts to cognitive science. (1) We can model brains purely computationally at a lower level of organization than originally envisioned. This opened the question of the appropriate level of analysis for mental systems, something that had previously been taken more or less for granted. This topic is pursued in chapters 2 and 3. (2) How we actually work differs quite often from the strategies various computers use in solving problems. These differences become important not only for therapeutic reasons, but also because cognitive science at bottom is a science about *us*. Computers comprise but one tool among many we use to divine the basic principles behind thought. This theme is echoed in chapters 6 and 7. (3) It is quite difficult and artificial to separate the study of one domain from another, since everything influences just about everything else in the brain. Hence, the ways in which we had originally carved our cognitive capacities up for study might be mistaken. This point is discussed in chapter 5.

The point of disagreement between myself and others is over how useful the brain sciences are and in what respects. I believe that these facts hugely alter the face of cognitive science. However, my reading of the current state of affairs is that many philosophers of mind have simply tacked neuroscience onto their list of what counts as a cognitive science without fundamentally reorganizing their notions of the field.[7] That is, their realization of the three points listed above, plus perhaps only a rudimentary knowledge of neuroscience, have led them merely to add an entry on computational neuroscience to their mental lexicon. This, I think, is a mistake.

What they have done mimics the currently popular textbooks in cognitive science.[8] In these books, we find chapters devoted to computation, language, reasoning, attention, memory, artificial intelligence, and psychological development, as well as a chapter on neuroscience (usually on vision, and usually the last chapter). Pedagogically, it makes sense to break the study of the mind into these (or similar) categories, since historically each has been studied separately, and each has developed under different research paradigms. It is simply easier to learn piecemeal.

However, *thinking* of the theories of cognitive science or its subject matter in this compartmentalized manner is not prudent. For all of these topics are intimately related, and all (for us) are related to the brain. It is simply a mistake to reduce meaningful symbols to formal patterns (to reduce semantics to syntax) and then remove those patterns from their culture, history, and biology. We are living, interactive creatures. We are designed to move through this world, seeking food and mates and avoiding predators and other painful things. Any science that purports to study some aspect of us has to take these facts into consideration.

My point is that we cannot (or perhaps, should not) detach an organism's cognition from the animal's strategy for survival within particular ecological environments. Despite the claims of the early serial models, nervous systems are not general purpose computers; they evolved to accomplish a certain range of specific tasks and their architecture supports those tasks. We all know this, and yet, the early von Neumann models push us toward pretending that the brain essentially is in the symbol manipulation business. But if we consider the brain from a more biologically realistic perspective, we can see that nervous systems are designed to move organisms appropriately in their environment. As evolutionary biologists are fond of pointing out, nervous systems enable organisms to succeed in the four F's: feeding, fleeing, fighting, and reproducing.[9]

I can give no serious argument for why I think this sort of bias toward the neuroscientific study of the mind/brain is superior, but adopting this perspective does offer several advantages. For example, the general organization of the brain makes sense if we assume that the nervous system exists for creating motor output. The cerebellum, an area crucially involved with motor control,[10] is connected almost directly to all areas of the brain. (See figure 1.1.) It inputs into sensory transmissions at all levels. It is connected to our reticular activating system, the system that controls arousal and attention. It is also connected via the thalamus to the basal ganglia and forebrain. With these connections, the cerebellum could alter the frontal cortex-basal ganglia interactions. Finally, it is connected to the hippocampus, the area responsible for laying down episodic memories, and via its connections to the hippocampus, it inputs to, and receives output from, the limbic system. Not only can our "motor control" center modulate sensory transmission, arousal, attention, cortex-basal ganglia interactions, and episodic memory, it can also alter our emotionality and social responses![11] All areas of our brains seem geared almost exclusively to coping with their functions as they pertain to problems of motor control.

Figure 1.1 *Connections of the Cerebellum*

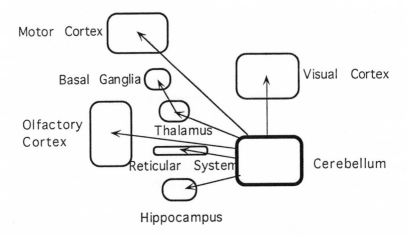

The brain puts much emphasis on the priority of motor tasks, and we should pay attention to this emphasis. If we do, then we reorient our essential understanding of what we are. Any abstract symbol manipulating we do becomes a matter of motor assembling. Because "thinking" would turn on the need to predict events in the extra-nervous world such that organisms can move successfully through that space,[12] we only process information insofar as doing so is relevant to some motor output. This, to me, is a very different picture of a cognizing organism than the one advocated by early cognitive psychologists.[13]

But I don't want to claim that cognitive science is simply cognitive neuroscience either. I do think that the brain is at the center of all of this, but theories in cognitive science are truly *interdisciplinary*[14]—they exhibit fundamental connections among previously disparate domains. To my mind, they exhibit connections between psychology and neuroscience in particular. Nevertheless, this is just my take on the current state of affairs. What is required to be an interdisciplinary theory in cognitive science is for it to span more than one traditional domain. Generally speaking, as I discuss in later chapters, this means that the theory will cover more than one level of analysis and organization in the mind/brain in its *explanans*.

To speak less from my heart: cognitive science is the study of information processing, and insofar as some discipline studies that, then it is part of cognitive science. (A computational approach, though dominant, is not required.) I shall try to do without explicating the subject matter in any detail; it changes as the science grows and develops, as we learn more about our cognitive abilities and their connections to the rest of our psyches and the world. I fear that any attempt to constrain or rein the topics would only make any analysis seem artificial and dated.[15] Having said that, let me now proceed to date this book. The disciplines currently involved to some degree or other in cognitive science include: anthropology, biology, computer science, engineering, linguistics, mathematics, philosophy, psychiatry, psychology, neuroscience, and sociology. And the list keep expanding as we realize that information processing is more complicated than artificial intelligence personnel originally thought and how many disciplines actually study this in some guise or other.

Contra Stillings et al. (1987), the convergence among these disciplines is not over the questions asked about mentality. (Indeed, as I argue below, the questions asked are very different in different domains for historical and sociological reasons.) Nor is it in a common research framework.[16] The frameworks differ as the domains differ. What they do share is an interest in explaining how we process information, period. But how they explain it and what counts as an information process is not uniform across the fields. My task is to explicate how one can take these diverse beginnings and still come out with coherent interdisciplinary theories. My answer will revolve around the common explanatory patterns one finds in cognitive science.[17] My secondary task is to convert (perhaps) a few fence sitters into believing that the brain has to be at the center of any serious cognitive science. That is, it will be to illustrate by way of example that most of the common explanatory patterns involve the brain in some way or another.

This is why I fashioned the book as a "how to" manual, for it is partly descriptive and partly normative. I describe how cognitive science is actually done, at the same time that I implicitly recommend how it should be done. Ultimately, I do not believe these two projects are that different, since instances of the successful interdisciplinary theories in cognitive science have already been done properly.

But before we can work our way to what counts as an interdisciplinary theory, I need to lay some theoretical groundwork. I begin in the next chapter by explaining a bit of the metaphysical relationship between the mind and the brain. In particular, I focus on how to understand mental causality in a physical world. I argue that the real problem is not defining causality but, instead, is deciding which level of analysis to privilege in any explanation. This decision ultimately turns on contingent facts, local to the particular investigation. I return to the question of levels of organization and analysis in chapter 3 and spend more time developing accounts of the types of hierarchies one finds in the cognitive sciences and how one should use these hierarchies in explaining mental or biological phenomena.

Chapter 4 introduces computationalism and functionalism, two popular methodologies in cognitive science. I argue that both of these have strongly pragmatic dimensions as well that belie using computer analogies as primitives in theory building. As I explain in chapters 4 and 5, much of science relies on a bootstrapping method, which in turn is determined by the history of the inquiry. So, for example, our needs and goals in developing an explanation determine the boundaries of the physical system we investigate. We then rely on previously accepted theories to determine which functions a physical system computes, as well as to give a semantic interpretation to the arguments of the function.

Indeed, most of this book emphasizes the pragmatic aspects to scientific pursuits. Theories are accepted as an answer to some specific questions, which have been posed against a background of common assumptions, and with respect to specific alternatives. In addition, available methodological and empirical techniques influence what level of description one can give a physical system and consequently influence the types of legitimate questions one can pose. The bottom line is that theories are tied to a particular scientific community, operating during a particular time, with particular players.

As I argue by example in chapters 6 and 7, these pragmatic aspects of science entail that it is difficult simply to import data or theories from one investigative domain to another. Indeed, classical notions of theoretical reduction simply can't work. It would be a rare case in which one theory from one field could explain the success of another theory in a different field, since the players, the background assumptions, the history of the discipline, and the contrast class of the questions asked would be different as well. Still, I don't want to maintain that the disciplines involved in the cognitive sciences are completely independent. Instead, something like the notion of "explanatory extension" captures the two-way dependency relations among autonomous fields. A multi-disciplinary approach to problem solving means that we may use another discipline for collateral support, inspiration, and to help set the parameters of inquiry, but we cannot simply borrow data wholesale from other theories over the same state space. Such borrowings would represent an abuse of evidence because in order to import in such fashion, we must overlook important aspects of the theoretical assumptions behind the data gathering, assumptions that shape not only the very nature of the evidence but the nature of the abstract physical system as well.

I conclude that the best way to approach developing an interdisciplinary program would be to rely on "bridge sciences" for important connections. Such a program requires that at least some of the domains involved share fundamental assumptions. In the case study I examine, neuropsychology adopts the theoretical framework of some aspect of cognitive psychology in order to investigate psychological questions using neuroscientific techniques. This sort of "data borrowing" is legitimate because portions of the contrast classes, scientific audience, and theoretical vocabulary are in fact shared.

In sum: interdisciplinary theories in cognitive science are going to be messy affairs, operating on many different levels of analysis and description. In general, they will function as an overlapping set of related models whose explanatory power is based on a sort of etiological story telling of the development and occurrence of some attribute. The models refer to the exemplars of natural kinds, and the resultant theory, which is but a set of models and a list of general principles, maintains its coherency in virtue of these common principles. I explain by example how this is supposed to work. Though I focus on research in mnemonic processing for the examples, what I have to say should be taken as a general account of how to build a theory in cognitive science.

Let us now get to work.

Chapter 2

The Dilemma of Mental Causality

> If it isn't literally true that my wanting is causally responsible for my reaching ..., and my believing is causally responsible for my saying, ... then ... it's the end of the world.[1]

> That [the collapse of intentional psychology] would be, beyond comparison, the greatest intellectual catastrophe in the history of our species.[2]

Consider the following simple claims:

1. The physical is causally closed.
2. The mental and the physical are distinct.
3. The mental and the physical causally interact.[3]

All are reasonable. Premise 1 claims simply that materialism is true. All causal interactions are physical, and these interactions are enough to explain everything in our universe. Premise 2 is just an expression of the nonreducibility of the mental. It is now (more or less) accepted wisdom that mental states cannot be reduced to physical ones, though they are "realized" by them.[4] Materialism entails that the physical must instantiate the mental (unless you are an eliminativist, of course),[5] but because wildly different underlying physical configurations can underwrite type-identical mental states, we cannot identify mental state types with any particular physical types. Hence, we say that the mental "supervenes" on the physical.[6]

Nevertheless, it is also (more or less) common knowledge that the mental affects the physical (premise 3). I feel thirsty, so I drink water. I feel pain, so I wince. And so on. Moreover, assuming the influence of the mental on the physical is not just limited to common usage. Ever since cognitivism displaced behaviorism as the more popular research paradigm in psychology, mechanisms for behavior are generally given in terms of the mental moving the physical.[7] Though one can disagree over the cost of relinquishing these sorts of causal explanations involving the mental,[8] no one can dispute that they are endemic.

At a first pass, these premises are also fundamentally incompatible. If we are materialists, then it seems that we should simply do away with the mind, as it were. For anything that is explained using mental states would have another explanation—one that traces the *actual* causal history—using physical events. The mental becomes redundant, derivative, explanatorily superfluous; hence, epiphenomenal.[9]

But on the other hand, mental states appear to be separate from physical ones. Multiple realizability—the fact that any particular mental state could be instantiated by an indefinite number of physical configurations—tells us that no particular physical state is necessary for any mental one.[10] This precludes any sort of reduction between the mind and the brain.[11] But if the mental is distinct from the physical, and our minds influence our behavior, then our physical world could not be "closed."[12] So materialism must be false.

This of course is just the mind-body problem with which dutiful materialists continually struggle. Our metaphysics breeds epiphenomenalism, but our mentalism breeds a different ontology. And around we go. . . .

On a second pass though, the story is a bit more complicated. If we want to be materialists first and foremost, then we can say that some mental state caused some physical event just by noting that each mental token is identical to some physical token or other and that the physical world is causally closed. However, what a materialist cannot maintain is that it is the mental state qua mental that causes a physical change. (At least, a materialist cannot maintain this without additional labor, which I try to provide below.) That is, a materialist seems compelled to assert that every mental property M has some physical implementation c such that we can subsume $c \rightarrow e$ under some physical law (where '$\rightarrow$' denotes 'causes'). To pretend otherwise would be to deny the causal closure of the physical universe. But, as van Gulick writes, "once we acknowledge that there is such a . . . physical law subsuming c and e, like a young cuckoo in the nest of a robin, it 'greedily' grabs off the causal potency for itself" (1993, p. 241). The fact that M seems to cause some property N so that $M \rightarrow N$ is lawlike results from our more basic physical causal laws and the fact that *M* supervenes on the physical. LePore and Loewer conclude:

> The real locus of causal powers are the physical properties. . . . [*M*], so to speak, gets carried piggyback on physical properties and it is mere appearance that possessing . . . [*M*] determines *c*'s causal powers. The basic physical properties and laws determine both the causal relations among events and the nonbasic [lawlike relations]. . . . It is merely an appearance that the nonbasic [relations] . . . determine causal relations among events. (1989, p. 187)

But what materialists seem forced into concluding regarding the causal efficacy of mental properties qua mental appears to be fundamentally mistaken. There is an undeniable difference between someone breaking a glass by accidentally brushing up against it and smashing a glass in a fit of anger. In the first case, the person's cognitive state has little or nothing to do with the glass shattering, but in the second case, the mental state qua anger seems to be quite relevant to the broken glass.[13] How are we to understand the difference between the two cases? What is the proper way to understand the relation between the mind, the brain, and the resultant behavior?

This chapter is devoted to exploring these questions. In particular, I explore the more popular middle ground in which mental phenomena are claimed to be "as real as" other higher level properties. I argue that this position is inappropriate because it fails to answer the dilemma. In addition, it relies on an outmoded and implausible notion of theory. However, with a more sophisticated understanding of scientific theorizing and the relation between ontology and explanation, we will have a framework by which we can determine when mental states are causally efficacious.

Mental States as Higher Level Properties

With the assumption of materialism, we must hold that mental properties just *are* physical properties. That is, mental properties exist *at the same level of organization as* some of the physical properties—these properties might be fairly complex or abstract, but they are physical nonetheless.[14] Of course, the lower level physical structures may still be primary since they appear to be ontologically prior. Hence, we say that mental properties *depend* on physical ones (and not vice versa).[15] Materialism gives us something like a weak form of property "dualism" with the lower level physical properties determining the higher level mental ones. We can understand lower level P's as specifying a microstructural property of c that provides a mechanism for the implementation of M in c.[16]

Here is the question: If we assume that both P and M have lawlike links to N, and that P is a cause, should we say that M has a distinct causal role as well? Jaegwon Kim argues that we should lean on the ontological priority of the lower level physical properties and recognize that the only way to get mental properties or other higher level social facts is through a lower level physiological property.[17] He denies that mental properties are proper causal agents in explanation. Simplicity would favor P alone. We accept that if N occurs by being realized by P^*, then any cause of P^* must be a cause of N. We can see this, for example, when we treat pain by interfering with the body. Hence, if M is realized by P, then the causal powers of M are identical to (a subset of) the causal powers of P. Kim concludes that there is no such thing as actual (explanatory) mental causation. This effectively abolishes M.[18]

But there are difficulties with this sort of eliminativist picture. If we were to adopt Kim's view, then we would have to acquiesce that physics is the only science and that all we can legitimately discuss are vectors in Hilbert space. His argument must be incorrect, for it makes *all* distinct higher level properties causally inefficacious. It entails that the only causally relevant properties would be those defined in physics, and so all chemical, biological, and sociological properties must be inert.[19] For example, we would not be able to explain the death of AIDS patients in terms of a decrease of T-cells in their blood, for the biological property "death," the sociobiological property "AIDS patient," the biochemical entity "T-cell," and so on, are not the proper sorts of properties or objects that could engage in causal interactions.[20]

The different levels of organization in the world are not being taken seriously enough.[21] One and the same object—the eye, for example— can be and in fact is described differently depending on what sort of questions are being asked. We can talk about the eye in terms of its cognitive function, in terms of its anatomy, in terms of its physiology, in terms of its chemistry—and within each of those broader divisions we find a further hierarchy of descriptions. When discussing an eye's physiology, we can distinguish the rod from the cone cells and explicate their path to the retinal ganglion and how the different response patterns of the rod and cone cells affect what happens beyond. Or we can distinguish among the various types of rod cells and how they interact with one another in the retinal ganglion and beyond in terms of their individual response patterns. Or we can talk about the firing properties of a particular rod in terms of the influx and efflux of ions. And so on, with each "level" of description being legitimate with respect to answering certain questions about eye physiology, but not others.[22]

The picture of the world that emerges with the perspective of different levels of description and organization is obviously a layered one.[23] We can understand this world in terms of sets of entities that constitute the domain of particulars for each level of organization and sets of properties then defined over each domain or over sets of domains. Though causal closure would be a level-specific property, causal interactions could range across levels.[24]

As a result, causality becomes a promiscuous relation.[25] In this sort of "vertical" arrangement, causality becomes "transitive."[26] That is, whatever happens in the mind can be nothing more than whatever happens in certain brain areas (and perhaps the environment as well), and whatever happens in brain areas can be nothing more than the interactions of neuronal circuits, and whatever happens at the network level can be nothing more than the interactions of neurons, and whatever happens at the neuronal level can be nothing more than the interactions of molecules, and so on down. However, it is important to stress that this is not a reductionist position with respect to causality but, rather, just the opposite. We can think of causal interactions as operating on any level of organization.

M at some level is identified with a higher level P. Furthermore, these higher level P's have causal powers *at that level*. We can compare the relationship between M (or the higher level P's) and lower level P's with the relationship between physics and biology. The higher level (with respect to physics) is the only place in which biological concepts exist. For example, many agree that "species" or "gene" cannot be *defined* in terms of lower level properties or entities because the definitions are intimately tied to other properties and entities at the higher level.[27] Or, for an extreme example, consider chaotic phenomena. The sort of larger scale order that emerges in the scroll waves of concentration in the Zhabotinske reaction,[28] in the formation of Bénard cells of convection in fluid dynamics,[29] or in populations in ecology[30] cannot be expressed or reduced to the movements or interactions of the individual units that support and ultimately determine the higher level patterns.[31] Moreover, we can think of these higher level objects as denoting *natural kinds* because they engage in the right sort of regularities for science.[32, 33]

The causal powers at the higher level are not strictly derivative of any particular lower level property since we only get the properties that enter into these sort of regular behaviors at the higher level, which are or can be multiply instantiated in any number of sets of lower level entities. We cannot immediately conclude that mental states (or other higher level phenomena) are explanatorily epiphenomenal and should be eliminated from our explanations. Instead, mental states appear to be higher level physical properties that enter into theories just as easily and as frequently as any other sanctified regularity. At first pass, this multilayered view of the world overcomes the dilemma of the mind by explicating how the mind is physical (hence, potentially causal), yet not necessarily reducible to lower level descriptions. And it seems to give us what we want—autonomous sciences and a place for the mental in explanation as one of the higher levels of organization in a physical world.[34]

Privileged Regularities and Ceteris Paribus Clauses

We now have arrived at a useful middle ground. Mental phenomena are just as good and real and useful as any other higher level property. Our world exists as a nested hierarchy in which the different levels of organization follow different—perhaps fundamentally different—patterns of behavior and interaction. At each level, though, one may distinguish regularities in the observed phenomena that are ultimately used to ground models and theories that describe and predict the phenomena. Mental events are thus just one more type of (higher level) regularity that we observe. Lower level physical events are not explanatorily prior to the higher levels, nor are they clearly metaphysically superior to them.

Given the nested nature of our world, it is easy to see how the properties in the higher levels can supervene on the properties of each of the lower levels. However, there remains a gap between regular higher level properties and higher level properties *causally responsible for some course of events*, for not all supervenient properties are causal. More work must be done before we can answer when one level of organization contains the objects and concomitant properties *responsible* for some event. Audi (1993) points out, for example, that we might legitimately claim that Nixon was run out of office because he was morally corrupt. But that fact does not thereby entail that moral corruption qua moral property was causally responsible. Presumably, things like the Watergate investigations, Nixon's duplicity, the sentiment of the American public, and so on, are the sorts of things that actually caused Nixon to resign.[35] Perhaps more to our point, consider Pat staring at her sunburned nose in the mirror. It seems natural to claim that Pat's fair skin (among other things) is causally responsible for her reddened face; however, it is not responsible for her reflection's pink appearance. Nevertheless, the fact that Pat has fair skin supervenes on both Pat herself and her reflection. Why should we think that mental events resemble actual sunburns more than reflected ones? How do we know that mental events are responsible for some behavioral effects instead of being some illusory causal pretender?

Moreover, even though causal relations may turn out to be relatively ubiquitous, only some causal relations can be privileged in explanation. Even though causality may be transitive, explanation is not.[36] As Sober remarks, interdefinability does not mean conceptual equivalence. On two counts, then, we have to decide what sort of weight we should assign to the higher levels of organization in the brain or mind in explaining behavior. In particular, we need to answer whether there is an epistemologically privileged higher level of organization in the brain in explanation and how we would know this.

Fodor (1989) answers by arguing that we can claim that mental properties are causally responsible if they are subsumed under causal laws. For example, Freud could explain his patient Dora's nervousness, loss of appetite, and occasional loss of speaking ability in terms of sexual tensions that she feels with respect to her parents, Herr K. and Frau K., because this token of mental causation fits a lawlike pattern of sexual abuse causing abnormal behavior.[37] Exemplars of the causal laws Freudians might appeal to in order to explain Dora's discomfort include:

1. Unwanted sexual advances from authority or caretaking figures induce unresolvable conflicting desires.
2. These conflicts induce depression or hysterical symptoms.

Given that 1 and 2 fit Dora's circumstances, then, according to Fodor, we can say that the conflicting desires are causally responsible for Dora's behavior.

However, Fodor's recommendation without further discussion or elaboration begs the question. We want to know (among other things) whether the so-called intentional laws of our folk (or Freudian) psychology or our psychology proper *are* in fact legitimate causal laws and *not* merely convenient fictions. Are these perceived patterns *in fact* grounded in some causal relationship, or are they parasitic on something else?

But within the attempts to flesh out Fodor's suggestion lies a great controversy that goes back to Davidson's "anomalous monism" (1980). Donald Davidson (and others)[38] holds that only strict or basic or exceptionless laws support causal interactions. That is, only things like the laws of particle physics can provide the nomologically sufficient conditions for true causal transactions. Psychological laws, even psychophysical laws, are neither strict, nor basic, nor exceptionless. They are used to relate sets of events only in conjunction with ceteris paribus clauses. Hence, they cannot support true causal interactions. Hence, mental properties qua mental are causally suspect (anomalous). That is, the proposed laws 1 and 2 above would only be applicable in Dora's case if we assume that there are no other overriding conflicts, that Dora's development has been otherwise normal, and so on.

In response, Fodor (1989) denies that "hedged laws can't ground mental causes" (p. 72). We can see that ceteris paribus laws can do "serious scientific business" (p. 73) (where a ceteris paribus law has the form: "$M \rightarrow N$ ceteris paribus") because they hold nomologically or strictly whenever the ceteris paribus conditions are satisfied. We can see this because we can distinguish meaningfully between the claims "M's cause N's ceteris paribus," and "M's cause N's, except for when they don't." We can distinguish between unwanted sexual advances from authority figures inducing conflicting desires, everything else being equal, and unwanted sexual advances from authority figures inducing conflicting desires, except for when they don't. The real difference between the more basic laws and the laws in the special sciences is that the latter require additional or a mediating mechanisms in order to implement the causal transactions, while the former do not.[39]

But this debate over ceteris paribus conditions is a red herring because, in point of fact, *all* theories rely on ceteris paribus hedges. The real difficulty is that Davidson, Fodor, LePore, and Loewer are relying on a deficient notion of *scientific explanation*. If we modernize our notion of scientific theories a bit, the debate disappears. Indeed, with a better understanding of laws and explanation, we shall see that the answer to our dilemma turns on how to understand the relationship of causality itself within a model-theoretic framework.

It is simply a fundamental error to assume that the basic laws of physics (or any laws of any science) are not hedged in important and fundamental ways. Scientists have no intention of accounting for all the intricacies of their subject matter. Instead, they abstract away a small number of parameters from some collection of observed phenomena in order to form a *data set,* which is then used to explain and predict something (though not everything) about the phenomena themselves. These parameters are influenced by the goals of individual inquiry, the audience for whom the explanation is directed, the history of the study, and so on, and they may differ as each of the constraining factors differ.[40] To take a clear example from "basic science," classical particle mechanics uses point masses, velocities in frictionless environments, and distances traveled over time to characterize falling bodies. Theoretical physicists only want to explain the general pattern of behavior of moving objects; hence, they can rightly ignore the color of the body, the date of its falling, interference from gravitational attraction, and so on. They predict behavior based only on the position and momenta of extensionless points interacting in a vacuum. Engineers, who have different concerns and address different audiences, would probably want to include gravitational attraction and perhaps the times of the events in their calculations.

We can see this same picture of how science works in the "softer" sciences as well.[41] The genetic theory of natural selection characterizes evolutionary phenomena in terms of changes in the distributions of genotypes across a population over time as a function of the rate of reproduction, the frequency of crossover, and so on. Behaviorist theories in psychology describe the behavior of idealized organisms as a function of stimulus-response patterns and reinforcement schedules. Other examples include Chomskian theories of competence in linguistics, the Nernst equation in neurophysiology, and Treisman's cognitive theory of a master map of locations in attentional space,[42] all of which describe the behavior of abstract mechanisms under ideal conditions that only approximates the behavior of real phenomena in virtue of a few "fundamental" properties under normal conditions.

All scientists abstract away from the complexities of the actual world and define artificial domains isomorphic to the world in only a few aspects. Following Suppe, we can call these imaginary domains "physical systems": "highly abstract and idealized replicas of the phenomena" that characterize "how the phenomena *would have* behaved *had* the idealized conditions been met" (1989, p. 65). Scientists calculate the behavior of these physical systems, which they then use to explain interactions in the actual world.

Science does not apply its laws directly to observed or hypothesized phenomena but, rather, uses laws to explain the behavior of physical systems abstracted from the phenomena in such a way that the behavior can be correlated with the phenomena.[43] A successful correlation leads scientists to identify the attributes of the physical system with properties in the real world, thereby explaining them in terms of the posited laws. What we actually observe must be stretched and pruned such that we can talk about what we would have observed if only the few relevant parameters of the phenomena existed under ideal conditions. These statements of altered observations are used with the theory to make predictions about the physical system. The predictions are then converted into statements about real phenomena by just reversing the procedure for altering the original observation statements.

Of course, what I have articulated is nothing more than a version of the semantic view of theories (much more on this below and in the appendix).[44] What is important for the discussion now about ceteris paribus clauses is how semantic conceptions (and related views) define the scope of laws. Theories are interpreted to make universal statements about the set of possible objects that fall under the theories. The scope of proper theories are classes of natural kinds. Theories involving mental properties might encompass things like living creatures, or cordate organisms, or mammals, or humans and primates, or just *Homo sapiens*. Regardless, as long as these sets are describable by proper lists of natural attributes, they can be subsumed by proper causal laws in some physical system.

By restricting the scope of laws to the domains of the theories, the notion of a law that is "universally applicable" assumes the same meaning for laws in both the hard sciences and the "softer" ones. In sum, the laws in psychology and the other cognitive sciences are no different from any more "basic" law of particle physics or QM. All sciences prune their observations to conform to simplified and idealized circumstances; they then all implicitly hedge their theories by making their laws concern only the abstract physical systems. Theories in cognitive science and theories in physics are both devised to cover abstract physical systems, pared down and idealized versions of some aspect of the world. As a result, they both operate two removes from actual phenomena and both focus on correlating sets of data to build models. Their corresponding laws are sensitive only to these correlations, which may or may not correspond to how the world actually functions in all its messy details. Hence, we can see that whether and how ceteris paribus clauses or additional mediating mechanisms are wielded is inconsequential. The Freudian "laws" that unwanted sexual advances from authority or caretaking figures induce unresolvable conflicting desires and that these conflicts induce depression or hysterical symptoms are just as dependent on abstraction, omission, and reconstruction as the law of gravity or the conservation of momentum.

But saying that psychological laws and theories are just like any other "more basic" physical law or theory is no more helpful than claiming that supervenient properties are just like the instantiating properties. It does not answer our original problem. Suppose that idealized versions of c and e are subsumed by the law $M \to N$. If we be materialists, then we would have to agree that for this particular instance of $c \to e$, there is also a "more basic" law that likewise subsumes the events, perhaps idealized differently. How do we determine which law to privilege in explanation of behavior? Saying that psychological laws are just like any other accepted scientific law is not enough, and we have seen that Kim's use of simplicity is not telling.[45] What would be?

Let me clarify what I am asking. I grant Nelson Goodman's point that "regularities are where you find them, and you can find them anywhere" (1979, p. 82).[46] But I am assuming that, in building a physical system, we pick out which regularity or regularities are especially salient. *How* we pick out these patterns is a separate question and one that I presume turns on personal interest, the history of the inquiry, background theories, the shape of the query, and so on.[47] I leave that question aside for now, though I do return to it in the next chapter. What I wish to focus on for the moment is what happens *after* the physical systems are constructed and certain regularities highlighted.

I want to know: If it is the case that more than one model can subsume each particular $c \to e$, then how do we know which model to use? (Or are all equally applicable?) This is not just a question of which model best captures some regularity. Because different models may subsume $c \to e$ differently—that is, because different models may emphasize different aspects of the interaction and, as a result, may project its predicates differently[48]—which regularity we should be talking about *from the sets culled by science* is the issue. Will mental properties end up being *effectively* epiphenomenal in that models defined over those sorts of properties should not be used in explanation?

We can see this question very clearly in the timely case of Freudian analysis and memory repression. Should we understand Dora's disturbances in behavior and other similar abnormalities as being caused by conflicting "intentions" regarding sexuality and authority, or should we understand them as reflecting imbalances in the brain's endorphin levels?[49] Even if we assume that psychoanalysis is emprically adequate (and I am well aware that many don't),[50] perhaps it still should be disregarded since the lower level description and explanation of the unusual behavior is better, or ontologically prior, or more generalizable, or something like this.

Screening off Causes

In order to answer this inquiry, we must first notice how the notion of cause is used in model-theoretic accounts of science. I have suggested that science is engaged in correlating data sets. Physical systems are designed to capture the salient patterns such that we can then use them as a tool in predicting phenomena. If this is a correct portrait, then a causal connection (in science at least) refers to nothing more than an interaction among the variables in a model. In virtue of highlighting an important regularity through constructing a physical system, one has thereby pointed to a cause.[51]

What is important for our purposes is that, from this perspective, causal laws refer to relations among variables in physical systems; hence they refer to the general types of events, objects, or properties, and not their individual tokens. In addition, causality becomes probabilistic.[52] Causality becomes an expression of how likely one sort of event is to obtain, given that some other sort of event obtained. However, we can still use causal laws and presumed causal relations to make probabilistic predictions about how likely e is to occur, given c ($\Pr(e|c)$), or how likely N is to be instantiated, given M ($\Pr(N|M)$).

With the semantic interpretation of theories and a probabilistic notion of causality, how to understand the relationship between mental events and their physical instantiations becomes one of how to understand the relationship between two models of the same set of events $c \rightarrow e$. Certainly these models will generalize c differently, one in terms of property M, the other in terms of property P. They might even generalize *e* differently, one in terms of M^*, the other in terms of P^*. (Or there might be some generalization N neutral between the two models.) We can think of these two models as specifying $\Pr(e|c)$ as either $\Pr(M^*|M)$ or $\Pr(P^*|P)$, where M^* and P^* might be coextensive. The question before us is: which model presents a better explanation of *e*—the one that postulates $\Pr(M^*|M)$ or the one that postulates $\Pr(P^*|P)$?

To continue with our example of memory repression and sexual abuse, we can think of there being (at least) two models designed to explain these phenomena. One would generalize the cause (*c*) of Dora's loss of voice, decline in appetite, hysteria, and so on (*N*), in terms of repressed and conflicting desires (*M*). *N* might also be conjoined with additional symptomotology (such as identification with Frau K.) to form M^*. The other would generalize $c \rightarrow e$ (also described in terms of *N*) as a change in brain chemistry (*P*). Here *N* might be conjoined with additional factors (such as a depressed immune system) to form P^*. The sort of question I am trying to address is, Which model presents a better explanation of the changes in behavior, one that turns on repressed and conflicting desires increasing the probability of mental distress, or one that ties changes in brain chemistry to increasing the probability of various sorts of deficits?

Notice that now the question of how to understand mental causation is very similar to more general questions in the philosophy of science (especially philosophy of biology) concerning how to distinguish truly explanatory relations from mere artifact (more on this in chapter 3). The accepted wisdom there is that the relation of "screening off" determines which properties are the appropriate ones to use when framing a satisfactory explanation.[53]

In general, we say that *M* screens off *P* from *N* iff:[54]

1. $\Pr(N|P \& M) = \Pr(N|M)$
2. $\Pr(N|P \& M) \neq \Pr(N|P)$.[55]

That is, *P* adds nothing to *M* with respect to the instantiation of *N*, but *M* adds something to *P*.[56] To help clarify the connection between the probability calculations and predictability, consider the example of organismic selection. We say that the phenotypic properties (*M*) screen off the genotypic properties (*P*) from reproductive success (*N*) because changing the phenotype without changing the genotype can affect reproductive success.[57] Similarly, when discussing, say, the issue of levels of organization for physical systems, we might say that the higher level description of the informational patterns generated by individual firing neurons M screens off the lower level descriptions of the individual neurons P when accounting for some behavior N, just in case N is predictable from M alone, but N is not predictable from P alone.[58] A Freudian analysis of Dora would screen off a biochemical explanation if we could predict Dora's hysteria from known conflicting sexual desires, but we could not predict this outcome from only knowing that her endorphin levels had changed.

What is important to notice is that the screening-off relation is asymmetric across the various levels of organization, while causality is not. Hence, it presents itself as a likely candidate for a solution to the problem of artifact when choosing the correct level of analysis in explanation. Is it likewise a plausible candidate for a solution to the problem of mental causation in a material world? Is it the case that mental descriptions screen off lower level physical descriptions, or vice versa?

Let us consider a simple example first: pain. Suppose Terry has a severe headache and she winces as a result. Without pretending that there are complete theories of pain in either psychology or neuroscience, let us see how we might explain this phenomenon in terms of different levels of organization. We might say something to the effect that Terry's experience of pain caused her to recoil, or we might say something to the effect that constricting blood vessels stimulates various nerves such that (among other things) her brow furrows. Does pain screen off constricting blood vessels stimulating nerves, or vice versa?

The answer is not clear. Even though we are speaking of a particular instance of pain → wince, how to understand the explanation of that particular event depends on how we would generalize the wincing event. If we take the wince to be a token of some reaction to pain, then constricting blood vessels add nothing to the explanation, since there are other means by which to have a headache. On the other hand, if we take the wince to be a reaction to a muscle contraction, then pain adds nothing to the explanation, since head muscles can contract painlessly.[59]

To return to the example of Dora: Do conflicting desires screen off changes in the endorphin level, or vice versa? Again, the answer is not clear. Even though we are discussing a particular instance of conflicting desires → hysterical symptoms with Dora, how to understand the explanation of that particular event depends on how we would generalize the hysteria. If we take depression, the loss of voice, transient paralysis, and so on, to be tokens of some reaction to conflicting desires, then changes in brain endorphin levels add nothing to the explanation, since there are (presumably) other means by which to experience conflict. On the other hand, if we take depression, the loss of voice, transient paralysis, and so on, to be a reaction to changes in brain chemistry, then conflicting desires add nothing to the explanation, since brain chemistry can change without desires conflicting.

Which model to use in explanation does not admit to a principled answer. If we have a reductive bias, then we might be inclined to generalize over muscle contractions, nerve stimulations, and brain chemistry. On the other hand, if we lack that sort of bias, then we might be inclined to talk about pains, desires, and other sorts of mental events. And which sort of bias to have and what kind of generalizations are best cannot be decided a priori. It all depends on facts peculiar to the circumstance.[60]

Indeed, Freud is an interesting case to consider in this instance, since he began his career with a strong reductive bias and ended speaking mainly of mental causes. He started as a medical student searching for the substances that support mechanically conceived minds. As he realized that that project was simply too difficult for his time, he moved to other avenues of investigation, in particular, hypnosis and talking therapies. By the end of his career, he had all but given up on his original reductive project, though I don't believe that he ever thought seeking to understand the brain's causal powers was fundamentally in error.[61] But how Freud approached the study of the mind had less to do with which approaches he saw as correct prior to beginning investigation and experiment than with what was technologically feasible at that time, how he could support himself professionally, how he could help the most patients, and what others around him were focusing on.

So, I am not claiming that there is no way in which to make these sorts of decisions. Rather, how we decide to describe Terry's wincing event or Dora's hysteria depends on biases and preferences forged in the course of personal histories. It depends not only on which general questions we take ourselves to be answering, but also the context in which the questions arise, the audience with whom we are conversing, other answers that we have accepted to similar questions, technological and sociological limitations, and so on. Freud could successfully explain Dora's symptoms in terms of conflicting desires to her parents (and other interested laymen) as a respected psychoanalyst in upper-class Western society at the turn of the century. Today such explanations are a bit more difficult to run. Indeed, in the sociopoliticial context of Bush's Decade of the Brain, with its emphasis on pharmaceutical prophylactics, it would probably be much easier to account for Dora's behavior in terms of altered brain chemistry. Certainly, it would be much easier for a respected neuroscientist with the more sophisticated and invasive measuring devices available today to develop such an account.

Moreover, even though, say, psychologists and neuroscientists may have similar (sorts of) concerns regarding Terry or Dora, the answers that neuroscientists give to their questions may not be of much help to the psychologists, and vice versa. If one is attempting to teach Terry to control her pain using biofeedback, then knowing that firing C-fibers cause muscular contractions may not be useful information. On the other hand, if we are trying to control Terry's pain pharmachologically, then understanding the cause of the muscular contractions might be very relevant. Similarly, for psychoanalysts using a talking therapy, knowing that increased endorphin levels are correlated with hysteria and depression would be unhelpful data. However, for neuroscientists interested in the connection between brain chemistry and mood, postulating conflicting sexual desires would only confuse the issue.

I should stress that the uneasiness of fit between different explanatory models is endemic in cognitive science, and part of my project lies in articulating when and how the diverse models fit together as a single interdisciplinary theory. Obviously, I believe that they can, at least some of the time. The question is whether different models can cohere— despite there being huge differences in their respective explanatory aims—such that solid unitary theoretical frameworks emerge that can speak to the concerns of all the disciplines involved without straining.

The difficulty with this project lies in the pragmatics of explanation.[62] Psychology, neuroscience, and the other cognitive sciences operate in different contexts stemming from different historical developments, which leads to different investigative standards and methodologies, different canons of knowledge, and different central questions[63] so that what counts as an acceptable answer to similar sorts of questions will differ. We ask questions against a background of assumed facts and interests such that we want to know why N obtains instead of a particular alternative or set of alternatives (the contrast class). Explanations tell us *both* why N is the case and why the contrast class is false. The investigative context of a particular scientific domain determines which contrast class is relevant in posing the problem in the first place. Whether something counts as an explanation depends both on the audience the scientists are addressing and the background of the inquiry. In this way, explanations turn on a tertiary relation among possible theories, known and accepted data, and historical context.

So, then, if neuroscientific explanations are going to be true competitors to psychological ones, the contrast class for the two domains questions would have to correspond (this point is developed at length in chapters 5 and 7). But because psychology and neuroscience operate in such different academic environments, prima facie it is doubtful that they do. At least, we would need an argument that the contrast classes are importantly similar.

Ignoring the Realism/Antirealism Debate

How to explain something and what counts as a good explanation depend on a whole host of factors beyond the philosophical purview of this book. Much has been written on this topic in modern philosophy of science[64] and I certainly have nothing new to add here. Instead, let me focus on what my arguments are not designed to show by contrasting my position with other views. In this way, the move to reconceive the problem of mental causation in epistemic terms rather than metaphysical ones should be clearer, as well as the openendedness of this brand of scientific pragmatism. This should clear a path to a more detailed study of the levels of organization in the brain, which can then be used as a model for regimenting other hierarchies in cognitive science (e.g., the different levels of organization and analysis for individual and group dynamics in sociology or anthropology).

First, contra Dennett (1987, 1991), I need to emphasize that I adopt epistemological positions that have few metaphysical implications. That is, it is not the case that if we can legitimately and profitably generalize $c \rightarrow e$ in different ways, then there is no "deeper" fact of the matter (1991, p. 49). I agree that "there could be two different, but equally real, patterns discernible in the noisy world. The rival theorists would not even agree on which parts of the world are pattern and which are noise. . . . The choice of the pattern would indeed be up to the observer, a matter to be decided on idiosyncratic pragmatic grounds" (p. 49).[65] However, these sorts of disagreements carry no ontological weight such that there is an "issue to be settled" (p. 49). Given that our theories concern abstract physical systems, it is plausible—indeed, it is expected— that we might entertain fundamentally incompatible conceptions and explanations of the same event. Asking what grounds one might use to decide that issue confuses the epistemic project with a metaphysical one. The question of what is *really* out there (or whether there is anything out there at all) is no longer apropos.

One might question whether this sort of move of denial would not thereby commit me to *some* sort of skepticism about the ontological status of the mental.[66] I think that it does not (or at least that it doesn't in any interesting way). Whether any model involving mental causation actually corresponds to the world (and in a way such that we could know this) is just a question that recapitulates the realism/antirealism debate. Put in those terms, we can ask: Does a pragmatics of explanation thereby commit one to antirealism? I think not. Criteria for determining the truth of a theory or model operate independently of how the theories were forged. We believe a theory to be true, I presume, if it is explanatorily adequate, comports well with other accepted theories, is relatively simple, and so forth.[67] These issues are clearly separate from the pragmatic.

Suppose that we have two incompatible models of some set of events that entail incompatible properties or objects (even taking into account that models capture idealized and abstract physical systems). Obviously, at most, one of these could be true. If the pragmatics of explanation allows that both models are equally acceptable, perhaps it seems then that one cannot maintain a version of realism (even with a list of truth-conducive criteria) on pain of incoherence. However, in the remarkable event that both models are equally explanatory, comport equally well (or equally poorly) with other accepted models, and so on, all we should and can do is withhold believing that either model is true until something tips the balance in favor of one model over the other. But this particular position with respect to this particular case says nothing about whether one should be a realist or antirealist *tout court*.[68]

I notice in passing that quite often in science we deliberately use theories we know to be false (for pragmatic reasons). Though Einsteinian relativity has replaced Newtonian mechanics, Newton's "laws" are still used in solving elementary problems because they are simpler to use and get the job done well enough. It might be that, as Churchland (1981), Churchland (1986), Dennett (1987), and Stich (1983) seem to believe, our use of psychological explanations will turn out to be likewise prudential. These explanations are actually false, but we use them nonetheless because they are simpler and get the job done well enough. I have no idea whether they are right; time will surely tell. But regardless, eliminativist stories such as these cut no ice with the general issue of mental causation. Even if our *current* psychological explanations are incorrect, that says nothing about whether the replacement theories might not be true or about whether the new theories will quantify over mental states. Mental causation qua mental remains viable, even if we grant the eliminativists their arguments.

Second, claiming that there can only be pragmatic reasons for choosing one type of explanation over another keeps the playing field entirely open with respect to which sorts of reasons one might give for different sorts of behavior. Here I distinguish myself from Yablo (1992) and Dretske (1988), who both suggest that we use the mental level of explanation when we wish to distinguish meaningful behavior from mere molar bodily movements.[69] We can point to legitimate higher level explanations that invoke the mental (pain or desires) to explain "mere" bodily movements (a wince or paralysis), as well as to legitimate lower level explanations that use neurophysiological interactions (changes in endorphin levels) to explain "intentional behavior" (deliberately self-destructive activities). It is simply misguided to confine "mental" patterns to a single level of organization or allow them to be invoked in a single type of explanation. Our world is too rich and we are too clever to be so confined.

In other words, nothing I have said should restrict what counts as a mental (or cognitive) phenomenon, nor for when these phenomena are explanatory. The level of analysis for c may differ from that of e, and the level of analysis for the $c \rightarrow e$ link may be different still. Nevertheless, all may coexist in a single model for some abstract physical system designed to explain something putatively cognitive. This story about pragmatics in explanation, undetermined Goodmanian predicate projections, and multiple levels of analysis forms a basic explanatory pattern that I will repeatedly exploit throughout this book. Interdisciplinary theories will exhibit all of these characteristics, plus a few additional bells and whistles.

For now, though, we can say that we have arrived at a conception of mental causation in which mental properties are just as real as any other, but also in which we have the conceptual apparatus that allows us to decide when we should invoke those properties as explanatory, given our historical biases and investigative goals. In the course of developing this conception, we have moved from an ontological project (What is the mental?) to an epistemological one (When is it explanatory?). Nevertheless, we are still able to answer our original dilemma. The world is causally closed; the mental and the physical interact; however—despite considerations of supervenience and multiple realization—the mental and the physical are not distinct. The world is safe for a truly cognitive, but well-grounded, cognitive science.

Chapter 3

Hierarchies in the Brain

> [B]iologists are currently confronted by a... dilemma: If they insist on formulating... theory in terms of commonsense entities, the resulting laws are likely to remain extremely variable and complicated; if they want simple laws, equally applicable to all entities of a particular sort, they must abandon their traditional ontology. This reconceptualization... is certainly counterintuitive; its only justification is the increased scope, consistency, and power that results.[1]

I have been acting as though there are only two important levels of organization for cognitive science, the mind and the brain. This, however, is only an act. Certainly there is a great diversity of important levels of organization above the individual mind for explaining cognitive activity. Indeed, explaining the very existence of the hysterical symptoms so prevelant in turn-of-the-century Austria may require modeling communities of individuals.

I have always found it quite curious that the symptoms Freud became so famous for treating are almost nonexistent today. Only in the most extreme cases of abuse do we find individuals who lose their ability to speak or suffer from transcient paralysis. One hundred years ago, however, those symptoms were much more common. How can we account for this change? It is doubtful that the late nineteenth or early twentieth century was so much more unhealthy. Instead, it is much more likely that social conventions that govern how we express pain and outrage have changed.[2] Perhaps, to give a complete explanation of Dora's hysteria, we would also have to investigate her social community, in which individual actors and their structures form the basic unit of analysis. This higher level of analysis could then complement a Freudian analysis (more on this perspective in chapters 6 and 7).

And just as there are important explanatory levels of analysis above the individual, there are also many important levels within the brain. This chapter focuses on those levels and their relationship to one another. In particular, I aim to clear some conceptual ground in speaking about hierarchies in the brain, and in hierarchies in explanation in general. Though this chapter focuses on various intricacies in neurophysiology and neuroethology (both of which I think are importantly relevant for cognitive science), I believe that what I have to say can be generalized to speak about hierarchies found throughout cognitive science, all the way up to the structure and interaction of communities of cognizers. The orientation of this chapter merely reflects my own bias about where I think the meat of cognitive science is. At the end I try to set my own biases aside and speak a bit about how all the domains within cognitive science fit together. In any event, you should take my discussion of neuroscience as an extended example of how hierarchical theories work in all of the cognitive sciences. Some of the biological examples may get a bit technical for the novice, but I believe my general points should be clear and easily extractable from the details.

The Neuron

Historical and technological biases lead us to see the neuron as the central player in the brain. Historically speaking, this position was self-consciously adopted by practicing neuroscientists after significant debate. In the late nineteenth century, Cajal argued that neurons form the basic processing unit in the central nervous system against Golgi, who maintained that neurons formed a continuous "reticulum." In the end, Cajal's camp prevailed, and since that time, it has been assumed (more or less without question) that neurons qua individual cells, and the signals that pass among them, are the fundamental units of currency in brain communication.[3]

Technologically speaking, we have developed research techniques for studying single cells or small localized groups of neurons (patch clamps, single unit recordings, local field potentials, and various optical dyes) and for studying large areas of the brain (MFG, ERP, PET, lesions, microlesions, 2-deoxyglucose, and light microscopy), but we have few reliable ways to record brain activity at the "middle" level of organization. (See figure 3.1.) As a result, we know a great deal about how single neurons work and how the brain as a whole functions, but we have very little idea what the important properties of networks of neurons are and what these networks actually do.[4] These two contingencies constrain the way in which we think about the brain today. We see the brain as a mass of individual neurons. To be sure, we do see them as hierarchically arranged in larger structures, but the neurons and their firing properties are what most neuroscientific theories have historically centered on.

However, the level of the network in the brain is becoming extremely important, since it now appears that this middle level of organization may be *the* fundamental level for explaining cognition.[5] That is, our cognitive states and subsequent behavior seem to turn on patterns of neuronal firing activation across large numbers of individual cells. Nevertheless, we know very little about how to describe or investigate this level fruitfully.

Figure 3.1 *Spatial and Temporal Resolution of Techniques for Studying Brain Function*

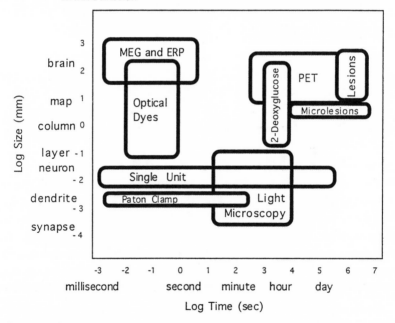

Schematic illustration of the ranges of spatial and temporal resolution of various physiological techniques for studying the function of the brain. The vertical axis represents the spatial extent of the technique, with the boundaries indicating the largest and smallest sizes of the region from which the technique can provide useful information. The horizontal axis represents the minimum and maximum time interval over which information can be collected with the technique (from Sejnowski and Churchland 1988, reprinted with kind permission of the publisher).

On the other hand, this deficit raises many interesting philosophical questions concerning how to identify the explanatorily relevant levels of organization among the many neuronal and informational hierarchies in the mind/brain. How exactly do we identify the hierarchical levels in the brain? Of the levels that we do identify, how do we determine which is the one, or which is the set, to study with respect to explaining any particular phenomenon? As a beginning in addressing these issues, this chapter explicates more precisely the types of hierarchies found in neuroscientific ontologies and their connections to questions of causality in scientific explanation. Hence, this chapter explores in greater detail many of the issues raised in the last chapter. I begin, however, by suggesting what this discussion is not by comparing my forthcoming discussion with certain metaphysical issues in philosophy of psychology.

The Methodological Individualism/Anti-Individualism Debate

The issue of methodological individualism or methodological solipsism versus a more holistic approach is a well-known and well-developed debate in the philosophy of psychology.[6] It also has counterparts in the philosophy of social science[7] and in the philosophy of biology.[8] A proper understanding of the general framework of this debate will provide a useful scaffolding for investigating how we are to understand the various hierarchies in the brain.

In essence, individualists and anti-individualists disagree over whether a whole is greater than the sum of its parts. Individualists say that it is not; anti-individualists say that it is. For example, in the philosophy of psychology, the individualists maintain that all we need to know in order to understand human cognition are the functional or causal relations among the stimuli inputs, the behavioral outputs, and the intervening mental states. The environment or context in which the thinker is located is irrelevant. The individualist holds that the cognitive economy of a person is determined solely by the sum of the mental states and their internal relations. The anti-individualist, on the other hand, believes that the environment or context is extremely important because it is what helps define the content of an organisms' mental states. Anti-individualists maintain that the cognitive economy of any individual is at least partially defined by the linguistic community in which that person is embedded. In this case, the whole of the individual's representations is greater than just their relations to one another and to proximate input stimuli and behavioral outputs.

However, this dispute (in part) turns on how philosophers understand "whole."[9] Psychological anti-individualists argue that mental events cannot be understood in isolation from one another; to be explicated properly, their relations to the environmental context as well as to each other must be included. What they mean when they say that the whole is more than the sum of its parts is that properties of the whole are not determined by local causal relations alone. In particular, distal environmental contributions are of upmost importance. However, psychological individualists agree with the anti-individualists that mental events cannot be understood in isolation from one another and that their character is fixed by their relations—yet they still insist that the whole in nothing more than the relations of these parts. The individualists accuse the anti-individualists of claiming that mental events are determined by *more* than the (immediate) interactions that individuals have with the environment. Anti-individualism then seems to amount to some sort of antireductionistic emergentism in which one must add some sort of supracausal elán vital to a set of brain states in order to get true mental representations.[10] And anti-individualists attack individualists on converse grounds; they claim that by denying a richer environmental context, the individualists are no better than rabid eliminativists.

I think that the appropriate response to this debate (at least for our purposes) is exactly the one Elliot Sober musters.[11] He points out that, in one sense, the whole is more than the sum of its parts, but in another sense, it is not. What makes the whole what it is—what makes a cognitive economy a specific unified set of mental representations—does turn on relational properties. In that sense, we might say that the whole is more than a mere aggregate of mental states. But at the same time, we must also realize that what makes the whole what it is is nothing added to the collection of parts above and beyond their relations to other things. In this sense, the whole is nothing greater than the collection of parts and their properties. Neither hypostasis nor an eliminativist approach need be correct; the anti-individualists and individualists are talking at cross purposes. Nevertheless, we can say without controversy that connections among the parts are important. Just *which* connections are the most important, though, should be a matter decided as empirical research develops—it is not for a priori philosophical speculation.[12]

This sort of debate (or nondebate) in philosophy can be easily and usefully translated into a discussion of how to determine the general methodological stance appropriate to studying of the brain, or any other complex object in cognitive science. Obviously, a purely atomistic approach of investigating isolated neurons exclusively is not likely to tell us how the brain as a whole works. We do know enough about the brain to know that how neurons are connected to one another is crucial. In this sense, the brain is greater than the simple sum of its parts. But to reify the higher levels beyond simply being higher levels of organization of the brain seems the mistake the emergentists made in the twenties.[13] At bottom, all the brain can be is a collection of neurons and their relations to things in the world. In that sense, the brain can be nothing more than the sum of its parts. So, the atomism/emergentism debate in neuroscience parallels the individualism/anti-individualism debate in psychology, only it runs along a vertical axis of increasingly higher levels of complexity over the same event space, instead of the more "horizontal" plane of the appropriate size for the event space in cognitive psychology.[14]

As I have presented them, these debates as metaphysical issues essentially disappear for both psychology and neuroscience. Dissolving this debate for neuroscience (and for any other "vertical" arrangement) amounts to claiming (again) that causality is "transitive." As I argued in chapter 2, whatever happens in the brain can be nothing more than the interactions of neuronal circuits, and whatever happens at the network level can be nothing more than the interactions of neurons, and whatever happens at the neuronal level can be nothing more than the interactions of molecules, and so on down. However, just as in chapter 2, it is not clear what sort of weight one should assign to the higher levels of organization in the brain, just as it is not clear where to draw the environmental boundary around psychological entities in accounting for mental states.

In general (and following Sober 1984, pp. 185–187), there are three sorts of epistemological difficulties remaining once the metaphysical dimensions of the problem are dismissed.[15] The first is methodological: What would be the most fruitful research strategy to understand the particular phenomenon in question? That is, which level or levels of organization are the appropriate ones to analyze in order to best explain the phenomenon? For example, neuroscientists discuss and explain the prefrontal cortex of higher mammals using several different levels of analysis and organization. At the highest level, they discuss the general function of the brain area based on evidence from gross brain lesions. To wit: the prefrontal cortex arranges goal-directed behavior since lesions to the prefrontal cortex impair goal-oriented reasoning, prevent using relevant memories to plan forthcoming projects, and allow inappropriate behaviors and improper social responses to continue. Most telling is that prefrontal lesions interfere with a patient's ability to perform tasks that depend on the capacity to recall an object after a few seconds' delay.[16]

But the neural underpinnings for the delayed-response task can be discussed more specifically in terms of particular brain regions within the lobe. Local lesions studies in the macaque and rhesus monkeys suggest that the "delayed-response" function can be located in a particular subdivision of the prefrontal cortex.[17] Moreover, we can discuss the delayed-response deficit at a lower level still, for a number of the specialized neurons fire only during the "memory" period of a delayed-response task.[18] These neurons first respond with the target stimulus, then continue to fire when the stimulus is no longer present, and finally, stop being active once the animal has to execute some behavioral response.[19] Furthermore, these neurons only fire during the memory phase when remembering the stimulus is required for completing the task. Presumably, even lower levels of analysis and organization are still possible.

Which of these levels of analysis is the appropriate one for explicating frontal lobe function, or does the explanation require several? How much detail is actually required? What is the correct explanatory story, and at which level of organization do we wish to privilege the causal interactions such that we say those causal interactions are necessary and sufficient ones? As discussed in the previous chapter, these are the sorts of epistemological questions we need to face before we can devise profitable strategies for research.

Second, there is the question of complexity: how much of the interaction of the parts is needed to explain the phenomenon successfully? For "vertical" relations, this is a question of the manner in which the parts are related across and within levels, not a question of reducibility per se.[20] To illustrate with a particular case, let me briefly mention the controversy surrounding theories of processing in the visual stream. Hubel and Weisel (1977) discovered what they called "simple" and "complex" cells in area 17 of the visual cortex. Simple cells have excitatory and inhibitory zones that respond to bars of light at a particular orientation; complex cells also respond to bars of light at a particular orientation, but do not have the excitatory and inhibitory zones. Since their discovery, there has been much discussion within neuroscience about how visual processing in cortex works. Some argued that as one traveled up the pathways of visual processing, the cells responded to more and more sophisticated and abstract stimuli until at the top there were cells that only responded to complete percepts (the so-called grandmother cells). If this were true, then in order to understand visual processing, all we would have to do would be to trace the feed-forward pathway of the cells and map their response properties. Others have favored more distributed representations, claiming that whatever these cells were actually doing, we have to look at all their connections—feed-forward and feed-back—to understand their processing task.[21]

Questions that we need to answer before we can claim a complete explanation is given include: How are the feed-forward and the feedback connections related? Do there then exist higher level patterns that can account for the behavior of the individual neurons or groups of neurons? Which of these connections or patterns should be privileged in explanation? All of these questions revolve around the complexity of the mechanisms necessary and sufficient for visual perception and how best to describe that complexity.

Finally, there is the need to distinguish type from token. It may be the case that we would use a causal-etiological story at a particular level of organization to explain individual instances of some phenomena, but then to explain the phenomena in general, we would use a different tactic at perhaps a different level. Consider, for instance, discussions of the connection between the lateralization of language and consciousness in the brain. Our capacity for language is generally thought to reside in the left hemisphere (for normal right-handed individuals) and it is hypothesized that language may be necessary for conscious experience. So if we could separate the left from the right hemisphere, the hemisphere nondominant for language might lose its connection to conscious thought (if it had any to begin with),[22] and by comparing and contrasting behavior elicited by each hemisphere, perhaps we could decide in which hemisphere consciousness is located. If language is in fact necessary for qualitative experience, then we should discover that the left hemisphere is the seat of consciousness.

As a general framework, this rather crude and high level mode of discussion of gross brain areas seems adequate. However, if we want to investigate this hypothesis by looking at individuals, then the simple but neat picture gets more complicated. On an individual level, it seems that a good way to investigate this problem would be to study hemispherectomies.[23, 24] However, developmental plasticity and individual differences remove any statistical significance of differential processing between hemispheres when considering people who only have one hemisphere.[25] Furthermore, there do exist patients with only a right hemisphere who, for all intents and purposes, have command of a language and appear conscious. In sum, the tactics involved in discussing individual instances of linguistic capacity and conscious awareness would seem to diverge rather substantially from how we might wish to discuss them as general phenomena (even though we have yet no complete explanation for either the connection between linguistic competence and consciousness in general or for the connection in particular individuals).

How to approach answering these sorts of questions in a principled manner is the topic of the remaining sections in this chapter. First I shall explore the types of hierarchies one might find in the brain, for to say that the brain (or any other object) simply has a hierarchical organization does not say enough. After suggesting what I take to be the correct way to understand the hierarchical arrangement of the central nervous system, I shall then turn to the issue of privileged causality in explanation, similar to the questions raised in the last chapter. I aim to answer the question, How do we know which *level of organization* is the appropriate one to investigate such that it should give us an explanation of the phenomenon in question? (This contrasts with the question of the last chapter: How do we know which *generalization* at a particular level is the appropriate one to make such that it gives us the best explanation? Not surprisingly, these questions [as is the question of chapter 4] are intimately related.)

Hierarchies in Neuroscience

What are hierarchies? Eldredge claims that they "convey the notion of rank—a series of levels" (1985, p. 140). Perhaps the most obvious (and most widely used) example is a chain of command. In a university, for example, the president operates at the apex of the organizational structure and at the highest level of power; under him fall the vice presidents, provosts, deans, associate deans, and so on down to the general staff. Each rank has dominion over those below it and the power structure determines the organization of the system. These sorts of hierarchies are *exclusive* in that the members at one level do not compose members or are parts of members at another level; each individual at each level is ontologically distinct from all the other individuals.[26]

Prima facie, exclusive hierarchies are not the sort we should find in the brain. It seems quite obvious that any higher level of order found in the brain will be composed of some arrangement of things at a lower level. In this case, the hierarchies we should consider should be *inclusive* ones (though this story too gets more complicated, as I explain below). These are hierarchies like the modern ordering of taxa: men are primates and primates are mammals and mammals are vertebrates and so on. But to say a hierarchy is an inclusive one does not narrow our discussion enough, for in the literature, there are at least four different types of inclusive hierarchy: constitutive, aggregational, embedded, and control.[27]

A constitutive versus an aggregational hierarchy is a distinction drawn by Mayr.[28] A constitutive hierarchy is the same thing as a "structural" hierarchy in which "members of a lower level . . . are confined into units . . . that have unitary functions and emergent properties" (Mayr 1982, p. 65). The smaller things are contained serially in progressively larger things, and this containment makes them what they are. So, we can think of the atom, macromolecule, organelle, neuron, lobe, brain, and so forth, as one instance of a constitutive hierarchy. The emergence theories of the twenties also would fit this definition.

Mayr opposes a constitutive hierarchy to an aggregational one, a hierarchy arranged by mere convenience: "Units at the lower level . . . are not compounded by any interaction into emerging higher level units as a whole" (Mayr 1982, pp. 65–66). Boxes of Christmas ornaments in the basement are one example of an aggregational hierarchy; so are galaxies. The smaller boxes in the basement are not what they are in virtue of being contained by the larger boxes; and stars do not receive their defining properties in virtue of being contained in certain galaxies (though being a member of a particular galaxy may help us pick them out in the sky). Though both constitutive and aggregational hierarchies constitute part-whole relations, the aggregational arrangement of convenience contrasts with constitutive hierarchies just in that the structure of constitutive hierarchy determines the function and properties of the higher levels.

Crosscutting this distinction is the distinction between hierarchies of embedment and hierarchies of control.[29] A hierarchy of embedment resembles a set of nested boxes (Marjorie Grene's analogy) that yield a classification. Grene uses Patterson's (1980) discussion of cladograms as her example of what this sort of hierarchy looks like. (See figure 3.2.) If we think of the cladogram as shorthand for a hierarchy of homologies, then we have more than simply a branching series (as it might appear to the uninitiated) but rather it is a set of nested boxes that classify features and organisms. Patterson explains how cladograms work:

1. Features shared by organisms (homologies) manifest a hierarchical pattern in nature.

2. Their hierarchical pattern is economically expressed in branching diagrams, or cladograms.

3. The nodes in cladograms symbolize the homologies shared by the organisms grouped by the node, so that a cladogram is

Figure 3.2

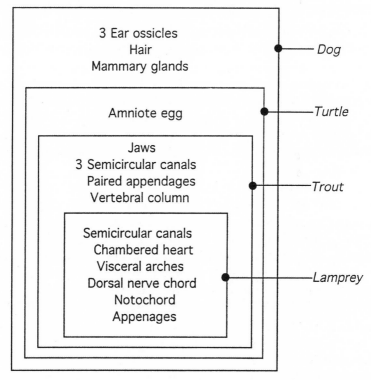

Five kinds of vertebrates are defined by one or more characteristics in the upper levels of the diagram which are considered evolutionary novelties. A cladogram thus rewritten illustrates the combination of a hierarchy of classification with an evolutionary hierarchy (adapted from Grene 1987).

synonymous with a classification. (1980, p. 110, as quoted in Grene 1988, p. 5)

However, as Grene remarks, "the synapomorphy is so interpretable only when the boxes are drawn around the branches" (1988, p. 5); in this case, the hierarchy is richer than simply a set of branchings: it is, as she puts is, a nest of Chinese boxes.[30]

Grene contrasts this sort of hierarchy with hierarchies of control. In a hierarchy of control, the upper level is "narrower;" it is an aggregate of elements that obey the dynamical laws for their levels but are nonetheless constrained by some arrangement that determines their functions and properties.[31] These hierarchies are opposed to sets of Chinese boxes, or hierarchies of embedment, in that the higher level limits the possibilities and the lower level sets bounds within which the upper can operate. For example, we are more than our skin, but control actually runs in the opposite direction.

This view entails that we would not be able to explicate the higher level solely on the basis of the laws of the lower level, for the higher level has its own set of defining properties. Using Keith Thompson's (1986) example, we say that tissue is smooth or rough, but its constituent cells are not. Therefore smoothness is a property that only appears at the tissue level.[32] Clearly, this is an antireductionist view, though one would not want to say that there are no important connections between the levels of organization. After all, the smooth or rough tissue is but made up of cells.

Grene likens a hierarchy of control to Aristotle's distinction between form and matter (which parallels his distinction between species and genus). "Footed animals ... can have two or four or six or eight feet. Footy matter, so to speak, can be shaped in more than one way. The form ... constrains the matter ... which has been organized in *one way or another*" (Grene 1988, p. 8). Form is identical to one arrangement of matter, and it is the arrangement of the matter that produces a novel system that then follows its own particular laws.

A more contemporary instance would be Pattee's example of DNA.[33] The four bases only form a genetic code when arranged in a few particular ways, though there are an infinite number of different ways that they could be arranged. Nonetheless a few special arrangements create a system able to convey information and carry out operations that most of the arrangements of the bases would be unable to do. In this type of hierarchy we can see that the higher level, the level of form, is "narrower," and the lower level, the level of the individual bases, has available many more instances or choices. A genetic code is an arrangement from many possible; it is just one that happens to work.

Notice though that with this type of hierarchy, the seemingly simple inclusion/exclusion distinction of Mayr breaks down. There is no obvious sense in which you would want to say that the higher level is contained in the lower; nor is the lower included in the higher, for arranged just so, they just *are* the higher level. That is why we want to say that Aristotle's form cannot exist except as an arrangement of the matter. And hence, it cannot be a classificatory system either; in this way, it is opposed to a hierarchy of embedment. But at the same time we do not want to say that it is an exclusive system, for formal patterns are not ontologically distinct from their instantiations. (This too is the point of chapter 2.) A higher level pattern is just one arrangement of the underlying stuff, but a president is not just one arrangement of a set of deans. And yet we still want to maintain some sort of nonreductionist stance (more on this issue in chapter 5). Life depends on *information*—the particular arrangement of the bases such that they form a *code*. Life is not simply an aggregate of macromolecules, for the *relations* among the bases are important.

The important point that Grene makes, and one that actually forestalls any reductionism, is that in hierarchies of control, information flows both vertically and horizontally. These are dynamical, multidirectional systems in which disregarding any of the neighboring levels excludes a complete explanation of a certain phenomenon localized to a particular level of organization. This horizontal and vertical flow of information is what makes the system of hierarchical control an "integrated, working whole" (Grene 1987, p. 505).

We now have three candidates for the type of hierarchical organization that might exist in the brain: constitutive hierarchy, a hierarchy of embedment, and a hierarchy of control. (I take it as obvious that we would not want to consider the aggregational hierarchy as a plausible alternative since that is simply an arrangement of convenience and the brain does exhibit more structure than stuff in a basement.) Constitutive hierarchies and hierarchies of embedment can be very similar. They both entail that the members at a higher level of organization are "broader" or more inclusive than the lower levels of organization. Though constitutive hierarchies are explicitly nonreductionistic and hierarchies of embedment could be reduced, they both explicate higher level units in terms of interactions of the members of the lower level—

the direction runs upwards, not downwards. Hierarchies of control work in an exactly opposite fashion. A higher level is more restricted than a lower level and the higher levels set limits on what the lower levels can do. Here control runs downward and the explication of the system is bidirectional. How do hierarchies in the brain work?

Interestingly enough, we actually find instances of all three hierarchies in neuroscientific descriptions. "Material" descriptions of CNS anatomy are often constitutive. Consider, for example, how the neostriatum is described.[34] (See figure 3.3.) The major components of the neostriatum are two large subcortical nuclei; the caudate and the putamen. These nuclei in turn are connected to the globus palladus, which projects to the subthalamic nuclei and the substantia nigra. In higher animals, the caudate nucleus and the putamen are structurally very similar and are separated by an internal bundle of neurons from the cortex to periphery (the "capsule"). (In lower animals they are essentially one and the same structure.) These nuclei serve as the input component of the basal ganglia. They receive input from mainly the cerebral cortex, the intralaminer nucleus of the thalamus, and the substantia nigra. The most important of these is the corticostriate projections. The entire cerebral cortex, including the motor, sensory, and associative cortices,

Figure 3.3

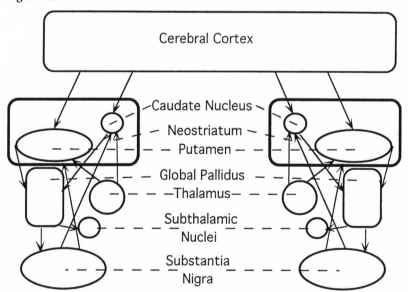

This schematic of a coronal section of the brain shows the nuclei of the neostriatum in relation to surrounding structures.

projects to the neostriatum. This projection is topographic so that particular areas of neocortex project to particular areas in the neostriatum. (There is overlap in the various terminations though.) The second projection, that from the intralaminer nucleus of the thalamus, terminates mainly in the putamen. The third major input, also topographically organized, is a dopaminergic projection from the pars compactor of the substantia nigra. Other minor inputs include projections from the amygdala, the raphe nuclei, and the hypothalamus.

The neostriatum then projects to the globus palladus whose entire output is to the subthalamic nucleus, which in turn projects to other parts of the globus palladus, and to the substantia nigra pars reticulata. (These segments provide the major outputs of the basal ganglia, which project to the ventral lateral and the ventral anterior thalamic nuclei, which in turn project to the prefrontal and premotor cortices.)

Ninety-five percent of the cells in the neostriatum are of one morphological class, the common spiney cell. They are inhibitory output neurons. The other efferent neurons, composing less than 1 percent of the neostriatum, are the spiney type II cells. (The remaining 4 percent are composed of three interneurons, aspiney I, II, and III.) Spines are present only on the dendrite in the common spiney cell and start approximately 20 microns away from the cell body. Each cell has about the same density of spines on all of its dendrites. Spiney type II cells have spines also on their body, but have a fewer total number of spines. These spines are used as sites for synaptic input to the neurons.

Notice the following three features of this description. First, the lower level of spiney cells as discussed in the paragraph above are confined into units; that is, they are what make up the neostriatum in just the same way that macromolecules make up organelles. Second, there are several clear hierarchical relations of constitution, viz., cells organized into nuclei, nuclei organized into areas, and areas organized into systems. Third, we can find a version of emergent properties; the properties of a spiney cell (e.g., is inhibitory) do not easily translate into the properties of the caudate or the putamen (e.g., receive inputs mainly from the cerebral cortex). These features represent the three defining properties of Mayr's constitutive hierarchies.

In contrast, "informational" descriptions of neurophysiology are presented as embedded hierarchies. Returning to the example of the neostriatum, we can see that the type of description of its function differs from a purely anatomical analysis in that physiological descriptions are classificatory instead of constitutive. The neostriatum is (in part) responsible for voluntary motor movement. We can think of essentially the entire neocortex as speaking to the motor cortex through the neostriatum. In particular, because each spiney cell requires many simultaneous inputs to its various spines to fire so that an action potential depends heavily on temporal and spatial synchronization, it is hypothesized that the neostriatum as whole uses a temporal code in which coincidence of events is most important to maintain its control.

There are essentially two rules that the neostriatum follows to ensure the necessary coherent timing. The first relates to topography (spatial distribution). The terminal fields in the caudate nucleus and the putamen more or less replicate the input fields of the neocortex. And topographic overlap in the neostriatum determines how much input each cell receives from the cerebral cortex. The second rule is that reciprocally interrelated cortical cells project to each other's spots within the neocortex. Hence, the cells receive overlapping input.

Since the neostriatum has an extensive collateral axon network, the lateral inhibitory network makes the neostriatum especially responsive to contrast. As suggested by other networks, these cells may be inhibiting their neighbors in order to enhance their own signal. Nevertheless, the question remains concerning exactly *what* the neostriatum relays. (Whatever its particular duty, it is at the least a very distributed network for some processing function.) One suggestion is that it relays the force component of ballistic movement. (If so, then the neostriatum would require no feedback loops from the motor cortex, and it in fact has none.)

An embedded hierarchy makes a nested classification. Physiological descriptions of the neostriatum do so as well. Each level of organization and its broad purpose are defined by the hierarchical description. For example, at the higher level of brain area, physiology has narrowed the neostriatum's function to one—motor control—in virtue of its connections to other regions in the brain. Again, at the lower level of individual cells, scientists classify the spiney cells' function via their relation to the nuclei. At a lower level still, we can discuss whether an individual cell fires, and whether it does depends on the timing of many inputs, which are determined by the spatial distribution and the receptive fields of the contributing cells. And so on, with each description serving to classify the function or behavior of the various parts of the brain through relation to its place in a hierarchy.

But the most important type of description for neuroscientific explanations— those that describe the relation between the material and the information it carries— reflect hierarchies of control. I offer

Heiligenberg's description of the jamming avoidance response in the gymnotid fish as evidence.[35] I chose this example because it is widely regarded as one of the most complete neuroethological accounts of animal information processing to date. I suppose one may dispute whether electric fish are truly cognitive, but I still take his research to present an exemplar of the *type* of model one would like to have of a thinking brain.

The jamming avoidance response (JAR) is a shift in an animal's electric organ discharge (EOD) frequency away from that of a neighbor's. Such a move decreases interference in electrolocation from the EOD of other nearby animals with a similar discharge frequency. Interestingly enough, for the JAR, gymnotid fish calculate the frequency difference between their EOD's and their neighbors', and its sign, without reference to their own electric organ pacemakers; that is, they solve the JAR problem on the basis of sensory input alone.

Speaking generally, the JAR works as follows. The fish's own signal mixes with a neighbor's similar frequency to produce a nearly sinusoidal signal whose instantaneous amplitude |S| (measured at the peak of the signal in each cycle) and instantaneous phase H (measured as the difference in timings of the zerocrossings of the two frequencies) vary at a rate equal to the difference frequency Df. If we plot |S| versus H on a Cartesian graph, the sequence of points forms a circle. (See figure 3.4.) This circle rotates counterclockwise with positive Df's and clockwise for negative, while the rate of rotation corresponds to the magnitude of Df. By "reading" the direction and rate of rotation, the fish determines how it must shift its own EOD frequency to avoid that of its neighbor's. A counterclockwise rotation means a downward shift; a clockwise rotation, an upward shift.

To evaluate these differences in phase, the fish compares the timing of zerocrossings in different parts of its body surface. If two areas receive inputs "contaminated" to different degrees from the neighbor's signal, then the fish can determine the sign of Df unambiguously. And as long as the animal's own signal outweighs its neighbor's in a sufficiently large area of body surface, pair-wise comparisons will always yield a net input of the correct sign to the pacemaker. Electric fish compare any two areas of their body surface in this way, and some large set of pair-wise evaluations control the JAR in a distributed, democratic manner.

More specifically, the fish has two types of tuberous electroreceptors, T-units and P-units, scattered over its surface. T-units are phase-locked to the timing of the zerocrossing of the signal, firing one spike on each EOD cycle, so the difference in timing of the T-unit spikes from

Figure 3.4

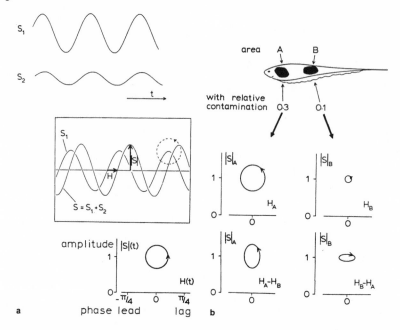

Figure 3.4a The addition of two sine waves, S_1 mimicking the animal's electric organ discharge and S_2 of similar frequency and smaller amplitude, mimicking the electric organ discharge of a neighbor. The center shows an oscilloscope display triggered by S so that S_1 appear stationary. Simultaneous display of the added signals, $S_1 + S_2$ yields a nearly sinusoidal signal whose momentary amplitude |S| and phase H, relative to S_1 as indicated by the dashed circle. The graph at the bottom shows a Lissajous Figure display of |S| versus H in a two-dimensional state plane. The nearly circular graph rotates in the counterclockwise sense for positive Dfs and in the clockwise for negative Dfs, and the rate of rotation is the absolute value of Df. The mean value of |S| is the amplitutde of S_1 which is considered unity. The mean value of H is zero which corresponds to the timing of the positive zero-crossing of S1. A positive H implies that $S_1 + S_2$ lags with respect to S_1. 2π denotes the period of the S_1 cycle, which is 2 ms if f_1 is 500 Hz.

Figure 3.4b Information about phase can be obtained by comparing areas of body surface with different amplitude ratios between the interfering signals, S_1 and S_2. Let the animal's electric organ discharge or its substitute, S_1 in areas A and B be contaminated by the foreign signal S2, by 30% and 10%, respectively. The stimulus modulation graphs, |S|$_A$ versus H_A and |S|$_B$ versus H_B have radii equal to the local amplitude ratios between S_2 and S_1 and rotate synchronously and in the counterclockwise sense for positive difference frequencies (Dfs). By replacing the local phase modulations, H_A and H_B by the differential phase modulations, $H_A - H_B$ and $H_B - H_A$, elliptical graphs with opposite senses of rotation are obtained. While area A thus decelerates the pacemaker, area B accelerates the pacemaker, in accordance witih the positive sign of the difference frequency Df. Note that the animal has no access to either H_A or H_B alone, but that it can only evaluate differences between such phase values by comparing the arrival times of spikes from T-type receptors (from Heiligenberg and Rose 1985, reprinted with kind permission of the publisher and Dr. Gary Rose).

two areas of the body surface reflect differential phase. P-units fire inter-mittently, and their rate of firing reflects the local amplitude of the sig-nal. Afferents from both types of units project primarily to three soma-topically structured maps of the electrosensory lateral line lobe (ELLL) of the hindbrain.

The afferents from T-units mainly converge on the spherical cells in the ELLL, forming electrotonic synapses. The spherical cells fire one spike per EOD cycle, which reflects the mean arrival time of the T-unit spikes within the receptive field of the cell. (Because of this averaging, the spher-ical cells record the timing of the zerocrossings with even less jitter than the T-unit receptor afferents.) The spherical cells of the ELLL then project to lamina 6 of the torus semicircularis of the midbrain, which contains a single map of the fish's electrosensory body surface. Here differences in timing of the zerocrossings across the body surface are computed. The circuitry in lamina 6 reflects apparently random comparisons of phase references between sets of two points from the body surface. It thus codes the differential phase between the two points by comparing a "local" phase with some "arbitrarily" chosen "reference" phase.

The main afferents of the P-units, on the other hand, form excita-tory synapses on the basiler pyramidal cells (E-units) of the ELLL—which are excited by a rise in amplitude within their receptive field—and on granule cells—which inhibit the nonbasiler pyramidal cells (I-units). (I-units then are excited by a decrease in amplitude within their receptive fields.) Both E-units and I-units project in somatotopic order to laminae 3, 5, 7, and 8 of the torus semicircularis. (They also send col-laterals to the nucleus praeminentialis of the midbrain, which is the basis of a recurrent, descending input back to the ELLL and serves as a gain control for the amplitude-coding system there.) Vertical interac-tions among the laminae integrate the phase and amplitude informa-tion in a spatial map. It allows for simultaneous evaluation of spatially related patterns of amplitude and phase change within the local neu-ronal circuits of the torus. (See figure 3.5.)

Some of the cells from the laminae project topographically to the tectum. Hence, more spatial computations of the phase and amplitude information can be carried out there. Presumably, the tectum combines (through 'and'-gating) inputs from the amplitude-sensitive neurons with those of the phase-sensitive neurons in order to discriminate the direction of rotation. The crucial point to note is that one phase input must come from the same area in the body surface that provides ampli-tude information, while the other phase input (the reference point) can come from anywhere else. From there, the exact route to the pacemaker in the medulla is still unknown.

The JAR is a highly distributed process. That is, there are no "control" neurons that individually beget particular behavioral responses.

Figure 3.5

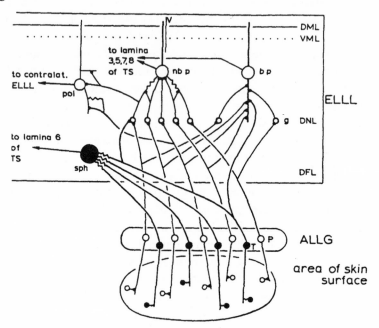

The synaptic organization of P- and T-type electroreceptive primary afferents in the electrosensory laterline lobe (ELLL). T-type afferents form electrical synapses upon spherical cells (sph), which in turn project to lamina 6 of the torus. In addition, collaterals of T-afferent synapse on targets originally assumed to be solely contacted by P-type afferents. P-type afferents form excitatory chemical synapses upon granule cells (g) and upon basilar dendrites of basilar phyramidal cells (bp). Basilar pyramidal cells also receive inhibitory input from more distant granule cells, which in turn are excited by P-inputs from the periphery of the receptive field. Nonbasilar pyramidal cells (nbp) on the other hand receive inhibitory input form nearest granule cells and electrical synapses from more distant granule cells, with the latter inputs bein inhibited by more centrally located granule cells. Both types of pyramidal cells project to laminae 3, 5, 7, and 8 of the torus. Within the dorsal and ventral molecular lays (DML and VML) the dorsal dendrites of pyramidal cells are contacted by parallel and vertical (V) fibers which originate in the lobus caudalis of the cerebellum and in the nucleus praeeminentialis and provide descending recurrent electrosensory inputs. Polymorphic cells (pol) receive P-afferent input and project to the contralateral ELLL. ALLG is the anterior lateral line nerve ganglion which houses the somata of primary afferents (from Heiligenberg and Rose 1985, reprinted with kind permission of the publisher and Dr. Gary Rose).

Rather, the representations of many and various sites on the body surface cumulatively contribute to the JAR frequency shift. Hence, the JAR is an example of a true biological democracy, not a "pontifical cell" oligarchy. And because of the distributed nature of the process, we cannot predict or explain the JAR on the basis of individual cells alone—we need to know how they interact, and more importantly, we need to know the type of cumulative pattern they produce.

Notice that this pattern is but just one way in which the cells could have fired, since the pattern reflects averaging over a large number of firing cells. Moreover, it is the information carried in any particular pattern that is so important, for that determines how the fish "reads" its electrical discharge with respect to others and how the fish subsequently behaves. Hence, we should say that the hierarchy discussed here is one of control. Actual control of the behavior is determined by the patterns, and the contribution of any single neuron could be eliminated without changing the resultant behavior. As Grene suggests, in these sorts of hierarchies, the direction of control is downward, though the explication of the system is bidirectional.

Let us focus for the moment on the level of information transmission in the electric fish. Even if we can agree that Heiligenberg's description captures a hierarchy of control—and even if we could further agree that neuroscientific explanations should be couched in terms of hierarchies of control in general—we still have to face the question of what the epistemological status of these higher level patterns are with respect to explanation in neuroscience (similar to the question of the ontological status of the mind with respect to the brain in the previous chapter). Are they more fundamental than the individual cells? Are neurons like worker ants, in which no single ant is necessary for the system to run? If so, then what is more important in the brain is not the firing of the neurons but the information that they carry. These systems would necessarily be hierarchical and the arrangement of the elements either constrains or controls (or both) the behavior of the system as a whole. In these cases, we can think of the basic elements (the neurons or whatever) as the material out of which the system is composed, and their arrangement as the boundary conditions for the behavior of the system.

On the other hand, neurons may be more like queen bees, such that each is specially designed and required for the tasks of its "colony." In that case, what is more important for the brain is the activity of the individual neurons. (Of course, there is also the possibility that some other level of organization is the most important for explaining some particular phenomenon—the influx and efflux of molecules through the cell membranes, local columns or hypercolumns of neurons, areas of the brain, or the entire CNS considered as a single unit.)

"Privileged" Causality in Neuroscience

How do we determine which levels are the appropriate ones in an explanation? Ernst Mayr (1961) has identified four types of causes used in a complete explanation. There are ecological causes, genetic causes, intrinsic physiological causes, and extrinsic physiological causes. We ask, Why do electric fish change the frequency of their electric discharge? And there are four sorts of answers we might give. (1) The fish, relying on its electrical discharge to locate prey, must be able to differentiate things that are edible from other electric fish. Hence, they must alter their discharge so that no fish in the same region discharges at the same frequency. (2) The fish, over the course of its evolutionary history, has acquired the propensity to change the frequency of its electrical discharge in the vicinity of other electrical fish because having that ability contributed to its ability to survive. (3) The fish changed the frequency of its electrical discharge because it read the rate and "rotation" of the discharge frequency and the rotation indicated that the fish should alter its output in accordance with the direction of rotation. (4) The fish changed the frequency of its electrical discharge because it was in the vicinity of another electrical fish that discharges at the same frequency.

Another way of parsing the types of causes used in explanation follows (most recently) Dretske (1988). We can think of the ecological and the genetic causes both as ultimate (Mayr's term) or structuring (Dretske's) causes—that is, they explain why over the course of evolutionary time the system has become structured the way it is. The two physiological causes are more proximate—they account for the events in the lifetime of the fish that triggered the system to behave the way it did. (These distinctions also roughly parallel Aristotle's final and material causes, Kant's teleological and mechanical causes, and Descartes's and Newton's primary and secondary causes.) Both sorts of causal explanation are needed for complete understanding. That is, to explicate the occurrence of some phenomenon, you need to know why the system is structured the way it is and how it behaves under particular circumstances.

Not surprisingly though, neuroscience in the main is concerned with triggering causes; in particular, it is concerned with the internal physiological causes of some event or state. The other three sorts of causal explanations form a background on which the physiological explanation can be given.[36] Nevertheless, within triggering cause explanations in neuroscience, one causal chain should be emphasized over the others as *the* chain that made the difference in this particular case, depending on what exactly is to be explained with respect to the contrast class, the professional audience, the preestablished biases that shape one's intuitions, previously accepted theories that form the immediate background for discussion, and the technological resources at one's disposal.

As should be obvious from the example, neuroscience accounts for phenomena by outlining a relevant "causal etiology" in which certain causal chains in the ubiquitous causal network are privileged as the most relevant.[37] Outlining relevant mechanisms is the appropriate approach to take because the brain is too complicated to expect helpful quantitative theories that allow for explicit derivation of explananda from explanans. In the more mathematical sciences, we can see examples of explanations that are very close to the "covering law" model of explanation: we can literally compute the explananda from the laws describing the behavior of the system and particular inital and boundary conditions. However, in the mind/brain sciences, these techniques wouldn't be helpful. The mechanisms responsible for behavior can be unpacked across many levels of organization in the brain.[38] Here a strategy of "decomposition" and "localization" is much more appropriate.[39] In neuro-explanations, we develop systematic connections between the data to be explained and various loci of causal interactions in the head. In doing so, we trace a causal history of the mechanisms responsible for the whatever it is we want to explain.

To take an example from neurobiology, when accounting for the choeric movements of Huntington's disease, we get a fairly detailed picture of the functioning of the cholinergic neurons and the neurons that synthesize gamma-amino-butyric acid (GABA-ergic neurons) in the striatum, followed by a history of their death in Huntington's patients using data based on CAT scans, PET scants, and magnetic resonance imaging. This profound loss is then connected to a disinhibition of the nigrostriatal dopaminergic system and an over-excitation of the remaining striatal neurons, and a resulting abnormal pallidal output to the thalamus (see figure 3.6). We finally get an outline of the connection

Figure 3.6.

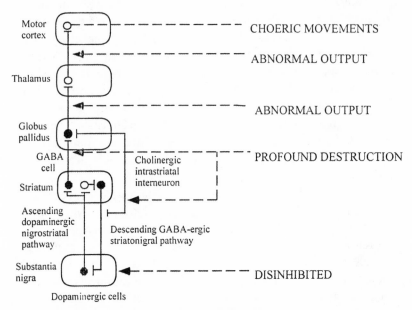

Interaction of neurons that use GABA, acetylcholine, and dopamine in the striatum and substantia nigra (the Dopaminergic-Cholinergic-GABA-ergic Loop), with indications of the effects of Huntington's disease. (Black neurons are inhibitory; white are excitatory.)

of the thalamus to motor output via the basal ganglia, a disturbance of which is tied to abnormal choeric movements.[40]

Here we do not see equations that indicate systematic connections between the pharmacology of the brain and involuntary movement; rather, the general mechanism of the disorder (an imbalance in the dopaminergic-cholinergic-GABA-ergic loop) is unpacked in a series of more or less detailed causal stories documenting systematic connections between factors of the mechanism with specific characteristics of the disease. These causal accounts play the same role as the mathematical derivations in physics or chemistry—they both detail a systematic dependency.

Neuroscience tries to trace the particular forces at work that produce the explanandum, even though there may be other abstractions that are just as predictively accurate, but conform less well to the dynamics of the system. Neuroscientists work hard not to confuse mathematically predictive apparatuses with accurate descriptions of the interacting causal forces (this theme is discussed in more detail in the next chapter) though they are perfectly happy to use to former to inform the latter. (I take this strategy in neuroscience to contrast with popular understandings of how physics and the other hard sciences proceed.)[41] As a result (and as you can see in the examples presented above), neuroscientific explanations are replete with causal details, perhaps at the expense of useful generalities. How should we understand neuroscience devising these causal history chains in a principled manner?

It has been suggested that when discussing any type of causal interaction, we look at three levels of organization:[42] the focal level at which the phenomenon in question occurs, the level immediately lower than the focal level, and the level immediately above. In evolutionary biology, if we take organisms reproducing as the focal level and the phenomena to be explained, we also look toward the genes or the initial conditions for reproducing, which constrain the path of development for the organism (the lower level), and the deme, which limits the activities of the constituent organisms (the higher level). These three levels of organization acting in concert account for the trajectory of the focal level through phase space. When accounting for some brain state or behavior, if we take the firing patterns as the focal level, we also should look to the individual neurons as the lower level that constrains the development of the patterns and the entire cognitive economy as the higher level that limits the effects of the firing activity as a whole. On the other hand, if we take the individual firing neuron as the focal level, then we should look at the influx and efflux of molecules across the cell membrane as the lower level that constrains the action potential, EPSPs, and IPSPs of the cell, and the area or circuit in which the cell is located, which limits the effects that the potentials may have. (There are, however, at least two exceptions when engaging in causal explanations in neuroscience in which this strategy will not work. First, if we are focusing on either the highest [the brain itself or the total cognitive economy] or the lowest level [molecular movements] of organization possible with the neuroscientific paradigm, then we cannot consider three separate levels of organization. And second, it is possible to get remote effects. That is, the highest level of organization may directly effect the lowest; for example, when the organism dies.)

Now the problem is to discover what the focal level should be for any given explanation, given that causality is transitive. That is, we grant that all the relevant causal information at the higher level can be represented in a complex description of neuronal firing propensities (or at even lower levels of description), but that does not mean that we want to say that the privileged causality for explanation operates there. As we saw in chapter 2, it is still an open question which "privileged" causes propel the changes in an organism's behavior.

Another way of looking at the problem is that we want to avoid the problem of artifact when selecting the focal level. We can see this difficulty most clearly in the so-called bookkeeping fallacy in evolutionary biology. The question there is whether we should understand the genes as only measuring natural selection's progress, while the organisms are the pertinent unit of analysis. As Grene remarks, "Genes may be good at bookkeeping, but it is Father and Mother Organism that run the family business" (1987, p. 504).[43] Or are organisms merely the by-products of natural selection operating entirely on the genes, as G. C. Williams has most famously suggested?[44] How do we decide which is the correct level of analysis (the gene or the organism) for explaining selection, and which effects are merely by-products or artifacts of a privileged cause operating at a different level of organization?

As discussed in chapter 2, the solution given most often to this general sort of question is that, within certain limits, we should use the relation of "screening off" to determine which variables are the appropriate ones to use. When discussing the issue of levels, we could say, for example, that the higher level discription of the informational patterns generated by individual firing neurons screens off the lower level descriptions of the individual neurons themselves when accounting for some higher level behavior, characterized in the reference class of neuroethology, just in case the behavior is predictable from only the higher level description of the informational patterns as characterized in neuro-ethology, but the higher level behavior is not predictable from only the lower level descriptions of the individual neurons in neuro-ethology. The point that bears repeating from our discussion in the last chapter is that the screening-off relation seems to be a likely candidate as a solution to the problem of artifact when choosing the correct level for analysis.

And, as before, where we look for artifacts depends a great deal on our original biases. So, for example, some believe that biology has a reductive bias,[45] in which case we would chose the lowest level of organization possible for an explanation unless some variable at a higher level screens off the causal chain. Another way of making the same point is to say that if we have a reductive bias, then we should chose as our level of analysis the lowest level of organization in which we can successfully predict the phenomenon.

At the moment, however, it is not immediately clear where our biases should lie in neuroscience. As I stated at the beginning of the chapter, neuroscientists have historically been biased toward reducing behavior to the interaction of individual neurons. In this case, for example, if the firing pattern over some brain area is a linear function of the sum of the IPSPs, EPSPs, and the spike trains of the individual neurons, the higher level patterns will not screen off the properties we care about from any input/output algorithm that can be derived to explain a single cell's interactions. On the other hand, if the firing patterns are not simple linear sums of the underlying activity, as current trends in research appear to indicate, then we need to look to the higher level as the proper level for explanation (regardless of historical bias) since the behavior of the system would not be easily predictable from the study of single neurons alone.

However, as Godfrey-Smith (1992) has recently pointed out, we should be cautious in adopting this sort of strategy too quickly. He showed that for the units of selection debate at least, additivity as an artifact may exist either above *or below* the chosen unit of selection. In this case, one should not automatically jump to the higher level of organization for explanation. We need to heed the earlier suggestion that we pay attention to three levels of organization: the presumed focal level, the one above for controlling constraints, and the one below for boundary conditions.

I believe that Heiligenberg's story about the electric fish's JAR bears these remarks out. Two factors about his research make it extremely important. The first is that the explanation does look to all three levels when explaining the JAR. Since frequency adjustment is determined by information distributed throughout the CNS, we look to the higher level of pattern distribution as the informational component that ultimately controls the animal and constrains the activity of individual neurons. How the individual neurons are constructed and parameters for their action potentials form important boundary conditions in the account of the electric fish's response. Nevertheless, both of these levels of organization subserve the focal level, the level of the individual neuron and its connection to other neurons, which accounts for how the electric fish is able to do what it does.

However, second, if we consistently find that we use the higher "informational" level of organization in explanation, then our biases should switch and we would first begin by focusing on that higher level, since that would now be what is the most productive approach. In this case, we would then be predisposed (though not bound) to look to the lower level when confronted with anomalies. But if this were to happen, the story about the electric fish need not become obsolete. We now have enough information about the electric fish that we can switch perspectives in our explanation fairly easily.

We would now claim that the distributed informational level is the focal level and the mathematical apparatus what predicts the JAR accurately describes the privileged causal mechanisms. However, these mechanisms would be bound by the connections among the individual neurons just as the genetic code is bound by the types of triplets that actually exist. We would also now embed this information level in the overall cognitive economy of the electric fish (such as it is) as a constraint on what the response may do. Our explanation would also shift from token accounts to type accounts. That is, when concentrating on the informational level as the focal level of explanation, we are explaining how electric fish, or whatever, behave in general. Particular individual differences would be washed out as the particular individual connections among neurons (which do differ across fish) are deemphasized.

Our focus and our explanation shift as our biases do, but the data themselves do not change. How we use the observations depends on how we are predisposed to understand the brain in the first place. What we consider an artifact and what we consider a real causal interaction depends on our reductive intuitions. These are changing. As Hull intimates in the opening quotation, neuroscientists are soon going to have to face the question of the type of theory they wish to pursue. They will have to decide whether to trade accuracy with extreme complexity at the lower level for increased generality with decreased precision at a higher level.

Explanation in Cognitive Science

The last chapter argued that much of how theory building proceeds in cognitive science is determined by local historical and social facts, as it is elsewhere. Nevertheless, reconstructions of the types of explanatory paradigms used in the mind and brain sciences are still possible. The most complete explanations in neuroscience rely on a control hierarchical approach to understanding the brain, use multiple levels of organization in analysis, and systematically exhibit either a reductive or an antireductive bias in which levels to priviledge causally. Neuroscientists give causal etiological explanations in which they trace the mechanisms hypothesized to be responsible for a particular behavior and their interactions over time. These explanations proceed with rich details, perhaps at the expense of simplicity and elegance.

These sorts of explanations are also given in the other cognitive sciences. For example, anthropological and sociological theories also proceed by tracing the relevant causal mechanisms for some higher level psychological or community property. Though the explanatory mechanisms can exist at the lower levels (relative to the phenomena to be explained), in the main the disciplines stress antireductionism and often give accounts couched in terms of group dynamics. Returning to the example with which we began this chapter, we can see that explaining Dora's symptoms sociologically might depend on such things as the local social and political climate and how these factors affect how individuals are raised to express their unhappiness. Similarly, Bruno Latour accounts for "rational" scientific activity in laboratories in terms of inherent power structures,[46] and Ed Hutchins explains choice in navigational strategies in terms of how information can be efficiently stored and retrieved from the environment.[47]

Nevertheless, even though these explanations turn on higher level regularities, they are also sensitive to the cognitive limitations of the individuals involved, as well as to the constraints the larger environment engenders. They are complex stories told of complex events and defy easy assimilation into the more traditional D-N models of theorizing. Instead, they all try to decompose the complexities into (complex) sets of simpler events and then localize those simpler events in the state space of explanation.

Psychological theories, the presumed paradigm of cognitive explanation in cognitive science, follow similar strictures. They are said to rely on a *functional analysis* of the system under investigation, in which complex intentional states are broken down into component parts and the interaction of those parts then explains some mental or behavioral event.[48] These theories usually explicate the mechanisms involved as entities existing on the same level of organization of the phenomena to be explained; in this case, the component parts are just simpler devices than what is mentioned in the explanandum. For example, Shiffrin and Schneider's dual processing theory,[49] Treisman's feature-integration theory,[50] Forester's theory of implicit and explicit processing,[51] all involve divisions between the automatic processing of data in parallel and a subject-controlled, serial manipulation of information.[52]

Chapter 4

Computationalism and
Functional Analysis:
A Pragmatic Approach

[I]f the dispositionalist attempts to define which function I meant as the function I am disposed to give for
arbitrarily large arguments, he ignores the fact that my
dispositions extend to only finitely many cases. If he
tries to appeal to my responses under idealized conditions that overcome this finiteness he will succeed only
if the idealization includes a specification that I will still
respond, under these idealized conditions, according to
the infinite table of the function I actually meant. But
then the circularity of the procedure is evident. The idealized dispositions are determinate only because it is
already settled which function I meant.[1]

The aim of natural science is to discover and characterize features that are intrinsic to the natural world.
By its own definitions of computation and cognition,
there is no way that computational cognitive science
could ever be a natural science because computation is
not an intrinsic feature of the world. It is assigned relative to observers.[2]

Perhaps, if nothing else ties the diverse disciplines together in the cognitive sciences, it is a broad commitment to computational theories of
cognition and functional analysis as an explanatory strategy. Cummins
and Schwarz (1992) suggest that "the working hypothesis of most of
current cognitive science is that systems are cognitive in virtue of computing appropriate functions." As time has gone by, we have discovered
that these (once presumed) simple distinctions become more compli-

cated as we take into account various pragmatic factors related to the actual practice of an interdisciplinary science. Here I try to present both the more traditional versions and their modern complications in order to lay a foundation for building interdisciplinary computational theories in cognitive science. What counts as a computation and how it relates to cognitive function are important questions for scientists interested in understanding how the mind or the brain thinks. The first third of this chapter tries to answer the first question and the second third sketches a reply to the second. The final third considers how psychological computation and function relate to underlying neurophysiological structure, which then sets the stage for chaper 5, an indepth examination of the difficulties of intertheoretic reduction in the "softer" sciences.

In brief, this chapter argues that pragmatic aspects of explanation ultimately determine how we can answer those questions. It does so by examining what is needed to make rigorous the notion of computation used in the (cognitive) sciences. I proceed by (1) outlining the connection between the Church-Turing Thesis and computational theories of physical systems, (2) differentiating merely satisfying a computational function from true computation, and finally (3) relating how we determine a true computation to the functional methodology in cognitive science. All of this discussion will be directed toward showing that the only way to connect formal notions of computation to empirical theory is in virtue of a pragmatics of explanation. However, once the connection is made, we are left with an extremely powerful explanatory strategy for cognitive science.

Formal Accounts of Computationalism[3]

To understand what is meant by computationalism and how it applies to cognition, I use three competing perspectives to triangulate onto the notion: formal accounts of computations, intuitions about what we compute qua cognizers, and comparison with other systems that we nonproblematically assume to compute. The standard approach in philosophy to account for what computationalism means in the cognitive sciences relies heavily on the Church-Turing thesis, drawing parallels between proof-theoretic schema in first-order systems and actual physical computing systems.[4]

In an analysis of our everyday notion of computation, Church (1936) conjectured that every computable function is recursive. In particular, he suggested that the class of effectively decidable functions over positive integers (a function computable in a finite number of steps) is identical to the class of lambda-definable functions, which he and Kleene had proven to be identical to the class of (general) recursive functions (roughly mathematical induction, as defined by Gödel [1931, 1934]). Turing (1936) supplemented that hypothesis with his suggestion that a function is computable if and only if there exists some mechanical procedure for computing it. The theorem entails that the set of recursive functions is identical to the set of functions that can be computed by a universal Turing machine.[5] Taken together, Church's thesis and Turing's theorum link our intuitions about what counts as a computation with a well-defined formal account: Any effectively computable number-theoretical function is recursive and hence decidable by a purely mechanical procedure.

However, it is far from clear that the Church-Turing thesis would apply to systems in the physical world (as we would need it to in order to use the thesis as a foundation for computational theories in science). Scientists interested in developing mathematical models of actual phenomena try to discover the mathematical relations that exist among two or more *real-valued* magnitudes of the physical system under study. Gödel et al., on the other hand, defined recursive functions as ranging over the *natural numbers*, and Church's original conjecture has not been extended to include all the real numbers. At first pass, the model-theoretic descriptions of physical systems that scientists develop and use do not fall under the mathematical definition of the class of recursive functions.

Nevertheless, for the purposes of scientific explanation, we can understand the functions on the reals that scientists use in terms of the natural number definition of recursion as follows: a function on the reals is recursive if and only if it can be approximated by a natural number function to any degree of accuracy we want.[6] This sort of approximation is not out of line with normal scientific practice: given the general noise in measurement, any data points are already going to be plotted with error bars. Approximating a function on the reals by a natural number function would be legitimate as long as the natural number function remained within calculated error.

However, understanding recursive functions in this manner raises an obvious question: How do we decide which function a physical system is actually computing? Since we can only approximate values in any actual measurement, and since there are an infinite number of possible approximations and of functions that more or less capture those approximate measures, scientists would seem to be unable to describe or explain some phenomenon using a unique set of mathematical relations. This point is stronger than merely that if there are no restrictions on how the states in a physical system get generalized nor on the interpretation of the system itself,[7] then every designated physical system computes every function. Rather, the point is that even if the interpretations of the physical system and its states are precisely fixed, then what function the system is computing is still undecided.[8]

Consider the following trivial case.[9] Suppose we have an electrical circuit under an interpretation that maps the sequence of electrical pulses I at a specified input point to the natural number i, and the sequence of electrical pulses J at a specified output point to the natural number j. This circuit would then compute the identity function (on the natural numbers) as long as $I = J$. (Hence, $i = j$.) Notice though that we are interpreting an obviously finite system as computing an infinite function. Eventually, the wires will rust, the power will cease, the circuit will be interrupted, or something else will happen, and yet we want to maintain that the system computes the identity function for *all* natural numbers. How can we do this? The only way to extrapolate thus is under the assumption that the system would counterfactually continue to obey (a subset of) the same physical laws that it does now in the actual world were the system to exist indefinitely (ceterus paribus).

However, there seems to be no a priori reason why we should base our hypothesized computation on counterfactual considerations at all. Why not just claim that the device computes identity for a finite subset of the natural numbers (viz., the subset mapped to the actual I_1, I_2, I_3, ... I_n and J_1, J_2, J_3, ... J_n that the circuit realized), otherwise it maps i to 0? Given suitable time and imagination, it seems that one could devise any number of possible functions that the system could compute equally plausibly.

Stabler (1987) suggests that the proper way around this difficulty is to relativize the system to the conditions of "normal operation." He points out that the counterfactual scenario "is not trivial; it is a substantial empirical claim supported by our physics" (p. 10). When the circuit ceases to function, then it no longer satisfies the condition of normal operation, so its behavior should henceforth be disregarded. Hence, "fixing the conditions of normal operation is crucial for making determinate claims about what function a system is computing" (p. 10).

How then do we determine the conditions of normal operation? Stabler allows that providing an answer goes "beyond the scope of [his] paper" (1987, p. 20); however, an answer must be given before we can rely on this distinction unproblematically. What separates the counterfactual in which the circuit's behavior is mapped to the identity function from any other counterfactual or actual behavior that is mapped to some more gerrymandered function? Since we rely on scenarios contrary to fact to identify the functions that a physical system computes, what picks out one possible scenario as a "normal operation," and the others as not?

I submit that there is no principled answer. We take counterfactual considerations as fundamental to our computational hypotheses; that is, we rely on more than the actual data gathered—or even the possible data that could be gathered. Moreover, any possible world we entertain in order to expand our intuitions about what the system is doing is necessarily going to deny one or more principles of physics (the one Stabler advocates denies entropy). I see no principled answer for which single possible world (once we have narrowed the choices to the close possible worlds) is the appropriate stand-in for the continuation of normal operations, given that none will be identical to the actual world.

Nevertheless, though there (may) be no principled way of deciding which natural number recursive function best captures the activity of some system, scientists still assign a unique computational interpretation to the measured relations. They do so based on their own understanding of how the physical system relates to other accepted theories. So, returning to the simple circuit example from above, we can see that asserting that the circuit calculates the identity function is the appropriate move to make because this hypothesis dovetails the best with our understanding of other similar physical systems, for example, simple calculators, other simple circuits, other systems that instantiate the identity function. This sort of comparison among proposed hypotheses and accepted theories determines which possible world to choose as the appropriate extrapolation of the actual world and determines which physical laws are the most important to preserve across worlds.

Continuing the theme of the previous two chapters, I claim that how scientists choose to use the previously accepted theories reflects pragmatic considerations on their part. These decisions depend on the historical circumstances of the inquiry, the technological limitations in measuring magnitudes, and the types of questions the scientists hope to address.[10] (This point will also be addressed in the next chapter.) By constraining proper scientific theories and explanation in this way, we can both complete Stabler's account and overcome other well-known and more general problems with unrestricted reconstructed views of scientific theory.

As mentioned in chapter 2, it has been clear for some time that explanation and theorizing in science require more than simple deduction from covering laws and initial conditions. Important for our purposes here is the fact that classic accounts cannot overcome the problem of irrelevant factors.[11] That is, it cannot determine which factors are important to preserve in counterfactual abstractions and which are irrelevant for any particular case. If we observe a subject reporting seeing pictures of orange carrots and blue lakes while seated in a room, we are not inclined to say that the chair is causally relevant for the subject's responses. Even though we could give some "explanation" of that behavior from the instantiation of Treisman's feature-integration hypothesis by this subject positioned in a chair, we would still maintain that the furniture is not a relevant factor in determining that this system "computes" the feature-integration function. In an abstraction of the event that includes only the physical facts needed for theorizing about feature integration in subjects, the chair would be absent. Though we can derive covering law accounts by appealing to all sorts of things irrelevant for explanation, an hypothesis should pick out only the relevant factors operating in the event to be explained nonetheless.

While there is no consensus on how to solve these and other problems in explanation, there is at least rough agreement that we need a pragmatics of explanation[12] (although whether pragmatics alone can solve the problems is still debated).[13] As I have discussed, theories are derived from answers to why-questions of the (reconstructed) form "Why F and not $G, H, I, \ldots$?" (the contrast class). Investigators ask these questions against a background context (which contains at least a subset of the statements accepted by the interested scientific community) and in an ongoing dialogue with their colleagues, so that the question is genuine if the background assumptions and the current practice imply that $(F \, \& \sim (G \vee H \vee I \ldots))$. The history of the inquiry plus current agent interactions set the contrast class, which then partially defines the factors relevant for theorizing. For any computational theory, these pragmatic aspects determine how scientists extrapolate or "bootstrap" their way to a true mathematical model once they have designated the proper interpretation function by highlighting which abstractions of the physical system are appropriate in determining its computational behavior.[14]

Computational Satisfaction and True Computation

However, this use of the Church-Turing thesis to approximate the behavior of physical systems doesn't quite capture our basic intuitions regarding whether a given system computes at all. For example, we believe that a falling stone, which approximates the distance function $D(t) = gt^2/2$, is not computing anything, though it can be described as satisfying some (computational) function. The falling stone contrasts with something like the simple circuit from above or a von Neumann computer, which also satisfy computational functions, but they do so by computing them. The broader notion of mere *computational satisfaction* needs to be differentiated from *actual computation*, which is more closely associated with the notion of a Turing machine qua computing device. To pull these two ideas apart, I shall first define the broader notion of *computational satisfaction* and then supplement this definition with additional constraints to narrow the scope of the criteria to *actual computation*.

I suggest that we understand computational satisfaction in the following way.[15] Since physical systems operate via physical properties, and since functions and numbers are abstract mathematical concepts, we as outside observers interpret a physical system as instantiating some mathematical function. For example, a physical system satisfies the identity function (or the distance function) if there is an interpretation function that maps the physical processes of the system onto the identity function (or the distance function). From these sorts of considerations, I arrive at the following conditions for satisfaction of a function:

(S1) A system satisfies a function by transferring tokens (the inputs *I*) to other tokens (the outputs *O*).

(S2) The process occurs over time, with the inputs always preceding the outputs. In addition, the inputs and the process that relate the inputs to the output determine the outputs for that system ($P: I \rightarrow O$).

(S3) There is an interpretation function that maps the inputs, process, and outputs onto an algorithm ($P(i, o) = f(A)(f^{-1}(i, o))$).

Now we need to narrow this definition of computational satisfaction so that we are able to say that a falling rock satisfies some function, but does not compute it, and a digital computer both satisfies some function *and* computes it. That is, we need to supplement these conditions for satisfaction with additional conditions of satisfaction such that we would have true computation. I posit the following two criteria.[16]

The first is that *only the processes taking place within the bounds of the system, plus previously accepted natural laws, are causally relevant to the behavior of a true computational system.* Intuitively speaking, only the processes internal to our simple circuit and only the processes inside the computer determine their outputs (given some input), but no changes within the stone cause it to move. From this difference in internal mechanisms we can conclude that circuits and computers can actually compute functions but rocks can only satisfy them.

However, this distinction is not that facile—it is only how *we understand* what falls within the bounds of some physical system that determines what *we count* as "internal processing." Since the demise of positivism, no one expects the structure of the world and therefore the boundaries of its systems to be completely transparent. How to partition the state space over which we define physical systems cannot be a completely objective matter.[17] Part of what determines how we partition the space must be pragmatic: our purposes in theorizing help us to choose the appropriate boundaries in our description of the world. And once we decide on the systemic boundaries, we can then defer to scientific theory to tell us how to partition the system further, given our explanatory aims. We then embark on the extrapolation mentioned above, using antecedent theoretical knowledge to determine how we should partition our physical system, once we have decided on the appropriate boundaries based on the purposes at hand.

So, in order to maintain that a circuit is computing the identity function, we first have to isolate that system from its surroundings. That the circuit "begins" with measured voltage pulses as input, contains a wire that transmits the volleys, and then "ends" with a separate measurement of the pulses does not fall out of the world simpliciter. We must decide to delimit the system in this manner, and we do so because this individuation fits best with how we have partitioned other state spaces, given our explanatory aims. For example, we could have decided to count only the neutrons in the wire as the relevant physical system. However, we believe that this partitioning would not help explain what we presumably had in mind, namely, the systematic relationship between the electrical inputs and outputs. And we suspect this fact to be true based on our experience of other explanations given regarding the behavior of electrical circuits.

The second criterion that distinguishes actual computation from computational satisfaction also turns on pragmatics. *We assign a computational function as an explanatory strategy in accounting for an actual computing system, while we do not for some system that merely satisfies the function.* In accounting for the behavior of some computational behavior system, we answer the question, "Why did *F* occur?" by answering the question, "How did *F* occur?" That is, we explicate how the interaction of the computing system's basic components generated *F* in order to explain why *F* obtained and not the contrast class (*G, H, I* . . .). So, in cognitive science, we can explain why *F* behaves the way it does by analyzing the capacities that produce *F*. In these sorts of explanations, it is not always necessary to specify which function is being computed; it may be enough merely to describe the internal dynamics of the system.

In three ways then do pragmatic decisions determine how to understand computationalism in general and how to assign a unique function to some computing system. First, we delineate the boundaries of the physical system under study by using fairly unprincipled decision procedures based on what we hope our theory to accomplish. Second, we overcome the general underdetermination of theory by evidence in concluding that the physical system satisfies (or computes) some function by relying on what we already believe to be the case about similar physical systems. Third, whether the assignment of a function to a physical system counts as an explanation depends on the contingent interests of the relevant community. At rough first pass, then, we can say that computation occurs in a physical system if it satisfies (S1)-(S3), if only processes internal to the system are relevant for the computation, and if the description of the dynamics of the system's components constitutes an explanation of the system's behavior.

Functionalism and Functional Analysis

The criterion of computation as explanation essentially amounts to adopting the strategy of functional analysis or functional decomposition. Loosely speaking, *functionalism* is the view that the various states of some system can be understood in terms of their functional or causal role with respect to input to the system, the output from that system, and the other states within the system causally connected to the states to be explained. Correlatively, *functional analysis* is a type of explanation in which some system is decomposed into its component parts and the workings of the system are explained in terms of the capacities of the parts and the way the parts are integrated with one another. The component parts and their interactions are specified entirely in terms of causal relations. That is, the parts are picked out by their causal role in a stream of inputs to outputs, and they display that role in virtue of their causal or "functional" connections to other surrounding component parts.[18] Though the inspiration for this type of explanation comes from computer science and attempts there to describe the abstract states a virtual machine passes through when it computes some function, it need not be tied to any particular computational model.

The earliest accounts of functional analysis refer to a flowchart of the algorithm some system is computing as the "functional description."[19] The true virtue of the notions of effective computability and the Turing Machine for cognitive science is the ready solution they present to the problems of behaviorism and the identity theories.[20] Behaviorism turned out to be circular as a psychological theory because it could not reduce descriptions of mental states to pure S-R behaviors without first assuming some mental states. Unfortunately, the identity theories originally proposed to cope with behaviorism's downfall entailed that even slightly different configurations of underlying wetware caused completely different mental states, so that no two individuals nor the same individual over time could ever enjoy the same mental state. Both theories were unacceptable, and the answer that appeared in response to these difficulties was functionalism: we would do better to individuate mental states more abstractly in terms of the functional roles their tokens perform in mediating input/output relations. If we assume this standard approach in cognitive science, a functional analysis of some cognitive process would then amount to little more than specifying the program we as computers are running, and the cognitive sciences reduce to the study of the computational processes that construct and transform mental representations in the service of some behavioral goal.

More current discussions, however, borrow biological approaches to understanding functions[21] and suggest that teleology is important in determining what a computational system's components are and how to describe them.[22] In these cases, a component's function is relative to its computational purpose, which in turn is loosely tied to an idealized version of evolution and natural selection: the function of a component explains why the component is there (or why it continues to exist). Though cognitive processes are still thought to be analogous with computer programs, the "software" now exists in a functionally decomposable hierarchy of control.

For computationalists, this sort of teleological explication of functional components just amounts to specifying the relations among the inputs to the system, the internal component states, and the outputs of the system for each level in the hierarchy. Since (from a computational perspective) the teleological function of any component part is to actively compute some function, once we determine the function and the states over which it operates, then we have outlined all we need in explaining the behavior of the larger physical system. We can understand computationalism in cognitive science as tying together the different versions of functionalism and functional analysis one finds in the literature today.[23] In sum, a computational functional analysis as an explanatory strategy in cognitive science is designed to account for cognitive systems by describing their internal functional relations.

Philosophical Functionalism

For philosophy of mind, the hope is that we can use this approach to dissolve many of the mysteries of our mind. Decomposing our mental faculties into primitive components should let us redescribe intentionally defined mental events in nonintentional terms. That way, any psychological explanation of our behavior or thoughts would beg no questions concerning what factors are actually responsible for our mental life, and we should be able to overcome any charges of latent *homunculi* actually performing the explanatory labor.

In particular, the drive in philosophical psychology is to explain in nonmentalistic terms what mental states are.[24] Reducing or translating mental terms to physical ones (or at least to some type of nonmental ones) became important when the commitment to materialism threatened to eliminate the mental's role in explaining behavior.[25] Putnam argued that the very plasticity of the brain made a type-type identity between mental state and neural events highly unlikely. Nevertheless, in virtue of the assumption of materialism, some sort of token-token identity must be true.[26] At least, given our understanding of a mechanistic world, in order for a mental state to affect our behavior, it has to be causally connected to the physical world in an important way. But how? It does appear that each brain event is causally preceded by some other brain event, and that our descriptions of the causal nexus of brain events have no gaps in them such that some mental event (appropriately redescribed) needs to step in to round out the causal story. One ideological response to Putnam's concerns was the advent of philosophical or machine functionalism. Correlating mental events with some sort of causally defined abstract state seemed to overcome, or at least avoid, the explanatory problems associated with token-token identity.[27]

Some who are concerned to save mental events from the threat of epiphenomenalism take this type of functionalism to be an ontological thesis, that *all there is* to some mental state are its causal relations to other states, inputs, and outputs. These philosophers and cognitive scientists are concerned to answer more than just, "How did F occur?"; in addition, they want to know, "What are F's?." That is, they want to know how we should best understand what an F is. A functional answer to this sort of question is that F is a *functional state*: we can exhaustively define F in terms of its relation to appropriately defined inputs, other states of the system, and its various outputs.[28] The intuitions that guide these sorts of metaphysical claims are that a mental state's computational or functional role in the mental life of an individual fully determines what kind of mental event that state is, and that an explication of that relation in functional terms would exhaust the meanings of mental terms. A functionalist account then underlies the explanatory power of any mentalistic explanation because a functional individuation of mental events will also specify the essence of various mental states. A computational functional analysis then gives us insight into the nature of mental kinds.

However, the methodological considerations mentioned above (in particular, the fact that determining which function a physical system is computing turns directly on practical decision making) should force us to understand functionalism and functional analysis as *epistemological* theses: we can know a state only in virtue of its causal/computational relations. Given the centrality of pragmatic factors in building computational functional accounts, the best we can hope to say about any functionally defined state is that we understand it in virtue of a computational model, not that it and the computational model are equivalent. It is better to remain agnostic about the true essence of mental states and instead focus on how to describe mental states as fruitfully as possible.

An Example

Since the terms *functionalism* and *functional analysis* are bandied about quite often in philosophical circles, I wish to spend a bit more time on the concepts. Let me demonstrate how functional analysis works in a domain rather removed from the traditional cognitive sciences in order to make clear how broad and almost trivial the notion of functionalism as an explanatory strategy really is. To illustrate the methodological approach of a functional analysis, I offer the following analysis of a neuronal resting potential.

I chose this rather unusual example for three reasons. First, it illustrates how we might understand the notions of functionalism and functional analysis in the field of neuroscience. Since ultimately I will be arguing in support of an interdisciplinary framework that combines both psychological and neuroscientific perspectives (among others), it is important to emphasize fundamental methodological similarities between the two disciplines. (I take it that how computationalism and functional analysis should work in psychology are fairly well understood—at least, it has been well discussed.)

Second, and related to the first reason, I believe functional analysis to be ubiquitous in the cognitive sciences as they are practiced today. Even though the influx and efflux of ions in individual neurons operate at a lower level of organization than I believe relevant for capturing cognition, using this framework to understand these data illustrates how I think most hypotheses in psychology (and neuroscience) should be analyzed generally. After illustrating functional analysis in a relatively straightforward theory, we should then have the tools by which to understand the more complicated hypotheses and positions in the cognitive sciences. Indeed, many believe that the relationships among the inputs and the outputs are the *only* relevant data for explaining psychological phenomena.[29]

Finally, I hope to underscore a general theme of this chapter, that functionalism is neither a very strong nor a very controversial position. It should be clear after the following discussion that most theories in science, and especially in cognitive science, can be analyzed functionally. Once we move beyond the philosophical impetus for using rigorous functional analyses as an explanatory strategy, then functionalism is almost no longer an interesting position. (However, I must hasten to point out that I am not suggesting that *all* theories rely on functionally described states. Block (1980) suggests that our theories concerning matter and antimatter cannot be understood in functional terms since Ramsey definitions of matter and antimatter are causally isomorphic to one another.)

Here a few facts relevant to the example. There are four types of ions important to axonal behavior: Na^+ and Cl^-, which are concentrated more outside the cell, and K^+ and anions A^- (negatively charged amino acids and proteins), which are concentrated more inside the cell. When the ions across the cell membrane are in equilibrium, we find a resting potential. Using K^+ (the ion for which the cell membrane is most permeable) as an example, we can see how two opposing forces interact and stabilize. The chemical concentration gradient pushes K^+ out of the cell, while the electrical potential difference drives K^+ back into the cell (because outside the membrane is positive in relation to the inside). At equilibrium, the force of the concentration gradient that pushes the ions out is equal and opposite to the electrical potential difference that forces the ions in. (See figure 4.1.)

The Nernst Equation (for the element K)

$$E_K = \frac{RT}{ZF} \ln \frac{[K^+]_o}{[K^+]_i}$$

where E_K is the value of the membrane potential at which K^+ is in equilibrium, R is the gas constant, T the temperature in degrees Kelvin, Z the valence of K^+, F the Faraday constant, and $[K^+]_o$ and $[K^+]_i$ the concentrations of K^+ on the outside and the inside of the cell.

The axon then "computes" the function listed above (the Nernst equation) to determine this resting potential, or the equilibrium potential, of K^+. (Likewise, this equation can be used to find the equilibrium potential of any other ion present on both sides of a membrane permeable to that ion.) Put simply, the Nernst equation defines the causal relations among the elements of the system with respect to the axon. Moreover, it also defines the resting potential of a neuron solely in terms of the functional connections among ions. In this particular instance, these functional connections can be understood as place-holders for any elements that satisfy the relations described by the Nernst equation. We take the Nernst equation to explain the behavior of the resting potential of a neuron—when we ask why the neuron is behaving the way that it is (i.e., is at equilibrium), we take the relations sketched above to be an answer to that question. Thus we have a functional analysis of neuronal resting potential.

Figure 4.1

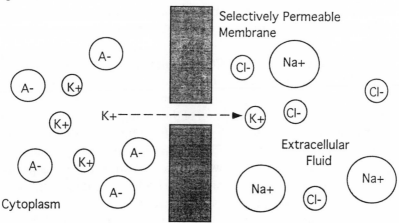

With a membrane selectively permeable to K+, the concentration gradient for K+ forces K+ out of the cell, and the electric potential difference moves K+ back in. The efflux of K+ helps to generate the cell's resting potential.

The Nernst equation also exemplifies the distinction between ontological and epistemological functionalism in that, loosely speaking, what we need to know for our theories about axonal resting potentials is captured in the function. It turns out that the Nernst equation for K^+ is a good, but not perfect, predictor of a membrane resting potential. The actual resting potential deviates from the calculated values for relatively low values of $[K^+]_o$. For example, the Nernst equation predicts that the resting potential should equal approximately 75 mV; but experimentally, we find that it is really about 70 mV. This difference is due to the movement of other ions (viz., Na^+) across the membrane. However, the voltage measured is still close to the Nernst potential of K^+ because cell membranes have more transport channels for K^+ and therefore are most permeable for K^+. Thus, the Nernst equation serves as the most useful approximation for an admittedly more complex interaction, and usually we take it to be enough to capture and explain equilibrium in our neuronal system.

Even though we know that, strictly speaking, the Nernst equation is wrong, we still use it in explaining neuronal behavior for pragmatic reasons. We could add complications to the equation to take into account the movement of other ions such that it would now accurately describe membrane resting potentials at low values, but to do so would complicate the equation beyond its usefulness. It is preferable to claim that the

Nernst equation "satisfices" because it gives us useful information in exchange for relatively minor labor. It doesn't capture precisely what we know actually occurs, but it is good enough to get the epistemological job done.

Adopting Haugeland's (1978) terminology, we can call this sort of functional explanation a *systemic* explanation. These explanations turn on a description of the "organized cooperative interaction" of the component parts. So in our explanation of the resting potential for neurons, we explain equilibrium in a cell by specifying the complex interdependent pattern of the influx and efflux of ions. It would not be enough just to list the component parts, how they are aligned, and their respective capacities. Instead, what is crucial for the explanation is how the pieces "depend" on one another—that the influx of K^+ depends on the electrical potential difference between the inside and the outside of the cell, and the efflux of K^+ depends on the concentration gradient inside the cell—and that this "cooperation" takes the form of the Nernst equation.

This kind of explanation contrasts with *morphological* ones. These explain the disposition or ability of a particular type of object solely by articulating the structure of the object and the various capacities of the structure.[30] The assumption behind these explanations is that any object with this particular structure and with these particular capacities would have to have the overall ability we are trying to explain. It is enough in these explanations simply to detail the component pieces of some system with respect to their concomitant capacities, for once we have done that, we have done everything we need to do in order to predict and explain the general function of the system or process in question.

To return to the resting potential example, we could thus explain how K^+ physically enters the cell by outlining the structure of a K^+ transport channel and detailing how that structure and its resultant capacities allow ions with a certain structure and with certain properties to pass through the channel, and that the ions cannot pass through the surrounding membrane because it remains impermeable to ionic structures in virtue of the properties of its own structure. To wit: because of the dipole moment of water molecules and hydrophilic nature of cations and anions, the ions in extracellular space are surrounded by electrostatically bound shells of water. However, the nonpolar hydrocarbon tails of lipids within a cellular membrane are hydrophobic, so a great deal of energy is required to strip an ion of its water coating and allow it to move among the lipid layer. In other words, the "waters of hydration" effectively prevent ions from moving through the lipid layer. Instead, the ions move through protein pores (the ion transport channels) that are embedded in the membrane. These pores not only are large enough to allow ions to pass through with their waters of hydration intact, they also are polar and, hence, attract water molecules as well.

In sum, the actual movement of K^+ through the membrane depends solely on the physical properties of the lipid layer, the transport channel, and cations and anions—the differences between hydrophilic and hydrophobic ions and molecules and the dipole moment of water. No real "interactive cooperation" among the component parts occurs or is required in the description of the event. Thus, this explanation is purely morphological or structural. Using functional analysis as an explanatory strategy for defining component parts functionally makes for systemic explanations, while purely structural descriptions are aligned with morphological explanations. The real difference between the two sorts of explanation, and the two types of description, is in the *interaction* of the parts vis-a-vis explaining the system as a whole, not in isolating the parts per se.

The Function/Structure Distinction

Functionalism and computationalism in cognitive psychology began with a computer metaphor. One of the attendant properties of the computer metaphor is a unitary distinction between software and hardware, which allowed scientists to visualize how a functionalist solution to psychology's behaviorist woes might go. When early cognitive scientists compared humans to computers, their attention was captured by the fundamental contrast between a machine's program, which could be instantiated in any number of different machines, and the material out of which the machine was made, the stuff that realizes the program in this particular instance.[33] As traditional reductionists, they concluded that psychology could be in the business of studying the programs of the mind (the function), while other disciplines could investigate the physical machines that run these programs (the structure).

We could map Haugeland's systemic/morphological distinction to this function/structure distinction, now so popular in psychology. In the main, those who study higher level cognitive processes believe that any explanation of those processes will be systemic, computational, and derived from a functional analysis of functionally described component parts. These explanations of some cognitive *process* stand in stark contrast to accounts of its *structure*, which instantiate the process and "[provide] the computational resources for realizing [the] cognitive processes" (Pylyshyn 1984, p. xvi). That is, as discussed above, our psychological (or mental) processes require a functional analysis for a proper explanation, which is fundamentally different from the token neural events with which we can identify the individual mental events. The systemic explication of cognition is opposed to any morphological account of underlying brain structure.

This underlying structure then is traditionally assumed to be more or less irrelevant to our higher level psychological processes. It has been variously thought of as the "biological substrate," explained in "physicochemical" terms (Putnam 1973),[31] the "physical constitution" or the "innards of the particular object" to which the "laws of nature" apply (Dennett 1971),[32] or as the "functional architecture," analogous to a virtual machine in a computer (Pylyshyn 1984). Thus structure seems to be whatever token physical events that allow or support the functional interactions among component parts of a system or larger process. Intuitively, we can think of the distinction as the difference between what systems *do* and what they are made *of.*

But regardless of how the distinctions are described, explanation in cognitive science now seems to depend on this distinction. Explanations of cognitive events qua cognitive events appear to require a functional analysis in order to overcome the charge of epiphenomenalism relative to scientific explanation and the difficulties associated with type-type psychophysical identity. In any event, nowadays, most cognitive scientists assume that the sorts of questions they ask with respect to information processing will entail systemic, functionally described, answers.

The computer metaphor is unfortunate, though, because it obscures the true nature of the function/structure distinction. Our world, and we in it, cannot be neatly captured in two levels of description: a functional one of programs and a structural one of physical implementation.[34] The monolithic distinction, in which psychology worries about the semantics and the syntax of information processing while others concern themselves with the physical mechanisms of the information processing machines, simply does not exist. The distinction between function and structure is neither as obvious nor as simple as it seems at first blush. In fact, *the distinction between functional properties and structural ones is arbitrary with respect to one's ontology. Instead, what counts as a functional property and what counts as a structural one turns on the sort of explanation one gives of the objects or processes*

involving the properties relative to the other sorts of explanations avail-
able over the same state space. To see how this prima facie oxymoronic
suggestion could make sense, let us return to the example of ionic flow,
which, as a morphological explanation of select ions passing though a
neuronal cell wall, is also a structural account of some biological process.

Even in this relatively simple example, what actually is functional
and what is a purely structural description are not entirely clear. For
even though how K^+ enters a cell membrane through protein pores does
depend (in part) on the physical arrangement of the molecules
involved, this is not the entire story. Ionic transport channels can be
divided into two categories: passive or active. Passive channels are
important in determining the resting membrane potential, as described
above. The channels are always open and, hence, appropriately sized
molecules pass freely through. Active channels, on the other hand, are
responsible for the action, receptor, and synaptic potentials. They have
a "gate" somewhere along their length such that they do not allow ions
through when the membrane is at rest. Giving a purely structural
account of the behavior and capacities of the passive channels does seem
the correct explanatory strategy to chose. However, because the gates in
the active channels are regulated by things like synaptic transmitters,
membrane potential, or various physical stimuli (in the case of receptor
cells), we cannot describe their behavior in purely structural terms.
Whether a gate is open, and for how long, depends on the interaction
of the gate with other biological components. So, not only do we speak
of the relative functions of the transport channels (whether it contrib-
utes causally to a resting membrane potential or it is causally connected
to, say, an action potential), but we also need a functional analysis of the
interacting component parts to explicate fully the behavior of active
channels. (Nevertheless, if all we are discussing are passive channels
with respect to resting potentials, it could still make sense to give a
purely structural analysis.)

The moral of this example seems to be that how and to what end we
are describing the parts that comprise some system is tied to the amount
of detail we want to include in our description of the component parts.
Our first description of K+ diffusion was indeed structural; however, as
we included more detail, the descriptions included functionally defined
interactions. But if we then restricted the scope of our account to
include only passive gates and resting potentials, our explanations
reverted back to being purely structural.

This discussion corroborates other suggestions that the function/ structure distinction is relative to the type of inquiry one is making. There is no obvious division of labor between higher level psychological descriptions and lower level neurophysiological descriptions with respect to functional or structural descriptions of their subject matter. Our world, and we in it, cannot be neatly captured in two levels of description: a functional one of processing algorithms and a structural one of physical implementation. Instead, the world is better explained in terms of a more complicated arrangement. Whether something counts as a functional analysis or a structural one depends on the type of questions asked and the sort of explanation given.

However, I would like to distinguish my view of the relation between structure and function from, for example, Lycan's or Churchland's.[35] They conclude that the level of "implementation" can be understood functionally from a lower level of analysis such that structural properties are functional ones from a different perspective. The physical instantiations can always be described functionally. My analysis is importantly different though. I claim that whether something counts as functional or structural depends on the questions we are asking and the amount of detail we include in our answer *from the perspective of a single level*. Whether we understand transport channels as functionally or structurally defined objects depends on how much detail we decide to include in our answer, irrespective of level of analysis. And the amount of detail will depend on the audience we are addressing, their background knowledge, and why they are asking the question in the first place.

Hence, as with functional analysis in general, I conclude that whether something counts as "functional" or "structural" depends (in part) on the pragmatic interests of those involved and not on how the world "actually is." Moreover, since the type of description or explanation we give ultimately depends on our interests and the intellectual milieu in which it is given, the original philosophical motivation to separate function and structure as a way to overcome problems with type-type identity in explanation is fundamentally misguided. Whether something counts as a functional or a structural analysis depends on the scope of questions asked. Because it is contingent exactly when research programs are carried out, whether we consider a description functional, structural, or both, is literally an historical accident. Hence, any putative difference in structure can be redescribed as a difference in function by including enough detail.

To summarize: a computational functional analysis in philosophy refers to a specific type of explanatory strategy in which all we need in order to account for some system is a description of its internal computational/functional relations. In this sort of analysis, the system is broken into simple component parts and how the parts interact to give rise to the outputs of the system is analyzed in terms of the parts computing some function or functions. Moreover, for an epistemological functionalist, this decomposition (exhaustively) defines the system *relative to the questions we are trying to answer about it*. That is, we can understand the components of the system fundamentally in terms of their relations to other components, the input to the system, and the system's output. Computational functional analyses in cognitive science are but methodologies; whether a physical system is actually computing turns on whether the description of the computation encompasses only processes internal to the system and whether that description explains that system. I have argued that both of these factors depend on the interests and aims of the people involved in the investigation. Since there is no reason to suppose that such pragmatic factors could ground any ontological claims, questions about the essence of computational systems are misguided.

Generally, philosophers of psychology have assumed that psychological theories separate the "programming algorithms" (or functions) from the stuff that instantiates them (the structures). Indeed, several philosophers and psychologists have maintained that a functional analysis precludes using morphological information as evidence for functionally defined entities. In particular, they have differentiated the questions psychologists ask from the investigations neurophysiologists conduct such that no neurophysiological datum could help answer any higher level psychological question about cognitive capacities. However, an interdisciplinary cognitive science must rely on at least some sort of connection between psychology and neuroscience.

Indeed, the phenomena cognitive scientists wish to explain are just too complicated and depend on too many different types of variables for us to capture on a single organizational level. The evidence supporting a multilevel functional analysis will come from many different domains that are only loosely connected via the relation of explanatory extension. The interdisciplinary theories in cognitive science encompass various levels of analysis, which in turn reflect different levels of organization in the physical system. Specifying the relevant connections between the "programming algorithms" at different levels and the corresponding state in the physical system leads us to a computational theory that mixes together "functions" and "structures" in a single theoretical model. In the end, an interdisciplinary theory based on functional analysis will lead us to functionally specified components in a computational model that look very different from what philosophers of psychology had originally assumed. In particular, the psychological level of information processing will not be a privileged level of analysis.

Chapter 5

Reductionism in the Cognitive Sciences

> If it turns out that the functional decomposition of the nervous system corresponds precisely to its neurological ... decomposition, then there are epistemological reasons for studying the former and not the latter. But suppose that there is no such correspondence? Suppose the functional organization of the nervous system cross cuts its neurological organization. Then the existence of psychology depends not on the fact that neurons are so depressingly small, but rather on the fact that neurology does not posit the kinds that psychology requires.[1]

> There is no firm data for any but the grossest of correspondence between types of psychological states and types of neurological states.[2]

Even though it is traditionally assumed that the structure of some physical system is supposed to be irrelevant to its functional description, interdisciplinary cognitive scientists rely on neurophysiological evidence to help support their functional analyses of cognitive processes nonetheless. They do so in roughly the following manner. They analyze some cognitive process or other as a systemic process and then compare it to some physiologically described neural process, which exists quite separate from any higher level functional descriptions. If they can draw parallels between the two levels of analysis and among the independently derived descriptions, they then use this parallelism to justify using evidence about underlying morphology to support arguments about instantiated algorithms. They base these sorts of arguments on the belief that if two descriptions are over the same event space, then they may use data supporting one description as evidence for the other. Using this form of parallelism, theories in neuroscience should be able to support theories in psychology, or in any other higher level domain. Indeed, this position reflects a fairly traditional reductionist position in the cognitive sciences: there is a lawlike correspondence between higher level theories and neuroscience, and this correspondence helps explain the accuracy of the higher level theories.

However, relying on a scientific domain other than the one that proposes the theory for evidence is a strange way to approach supporting functional or computational theories of cognition *exactly because* most of the higher level theories are functional. Because these theories *define* their explananda as a process that manipulates mental states according to some computational (or at least causally defined) algorithm, accepting even epistemological functionalism therefore seems to entail that a true reduction between, say, neuroscience and psychology is impossible. Since functionalism defines events or processes as a set of causal relations with respect to some set of inputs and outputs, then in which substance these causal reactions occur is irrelevant to describing the functional processes themselves. But without *some* sort of reduction, neurophysiological evidence would be inadmissible in supporting a higher level theory.

When confronted with this dilemma, the trend among philosophers of mind has been simply to argue that reductionism is wrong.[3] This argumentative strategy is unsatisfactory, because few positive replacements for the classical reductionist story are offered for the cognitive sciences,[4] and yet some are obviously needed. Here I attempt to fill that gap. In this chapter, I elucidate one way to understand the current relationship between psychology and neuroscience, taking these two (again) as stand-ins for all the disciplines that comprise cognitive science. (That is, once again, I believe that my points can be generalized to any two disciplines in cogntive science that you please, though I leave the generalizations to the discretion of the reader.) After outlining what philosophers of mind take reductionism to be, rehearsing two types of arguments traditionally given against reductionism in the "softer" sciences, and considering various replies to those positions, I present a positive way of conceiving current trends in the mind and brain sciences, using Philip Kitcher's (1984) notion of explanatory extension as a model.

Reductionism in Philosophy of Mind

Philosophers of psychology (in particular, Fodor and Putnam) base their conception of reduction on Nagel's (1961) classic formulation.[5] They claim that if neuroscience reduces psychology, then all the kind predicates in psychology are coextensive with kind predicates in neuroscience. Bridge principles can express nomologically necessary identities in such a way that every event that falls under a proper generalization of psychology will also fall under a bridge principle, and thereby also fall under the generalizations of neuroscience. That is, all the primitive terms appearing in the reduced theory either appear in the reducing theory or are associated with one or more terms in reducing theory via specified bridge principles. The bridge principles jointly exhaust the domain of the reduced theory: Each primitive predicate of the reduced theory is associated with an open sentence of the reducing theory via a bridge law such that if each predicate is satisfied by an n-tuple, then the open sentence is satisfied by the same n-tuple. Finally, the reduced theory is derivable from the union of the reducing theory and the bridge principles.[6]

Cleaving to the logical positivists' line, reductionists hold that the point of reduction is to explain the generalizations of psychology by reducing those generalizations to a more basic science. They presume that by explicating the physical mechanisms in virtue of which psychological events conform to the reduced generalizations, they will thereby exhibit the psychological generalizations just as special cases of neurological theories. This version of reductionism is much too strong to be useful, however, for even our "parade" cases of reduction cannot meet these conditions. Consider electromagnetic theory reducing physical optics.[7] We cannot, strictly speaking, deduce the laws of optics from Maxwell's equations once we specify the appropriate boundary conditions and the bridge principles, for at least two reasons. First, Fresnel's laws of intensity ratios end up with an additional factor in them when derived from Maxwell's theory. In practice, this factor is negligible in most cases, but theoretically it is very important, for it tells us that the behavior of light in part depends on the magnetic properties of the surrounding medium. Second, the perfectly legitimate concept of "black" in optics has no counterpart in electromagnetic theory, so it is impossible to formulate the nineteenth-century optical problem of calculating diffraction by a black screen in electromagnetism. *Strict* reduction fails here, yet no one claims that this is not an example of some *sort* of reductionism.

The conclusion that some (e.g., Schaffner) draw is that we can derive a theory closely resembling physical optics from Maxwell's theory, but not classically understood optics itself. That is, we have to "correct" the reduced theory T to T' before we can derive it from the union of the reducing theory and the bridge principles. T' "corrects" T if T' gives more accurate predictions than T over the same domain. (This revised version of reductionism leaves many crucial questions unanswered, most obviously: How much may T' correct T before T' stops being a version of T and becomes a different theory? I shall not try to resolve this issue here.)

The point to notice is that even a weakened notion of reduction still entails that there is some lawlike correspondence between the entities of the reducing and the reduced theories, and that this correspondence helps explain why (some version of) the reduced theory holds. The reduction shows the corrected laws of optics to be special instances of the more general laws of electromagnetism and, in virtue of this demonstration, helps explain why Fresnel's laws of intensity ratios and Snell's laws of refraction give the results they do and why the problem of black screen diffraction is a nonstarter. So, if psychology reduces to neuroscience, then for some version of most psychological kind predicates, there must exist coextensive neuroscientific predicates, and the generalizations that express this coextension help explain the accuracy of psychological generalizations.

Moreover, I have already noted that whether something is an explanation depends at least on the speakers, the audience, and historical circumstances of the inquiry, that explanation per se cannot be entirely divorced from the particular scientific community in which it arose. So if neuroscience is to explain psychology reductively, there have to be neuroscientific formulations of *all* relevant psychological statements: that is, if a question, "Why F and not G, H, I, . . . ?" is formulated and answered in psychological language, there have to be corresponding neurophysiological statements that express all the propositions involved, including the contrast class and substantial portions of the accept background context that determine the contrast class.[8]

Let us now turn to the issue of determining whether psychology reduces to neuroscience. To argue that psychology does not, one must show either that neuroscientific predicates coextensive with psychological predicates do not exist or that, if there be such correspondences, then they can't be used to reformulate the psychological explanations. The three arguments I rehearse below try to establish exactly these points.

Arguments against Reductionism

Generating arguments against reductionism seems very easy once one accepts psychological functionalism. Defining mental states solely in terms of their causal relations makes it possible to generalize across psychological events whose underlying physical descriptions have nothing in common, for these psychological theories could be instantiated by a number of different physical mechanisms. For example, anatomically and evolutionarily distinct neural structures underlie binocular stereopsis in the owl and the cat.[9] Systems can satisfy kind predicates of psychology but not the kind predicates of neuroscience, and this lack of correspondence prevents reduction between fields.

Furthermore, even if it were true that *humans* who have functionally identical mental states also have the same underlying neurological patterns, it would say nothing about the viability of reductionism. As Fodor argues, mental states are defined in terms of their functional roles, so "*whether* the physical descriptions of the events subsumed by [psychological] generalizations have anything in common is, in an obvious sense, entirely irrelevant to the truth of the generalizations, or to their interestingness, or to their degree of confirmation, or, indeed, to any of their epistemologically important properties" (1983, p. 133, italics his). Functionalism inherently denies a reduction between psychology and neuroscience.

These arguments rest on confusions about what reductionism amounts to, however. First, arguing from multiple instantiability to the impossibility of bridge principles depends on a notion of reduction that even paradigm cases of reduction do not fulfill.[10] Quite often reduction is relativized to a domain, and domain reduction is a normal part of science.[11] Consider the classic example of the reduction of temperature to mean molecular kinetic energy. This reduction holds only for gases. Temperature in solids is something else, and temperature in plasma is something else again. "Piece-meal" reduction seems intuitively correct as well. Suppose that scientists discovered that all psychological natural kind terms can be mapped directly to natural kind terms in neuroscience. Would we want to claim that a reduction had not taken place simply because there might be (or are) some creatures that our psychological principles would accurately describe, but our neuroscience wouldn't? I think not. Although perhaps not a matter for a priori decision, it seems likely that we would bite the bullet of chauvinism and argue that, amazingly enough, human psychology maps directly to human neurology.

Second, arguing from functional essentialism to a denial of reduction misconstrues what reductionism is. Reducibility between scientific domains per se makes no *normative* claims about either domain, for example, that the reducing theory should now set the definitional standards for the reduced domain. Rather, reduction merely sets out a relationship between the two domains.[12] Just because electromagnetism reduces physical optics does not mean that optics as a field no longer exists nor that how optics defines its terms is parasitic on electromagnetic theory. Likewise, if neuroscience ever reduces psychology, psychology could still functionally taxonomize its kinds. All that the reduction would add is a statement about the relationship between two sciences. Functionalism really cross cuts the issue of reductionism.

What seems to be behind the arguments from functionalism is the idea that psychology can't reduce to neuroscience because psychology and neuroscience worry about completely different types of questions. That is, even if bridge principles link psychology to neuroscience, neuroscience could not subsume *explanation* in psychology.[13] Different levels of analysis in cognitive science attempt to answer fundamentally different sorts of why-questions. Some questions revolve around the basic capacity of the system under investigation; other questions involve the processes subserving the capacities; and still others relate to the physical mechanisms that underlie the processes subserving the capacities.[14]

However, contrary to what the antireductionists often assume, there is no easy or obvious division of labor between psychology and neuroscience. As mentioned above, the monolithic function/structure distinction, in which psychology investigates function and neuroscience worries only about structure, does not exist. What counts as a functional description and what counts as a structural is relative to the amount of detail in a description. Moreover, at each level in the brain's hierarchy—the membranes, the cells, the synapses, the cell assemblies, the circuits, the networks, the systems, and even the gross behavior—neuroscientists answer questions concerning capacity, the processing subserving the capacity, and the physical implementation of the processing algorithm.

The next section examines these ideas using a specific example drawn from George Mandler's cognitive theory of emotion. Ultimately, I conclude that even complex nested descriptions of functions and structures will not give philosophers what they are looking for. Due to general theoretical underdetermination, neither higher level nor lower level descriptions *necessarily* constrain one another (though we still see some restrictions on allowable parsings of the state space and possible descriptions of the physical systems). The bottom line will be that the connections between the psychological and neuroscientific descriptions are messy and complicated. True reductions will not be possible; instead, the best we can get is the looser relation of explanatory extension.

I shall go on to suggest in later chapters that even if we develop this less powerful and less principled distinction, we would still be confronted with the fact that most of the data relevant to understanding individual cognition lie between the purely psychology and the purely neurophysiological descriptions (for those interested solely in the connection between psychology and neuroscience with respect to cognitive science). These middle level descriptions connect the higher level information processing models with the lower level neurophysiological theories and, hence, do much of the explanatory labor in interdisciplinary theories. Philosophers and psychologists should not underestimate the importance of these descriptions and corresponding accounts of underlying functionally defined components.

Cognitive Theories of Emotion: A Test Case

In order for neuroscience to reduce psychology, at least the two following rough conditions must be met:

1. Psychology contains primitive terms and predicates that can be associated with one or more terms or predicates in neuroscience via bridge principles.
2. A derivation of the generalizations of psychology from neuroscience would explain why the generalizations hold.

Fodor claims that "we do not know much about what psychological theories should be like" (1983, p. 149) and so trying to work out any correspondences between psychology and neuroscience is useless. I disagree. Ever since Wundt published *Grundriss der Psychologie* in 1873 we have had a very good idea what psychological methodology, explanations, and theories are. Just because all the theories are not well developed does not mean that they do not adhere to a certain explanatory paradigm. Therefore, I propose to examine each of the theses using current psychological and neuroscientific theories as data in order to work out a characterization of the actual relation between psychology and neuroscience. I shall begin by using George Mandler's (1984) cognitive theory of emotion as a test case for reducing psychology to neuroscience.[15]

Mandler argues that there are three aspects to emotional systems—arousal, cognitive interpretation, and consciousness. 'Arousal' refers to activity in the sympathetic nervous system induced by stimuli interrupting the behavior or the thought processes of some organism. It primarily serves as a warning device to let organisms know that they must seek more information from their environment. 'Cognitive interpretation' involves both innate structures that process incoming stimuli and more complicated evaluations of self via schemas. The experience of emotion results from an interaction of the sympathetic nervous system and a cognitive evaluation of the arousal in 'consciousness'. 'Consciousness', like arousal, stems from the need to alter the current pattern of behavior, but, unlike arousal, it supports the "quale" of emotion. Conscious experience of emotion involves continuous feedback: some stimuli trigger autonomic nervous system (ANS) arousal; organisms perceive this response and begin evaluating it; the result of the analysis leads to a particular conscious experience, which too can be evaluated and analyzed.

A key aspect in Mandler's theory is meaning analysis. Like other functionally characterized processes, meaning analysis entails that we assign meanings to things in virtue of the structure of the input to the system and the relation of what is activated to other cognitive structures. We know where we are and what our environment is like by assimilating analyzed sensory inputs into preexisting schemas, whose assimilation in turn can modify the schema. Any discrepancies between the expectations our currently activated structure engenders and the actual environment leads to arousal and the cycle of emotion begins.

Returning now to the conditions for reduction outlined above, I believe that (1) might hold for this psychological theory, but (2) definitely does not. Does Mandler's theory of emotion contain primitive terms and predicates that could be associated with one or more terms or predicates in neuroscience? The answer is yes. Consider just two of Mandler's principles: (1) the intensity of the emotional experience is proportional to the degree of autonomic arousal, and (2) if an ongoing action sequence is interrupted, then the ANS is activated. These principles meet the first condition, for each of their terms and predicates—'intensity', 'emotional experience', 'ANS', 'arousal', 'activated', 'ongoing'—are candidates for mapping to neuroscience.

The next question is whether terms and predicates like these could correspond to neuroscientific terms and predicates via bridge principles. Clearly, there will be a bridge principle that can link the term arousal in psychology with a term in neuroscience, for ANS arousal in psychology is just ANS arousal in neuroscience. It is less clear whether functionally defined terms like cognitive evaluation and consciousness can be linked to neuroscience. As the traditional argument goes, it seems they cannot because there is no neurophysiological similarity across individuals for either process that allows us to pick out *this* process from any other one. Though molecular biologists and neurophysiologists have been searching for almost two decades, they have yet to discover any conclusive evidence linking neurotransmitters or other chemicals to the various "qualia" of emotion.[16] Furthermore, work done in the sixties shows that there is probably very little physiological difference among different emotional experiences and that cognitive interpretation has a lot to do with how physiological responses "feel."[17] Since cognitive evaluation and the resultant conscious experience depends on the relative fit between incoming perceptual information and previously activated schemas, it is difficult (though not impossible) to see how one could find interesting structural similarities across all possible schemas in order to pick out instances of the relevant type of evaluation. One might list the structure of all schemas that an individual possesses at some time, and then claim that the neuroscientific term that corresponds to those schemas is the disjunction of the descriptions of all the structures. However, such a disjunction could not be used in a bridge principle because bridge principles must support counterfactuals.

The quick answer, as discussed in chapter 4 and section 2 above, is that these considerations say nothing about the reducibility of the terms cognitive evaluation and consciousness, for neuroscience is perfectly capable of using functionally defined terms. Neuroscience could simply import those terms and claim, like psychology, that when perceptual inputs exist in certain relation to other inputs and cognitive states, a particular meaning is assigned, and that when cognitive analysis is integrated (by whatever means) with the perception of ANS arousal, some emotion results. That is, like the term arousal, a bridge principle could easily link the psychological terms cognitive analysis and consciousness to corresponding terms in neuroscience because the terms in neuroscience would be intensionally *and* extensionally the same as psychology's.

One might reply that because Mandler's theory of emotion essentially defines these terms in virtue of mental content, the explanatory power of this theory turns on its ability to predict the content of the evaluative or the conscious state. The logical relations among the psychological state that fundamentally define the evaluative or conscious state cannot be explained in terms of the causal relation among neurophysiological events. Hence, neuroscience cannot just subsume these terms.

Of course, the assumption is that neuroscience cannot employ descriptions based essentially on content, but that assumption is false. Neuroscientists do produce theories dealing with content. Patricia Churchland points out that "neuroscientists do address such questions as how neurons manage to store information, or how all assemblies do pattern recognition or how they manage to effect sensorimotor control.... In doing so, they are up to their ears in theorizing ... about [content] ... and computations" (1986, p. 361). Hence, we have no a priori reason for ruling out neuroscience importing cognitive evaluation and consciousness from psychology.

In any case, the rub lies with the second condition. It is false that linking (or importing) terms and predicates in Mandler's theory of emotion to terms and predicates in neuroscience would *explain* any psychological generalizations. Consider Mandler's claim that "how I see, hear, feel, like, or examine" events in my environment "is fashioned by my biological limitations and my past experience represented in cognitive structures" (1984, p. 51). Remember, we understand how cognitive structures represent experience functionally in terms of the relations to those structures of past input, other structures, and resultant output. To take Mandler's example, we would then understand the relation between a real giant panda and our experience of it in terms of both our physical makeup and our cognitive-interpretive history. To explain why our experience is what it is depends on how our perceptual apparatus functions and on how we interpreted and remembered other experiences. So, these functionally understood cognitive structures are relevant in the answer we give to our question of why the experience is of a giant panda and not of something else.

Now suppose we have some bridge principles linking psychologically understood notions of biological limitations and past experience being represented in cognitive structures to neuroscience. Two sorts of links are possible. Either there are some neurophysiological structural similarities across tokens of perceptual apparatus or meaning analysis, in which case neuroscience could define those instances in terms of their structures; or there are no structural similarities, in which case the instances could still be understood functionally, as discussed above. I take it that we have every reason to believe that there are interesting

structural similarities to be found across tokens of perceptual apparatuses and that these similarities form the referential basis for neuroscientific terms that can be linked easily and directly to Mandler's "biological limitations." I also take it that we have no idea whether there are any
structural similarities in the case of meaning analysis.

Assume first that there are and that we get an easy link between the
neurophysiological similarities and the functionally defined psychological terms. Would this link now explain why the experience is of a giant
panda? The answer is no. Why is our experience of a giant panda as it
is? The past history of our cognitive interpretations as understood *functionally* provides part of the explanation. If we knew the morphological
structure underlying our cognitive interpretations down to the most
minute detail, it still would not change our psychological explanation
of the event because knowing the structure would not change the relevance of the functional explanation to the query, "Why is the experience
of a giant panda and not of something else?," as determined by the background context of cognitive psychology. Outlining the underlying morphology would only bury the higher level, systemic explanation of why
we experience the world as we do in a mass of irrelevant data.

So let us suppose instead that we have functionally defined "cognitive interpretation" in neuroscience by importing the necessary terms
and predicates from psychology. Would the links between neuroscience
and psychology now explain why we experience pandas as we do? Again,
the answer must be no. If the statements in neuroscience just *are* the
statements in psychology, then the description of the experiential event
must be the same in both fields. Furthermore, because the statements
accepted by the two scientific communities concerning "cognitive interpretation" are ex hypothesis the same, the background context and the
contrast class must also be the same. Hence, the explanation would be
the same as well. The one-step derivation of the psychological from
neuroscience would have nothing to add to the psychological explanation because the neuroscientific account would be exactly the same as
the psychological. Condition (2) does not hold.[18]

Explanatory Extension

If reduction is not the correct way to characterize the relationship
between psychology and neuroscience, we need to specify, insofar as
possible, what is. It does not follow, as Putnam seems to think, that

because reductionism failed, the two are autonomous. At least some of the terms and predicates used in both fields are the same, and it is possible to find neurophysiological structures underlying some functionally defined psychological terms. Patricia Churchland seems right when she claims that the mind and brain sciences "coevolve" and that the two sciences "knit . . . themselves into one another" (1986, p. 374) (although I suspect she is wrong in claiming that the two will "evolve toward a reductive consummation" [p. 281]). How can we cash out this metaphorical talk?

One sort of solution to the failure of reduction includes Mayr's (1982) use of hierarchies (cf., chapter 3) in which units at a lower level are combined into units at a higher level with different properties and functions. This idea reflects Wimsatt's (1976) levels of organization and roughly parallel Bechtel's (1982, 1983) account of the relationship between psychology and neuroscience in which he argues that psychological theories "describe the interactions of components whose operations are, in turn, studied by neuroscience" (Bechtel 1983, p. 325).[19]

However, these suggestions—though they present an adequate start in thinking about the relationship among levels of organization of the mind, brain, person, and community—gloss over the pragmatic aspects of explanation. Since what counts as an explanation depends on the context of the scientific inquiry, which in turn determines the contrast classes, we cannot simply assume that what one field examines could be *epistemologically* related at all to the concerns of another discipline. On the contrary, our discussion suggests that neuroscience concerns itself with *fundamentally* different sorts of questions and answers than psychology.

We need a characterization that can remain faithful to the different sorts of why-questions, with the different sorts of explanations they entail, as well as to the many levels of investigation both within and across neuroscience and psychology. I offer Philip Kitcher's notion of explanatory extension as a good model for helping us to elucidate the relationship. Explanatory extension does not require that the fields involved share historical contexts, reference relations, contrast classes, or explanatory goals. Rather, explanatory extension rests on the idea that one field can "illuminate issues that were treated incompletely, if at all," in another (Kitcher 1984, p. 358).[20]

There are two ways in which I see psychology and neuroscience working to extend one another in developing a framework for understanding cognitive science. On the one hand, one science can provide "a theoretical demonstration of the possibility of an antecedently problematic presupposition" for the other (Kitcher 1984, p. 361).[21] On the other, one science can conceptually refine the other by "[yielding] a specification of entities that belong to the extensions of the predicates in . . . [one] theory, with the result that the ways in which the referents of these predicates are fixed are altered in accordance with the new specifications" (Kitcher 1984, p. 364).

Some philosophers of cognitive science expect neurophysiology to provide a better way to specify some psychological attributes.[22] Neuroscience may give us a way to understand how various psychological entities function without resorting to unhelpful and vague metaphors. Psychology, of course, can provide the same service for neuroscience, as can any domain in cognitive science for any other domain. In general, the hope is that the other sciences will give us a way to identify the functionally defined items without having to rely solely on verbal reports or behavioral reactions to perceived phenomena. A combination of sciences should give our cognitive experiences better explicated underpinnings and fuller functional descriptions.

In the remainder of the chapter, I outline possible instances of both aspects of explanatory extension culled from the literature of psychology and neuroscience, and then use these examples to develop the notion of explanatory extension further and to argue that it fruitfully characterizes the relationship between psychology and neuroscience. The first example illustrates condition (1), that an extending theory theoretically demonstrates the possibility of some antecedently problematic presupposition of the extended theory. For our concerns, an antecedently problematic presupposition cashes out as some statement F_p which is implied by the union of the accepted background K of the extended theory and the theory itself, but for which there also exist reasonable counterarguments from other premises that the statement is false. This example is taken from current work in infant psychology and developmental neuroscience and deals with the structures necessary for memory processes. F_p is that retrieval is necessary but not sufficient for recall; K is Piagetian developmental psychology; and the counterargument comes from cognitive psychology, which holds that retrieval is not only necessary but also sufficient for recall.

Recall refers to accessing (bringing into awareness) a cognitive structure pertaining to a past experience not currently available through perception. Recalling something does not require a person's awareness that the event in question comes from past experience; it only requires that the person is aware of the event itself. We can contrast this term with the weaker notion, *recognition*, which refers to simply showing the effects of past experience on current behavior. Recognition does not require retrieval of information of a past experience from memory on the basis of some sort of cue; recall does.[23]

Infants apparently have the capacity for something more than just primitive recognition. Evidence suggests that they can passively recall information on the basis of external cues as young as seven months.[24] These early instances of recall are probably context bound and reflect the expectation engendered by conditioning. At this stage, the infant only has conditioned action responses and does not have the ability to explicitly imagine objects or events apart from the conditioned context. Thus, according to Piaget, their ability to be reminded is not *true* recall; deliberate recall and explicit imagining develop later.

Proponents of the Piagetian paradigm argue that there are two representational systems, declarative and procedural. Recognition can operate in both systems, but in order for us to truly recall an item, it must be stored in "symbolic" form in declarative memory. Procedural memory is only sufficient for some passive retrieval, and is not at all sufficient for true recall. As Jean Mandler states, "the sine qua non for recall is the ability to access stored information, that is, to bring it in awareness" (1984, p. 83). There is no reason to believe that infants can engage in this type of sophisticated processing, yet they still can retrieve some information from procedural memory.

In general, however, cognitive psychology argues that retrieval is not only necessary, but is also sufficient for all recall. Since developmental theory suggests that retrieval is only necessary, we have a fairly clear example of an antecedently problematic presupposition. This presents a good opportunity for another theory to step in and extend developmental psychology by showing how it is possible to get retrieval without recall; that is, how it is possible to have two memory systems. Work by Goldman-Rakic and others on the development of the prefrontal cortex does just that.

The frontal lobe is a rather late maturing system—it is not until one and a half to three years after birth that the prefrontal cortex approaches adult form in humans. Neuroscientists believe that in mature form, the prefrontal cortex organizes behavior for the achievement of goals.[25] As mentioned in chapter 3, damage to adult prefrontal cortex results in impaired synthetic reasoning, the inability to use past experiences in planning future activities, perseverance of inappropriate behavioral responses, and improper social affect. Most importantly, damage to the lobe in adults results in a loss of the ability to perform delayed-response tasks in both humans and primates. (This task reflects the capacity to recall an object after a few seconds' delay.)

There is now substantial converging evidence, primarily from local lesions studies in the macaque and rhesus monkeys, that "the capacity to perform delayed-response tasks depends on the bilateral integrity of the dorso-lateral prefrontal cortex" (Goldman-Rakic 1987, p. 377).[26] In particular, delayed-response function has been precisely localized to the principal sulcus (also known as Walker's area 46, and Brodman's area 9), a subdivision of the prefrontal cortex.[27]

As also discussed, the most intriguing finding is that a number of principal sulcus neruons fire in a pattern time locked to the delay period of a delayed-response task.[28] These neurons become active when the target stimulus is first presented, and then show increasing activity during the delay, and finally, cease firing at the end of the delay.[29] Furthermore, these neurons only increase their firing rate during the delay when the stimulus must be remembered in order to complete the task. These results provide excellent evidence that the prefrontal cortex plays a role in processing absent information; that is, it plays a role in retrieval and recall.

However, these neurophysiological results *cannot* be replicated in infant monkeys with still developing prefrontal lobes. Apparently, whatever the principal sulcus neurons are doing early in life has nothing to do with remembering important stimuli. Nevertheless, human infants are able to perform delayed-response tasks before their frontal lobes are mature, and infant monkeys can perform the task even with their prefrontal cortex oblated.[30] Goldman-Rakic argues that these results indicate that the prefrontal cortex does not assume its functional role in the cognitive system until relatively late in development and, prior to the frontal lobe taking over recall capacities, corticostriatal connections allow the recall needed for delayed-response tasks to take place. Exactly how this structure operates is not known, but neuroscientists suspect that it is linked to operant and classical conditioning in young primates and humans.[31]

So, in adults, retrieval may be necessary and sufficient for recall and such retrieval depends on an intact frontal cortex. Infants, however, may use a different mechanism than adults in storing information learned via conditioning.[32] This system, which is later supplanted in adults, does not tie retrieval inextricably to recall. Thus, neuroscientific research in the development of the prefrontal cortex demonstrates the theoretical possibility of the antecedently problematic presupposition F_P in Piagetian psychology, and in virtue of the demonstration, helps to extend the explanation given in infant development for the cognitive behavior of infants.

The second example illustrates condition (2), that an extending theory may conceptually refine the extended theory by better specifying entities that belong to the extensions of the predicates in the extended theory, such that proponents of the extended theory alter the ways in which the referents of these predicates are fixed in accordance with the new specifications. In this instance, the extension occurs in virtue of V. J. Ramachandran's work on our visual system perceiving shape from shading. This work refines discussions concerning the function of simple and complex cells in area 17 of the visual cortex.

Our brain uses many depth cues to move from the two-dimensional image formed by the pattern of light falling on our retina to our perception of a solid three-dimensional world. Some of these cues are binocular disparity, occlusion, perspective, and shading. Of these, the most important is shading, for we can perceive shape from shading alone. We can do this because our brains make the simplifying assumption that there is only one ambient light source. Further, it appears that shading serves as an elementary feature in perception, along with color and edges.[33]

The profound importance of shading cues for three-dimensional perceptions has raised the question of how our brains are able to use shading information to derive an object's shape. One would suspect, based on the processing's importance, that there is some neural system dedicated just to that purpose. Working on that assumption, Lehky and Sejnowski (1988) have created a neurally plausible computer simulation (a "neural" neural network) of shape from shading to see just what properties a dedicated system might have. Their connectionist network consisted of three layers of nodes: an input layer, a hidden layer, and an output layer. They designed the input layer to mimic the "center-surround" receptive fields of the retinal ganglia. They then trained the network to derive an object's shape from shading information by giving as input shading cues for a variety of objects with different points of illumination. The network guessed what the shape of the object was and a "teacher" function then adjusted the weights among the nodes based on the discrepancy between the guessed output and what the correct output should have been. After 40,000 trials, the network could correctly guess an object's axes of curvature from shading cues.

The surprise came when Lehky and Sejnowski examined the response patterns of the hidden layers. By determining what the receptive fields are in that layer, one might get a good idea of what the receptive fields of neurons dedicated to performing the shape from shading task could be like. It turns out that the receptive fields of the hidden layer units are very similar to those of the "edge-detector" cells of the visual cortex. The hidden units responded best to bars of various lengths, widths, and orientations and yet these cells were dedicated to performing a function that had nothing to do with bars at all.

The implication of this exercise is that the simple and complex cells discovered by Hubel and Weisel (1977) in area 17 of the visual cortex may now be functionally identified. Simple cells have excitatory and inhibitory zones that respond to bars of light at a particular orientation. Complex cells also respond to bars of light at a particular orientation, but do not have the excitatory and inhibitory zones. Since their discovery, there has been much discussion within neuroscience about how processing in the cortex must work. As mentioned in chapter 3, some argued that as one traveled up the pathways of visual processing, the cells responded to more and more sophisticated and abstract stimuli until at the top there were cells that only responded to complete percepts (the so-called grandmother cells). Others have favored more distributed representations, claiming that whatever these cells were actually doing, we have to look at them all at once to understand their processing task. The work by Lehky and Sejnowski provides the beginning of a clear answer to what the processing task may be. The cells in area 17 may be devoted to deriving objects' shapes from inputted shading cues.

Although the jury is still out and no one can say for sure yet what the function of area 17 is, we may be witnessing the development of conceptual refinement. It is not yet clear that psychology and the resultant computer simulation have functionally specified a group of entities that belong to the extensions of predicates in neuroscience dealing with the response patterns of neurons. It is even less clear that these results will alter the ways in which the referents of these predicates are fixed.[34] Still, it is clear how the move to conceptual refinement would work in this case—psychology could give a functional account of the simple and complex cells found by Hubel and Weisel thereby altering the way we conceive of the cells—and that some moves in this general direction are being made. As Ramachandran remarks, "The neurological events mediating the process in human beings are still mysterious, but insights from psychology can help to elucidate what the events may be and how they are organized in the brain" (1988, p. 83).

Again, we may have found an aspect of explanatory extension linking psychology and neuroscience. However, in this case, unlike the previous example, psychology would be extending neuroscience, and not the other way around. Psychology may have discovered a fundamental process in perception, and with the aid of neural network modeling, that process could be mapped to the response properties of area 17. (Notice however that what I have outlined is not a true reduction though, for even though work in another discipline may provide the referents for a term in psychology, it does not follow that the theory in psychology in which the term is embedded is now better explained or justified.) Explanatory extension is a bidirectional relationship in the mind and brain sciences. This bidirectionality is perhaps one important difference between the cognitive sciences and the strict biological sciences.[35] Furthermore, it goes against the common wisdom that one or the other science must be primary. (In the literature, one finds several arguments to the effect that discovering *what* the processes are must come before discovering *where* they are,[36] but this was not the case in either example. Discovery of location of process came before or simultaneously with discovery of the process itself.) The mind and brain sciences may literally coevolve, with each working to extend the other.

A second important point that this example also points out is a difficulty with argument from parallelism. In this instance of explaining perception, the lower level account, whether it be structural or functional, does not constrain the higher level descriptions to a unique solution. In this sense, it is possible to get multiple instantiation of higher level "functions" by underlying "structures." As mentioned above, a fairly popular argument in the philosophy of psychology is that psychology should disregard underlying stuff since the higher level events could be instantiated in any number of physical mechanisms. Laws in psychology would generalize over many different types of physical stuff, so the actual neural mechanism in humans are not relevant; the higher level generalizations do not tell us anything about lower level properties. This is just the problem of multiple realizibility for neuroscience and one reason philosophers often cite for the impossibility of reducing psychology by neuroscience. Here though, underlying physical descriptions do not constrain higher level descriptions either. As demonstrated by the alternative interpretations for the higher level function of area 17, it is not (yet) clear what the underlying structure, or even the lower level functional components, are instantiating. The nascent hope is that a fuller account of the lower level will eliminate the underdetermination of theory, but this sort of indeterminate multiple instantiability harks back to the underdetermination of functions discussed in chapter 4. What function we decide some components instantiate is determined in part by pragmatic and historical factors, including the interpretation we give surrounding components and other previously accepted scientific theories that parse the higher level physical system for us.

Cognitive psychologists generally assume that input from neuroscience will help narrow the possible interpretations they could give to functionally defined components. However, it is not at all clear that, in this early stage of neuroscientific research, neurophysiological evidence is able to do so. All we may ever have is partial or equivocal evidence, so simple arguments based on parallelism between functions across different research domains should be prima facie suspect. Knowing the underlying morphology in one domain (enough to answer that domain's questions adequately) may not thereby increase knowledge of parallel structures in another domain simply all desciptions are fundamentally underdetermined by the data, and how we chose our descriptions is relative to pragmatic considerations particular to individual fields. As should be clear by now, the connections among various levels of analysis are complicated and messy, and we are able to draw few generalizations about explanatory dependence, functional constraints across different levels in the organism's hierarchy, and the reductive connections among theories at different levels of analysis.

The bidirectional version of multiple instantiability also suggests that explanations from lower level to higher level descriptions, or vice versa, are not necessarily easy to make. This should raise serious questions about multidisciplinary arguments in general. If using data from related fields may not narrow one's search space, why should we complicate matters by bringing other disciplines in, except as a last resort or a final court of appeals? In the final two chapters, I try to answer this question by distinguishing between multidisciplinary approaches and true interdisciplinary theories.[37] I discuss how middle level descriptions, which are neither obviously purely functional nor structural (as traditionally conceived), are where most explanatory work occurs, and philosophers outlining the conditions for systemic explanations should not gloss over the importance of this level of description. Indeed, it is this intermediate level of description that actually connects the lower level neurophysiological models with higher level psychological theories, and allows multidisciplinary connstructions to become truly interdisciplinary theories.

For now, though, the bottom line is that we need to stop arguing over the reductionism/antireductionism issue in the cognitive sciences. Something is right about both sides: Despite Fodor's sentiment that we only have "gross" connections between psychology and neuroscience, there is unquestionably a close and interesting relationship among the mind and brain sciences. However, that connection does not reflect explanatory dependence. Psychology and neuroscience do rely on one another for evidence for some problematic entities or processes as well as for additional and more detailed support for their already developed hypotheses; however, nothing seems to suggest that any of these areas should merge or that they will need to rely on another discipline's advances for fundamental support.[38] Though they do share many important points of contact, the various scientific domains that make up the cognitive sciences are separate and independent fields of inquiry—each has its own history, with its own set of important questions, research techniques, explanatory patterns, criteria for error analysis, and so on. How or whether one domain will ultimately reduce another is simply the wrong philosophical approach to take.

A model of explanatory extension more adequately expresses the historical independence of the fields, as well as the complex connections that have been forged among them. Although the extending theory may indeed alter how we understand the referents of the extended theory, the change is neither significant enough to warrant replacing the extended theory outright, nor broad enough the count as a reducing correction. We are left with a fairly messy set of connections that can help to shape future questions and research projects but not force a fundamental change in identity. The examples I gave illustrate the range of evolutionary possibilities for rapidly growing domains of inquiry that may never be understood using simpler models of "partial" reductionism.

Chapter 6

The Dual Memory Hypothesis and the Structure of Interdisciplinary Theories

A cognitive approach to understanding behavioural development is essential, but . . . a traditional cognitive approach in isolation is, at best, inadequate. To take one extreme example, if a behavioural change were solely dependent on the maturation of a neural structure or pathway, then attempting a cognitive account of the processes underlying this change would not only be unncessary, but also may actually be misleading.[1]

We acknowledge that individuals may depend on their relations with one another for the appearance of distinctive human capacities; that the social entities individuals constitute may exercise a reciprocal influence on those agents, structuring their perceptions, motives, and opportunities; and that the discoveries of social science may lead to revisions in our intentional psychology, shaping our sense of what count for example as normal conditions.[2]

Here is a book intended to expound the modern theories . . . and to expound a new theory. In it there are nothing but strings that move around pulleys, which roll around drums, which go through pearl beads, which carry weights, and tubes which pump water while others swell and contract; toothed wheels which are geared to one another and engage hooks. We thought we were entering the tranquil and neatly ordered abode of reason, but we find ourselves in a factory.[3]

The straightforward function to structure reductionism traditionally assumed by philosophers of psychology and cognitive scientists alike is untenable. Neither the function/structure distinction nor reductive coevolution helps us understand the connection between psychology and neuroscience, nor do they help us analyze the use of evidence in an interdisciplinary field like cognitive science. Psychology and neuroscience, like the other investigative domains that comprise cognitive science, are joined in a complicated and nontrivial way, and the sucessful explanations that come out of cognitive science will rely on several levels of analysis over the same event space, each of which contains both systemic and morphological descriptions and each of which needs to share some fundamental guiding assumptions with the others.

This chapter documents an extended example of how a theory can not only combine various level of description and analysis, but also how a single explanation should encompass various experimental paradigms and research domains. It outlines the relevant data for building such a large scale multilevel theory and pulls evidence from developmental psychology, clinical neurology, neurophysiology, and cognitive pscyhology to develop the theoretical framework, though it focuses primarily on infant studies and what they can tell us about normal processing in adult memory.[4]

If we are seeking answers in other investigative domains, we need to understand what a strongly interdisciplinary approach is (as opposed to a merely multidisciplinary approach). It is one that relies on not only the evidence from more than one area, but which actively accepts the underlying assumptions of those areas as true and fundamental. This chaper also sketches how we should understand strongly interdisciplinary theories, given the diverse methodological frameworks that support them, by comparing them to Shaffner's notion of an overlapping interlevel theory and to the semantic conception of theories. I shall suggest that the semantic view of theories needs to be modified before it can serve as a philosophical reconstruction of interdisciplinary theories in cognitive science. In particular, it needs to better accomodate bridge sciences and the pragmatic factors in multidisciplinary uses of evidence.

Developmental Studies for a Dual Processing System

We shall begin with the distinction between recall and recognition in infants touched on in the last chapter. Evidence suggests that infants have two sorts of information retrieval systems. First, they appear capable of "recalling" information embedded in input-action loops. These S-R circuits are relatively noncognitive in that they are activated only in circumstances in which the stimulus input occurs. In other words, infants cannot freely and actively recall the information contained in these circuits unless the relevant input obtains. This retrieval system is obviously in place at birth, or shortly thereafter (more on this point below) and is later supplanted or augmented by a more sophisticated system. This more sophisticated system appears in older infants. Using this retrieval system, infants can recognize and actively recall information outside the contexts in which it originally occurred. Hence, the relevant data structures exist apart from any conditioned behavioral response. We can think of this system then as being relatively more cognitive in that older infants can control and manipulate their representations of the world.

These two distinctions, or distinctions like these, form the basis of the dual processing system hypothesis popular in cognitive science today. They recall the distinctions prevalent in the mid–1970s between automatic and controlled processing mechanisms in long-term store (LTS).[5] Shiffrin and Schneider, for example, distinguished between an automatic form of pattern matching that merely activated a learned sequence of elements and a controlled processing in which a temporary sequence of elements is created on the fly, as it were.[6] The former mechanism had few processing contraints, could operate in parallel, was largely unconscious and beyond the control of the subject's cognitive strategies. In contrast, the latter mechanism demanded conscious attention, could only operate serially, and was subject to the intentions of the subject.

At present though most cognitive scientists think (though not all, I should stress) that there are in fact two different mnemonic processing *systems* instead of two different types of *access* to the same underlying LTS. Part of the data I present below is designed to corroborate this point. For now, we know that Goldman-Rakic's neurophysiological explication of cortical development, which extends developmental psychology's distinction between recall and recognition, points to two separate processing and storage streams. Consequently, let us take as our working hypothesis that older infants (and presumably adults as well) have (at least) two separate mnemonic systems, one of which corresponds to conditioned S-R habits of behavior, the other to cognitively controlled but context independent manipulations of data.

Infants, of course, can be trained using operant conditioning paradigms. Presuambly, these tasks, as well as the habituation-novelty preference tasks I shall discuss in a moment, would activate the earliest
form of memory retrieval, the learned S-R habits of behavior. In the
operant conditioning training tasks for young (three- to five-month-
old) infants, general features of the task to be performed set their
behavioral responses. The particular attributes of any single item, or of
the testing environment itself, do not enter into the young infants' representations of the triggering input.[7] For example, infants were trained
to turn their heads to receive a squirt of milk (the R) when a tone
sounded (the S). On learning this behavior through repeated exposure
to the S-R link, the infants would continue to turn their heads when
the tone sounded, even though they were no longer hungry. They
would simply refuse to swallow. Even when quinine, a foul-tasting but
essentially harmless substance, was substituted for the milk in the later
versions of the experiment, infants continued to turn their heads and
accept the squirted liquid, despite having motivation not to.[8]

These results dovetail with Piaget's "AB error," the most common
type of forgetting studied in infant research, as well as the results from
various habituation-novelty tasks. Piaget noted that when infants
observe some object being "hidden" at location A, they can later locate
it. However, after finding the object at A several times successfully, they
will continue to search there even though the object is now placed at
location B with the infant watching.[9] For example, young infants will
repeatedly search for mother at door A if she leaves though that door.
After several trials, if the mother now exits through door B, the infants
will look for their mother at the previously learned door A, even though
they saw her leave though door B.[10]

In an habituation-novelty preference task, psychologists use infants'
innate preferences for attending to new and different objects as an index
for how much information the infants have recorded and are able to
retrieve about the world. Infants look at familiar stimuli less than new
stimuli. Hence, scientists conclude, the development of habituation
effects indicate that the infant has formed a memory for the known stimuli. This sort of behavior though does not require very sophisticated
information manipulations. Psychologists generally think of the infants'
performance in terms of facilitated processing, rather than as controlled
access to explicit knowledge of the previous occurances. For these differential attention effects in infants are unaffected by the length of time
between the original habituating exposures and subsequent novelty tests,

as one would expect with instances of actual learning.[11] Moreover, if there is a shift in the sensory modality used between study and test (from visual cues to auditory tests, for example), there is no habituation effect in six-to nine-month-old infants,[12] even though in conditions using only a single modality, the younger infants show reliable novelty preferences with changes in orientation, representational format, and motion.[13, 14]

This is not to say, however, that young infants can only operate using one modality at a time. Indeed, some cross-modal talk has to occur at least shortly after birth. Andrew Meltzoff and his colleagues have shown that infants as young as a few hours old can mimic the facial expressions of adults without any sort of visual feedback.[15] They conclude that there must be some mechanism for comparing visual and propioceptive representations present from birth. Lest one think that these mimetic capacities are somehow special and do not represent the norm in innate represenational capacities, Meltzoff and Burton (1979) demonstrated that very young infants (the average age in their study was 29 days) could recognize by sight objects only touched previously.

The traditional view has been that young infants have compartmentalized, modality-specific representations that become coordinated only after they begin bimodal explorations of their environment at around a year old. Now perhaps it is better to think of visual-action schemas being encoded as single units from birth.[16] Nevertheless, we can still conceptualize these schemas in terms of facilitated processing of S-R connections. Certainly there is no indication that these young infants can detach the information stored in the visual-action circuit in order to respond preferentially to auditory stimuli, say.

For a different sort of evidence that supports the general view that there are two separate processing streams in infants, only one of which is active at birth (or shortly thereafter), let us turn to the development of facial recognition in infants. It is clear that our talent for recognizing faces is quite specialized. Perhaps the best evidence for this is that we cannot recognize inverted faces as easily or as quickly as we can upright visages, with our competence decreasing by as much as 25 percent. Though we are not perfectly accurate, we are much better at recognizing and distinguishing other objects in inverted positions (different cars, for example). In these instances, our rate of success decreases only by about 10 percent.[17] Given the special salience of faces for our survival, and the importance of distinguishing among them accurately and rapidly, it is not too surprising that we should have developed expert systems dedicated to facial recognition.

Nevertheless, even though we may have a specialized processors for distinguishing faces, this expertise is clearly learned. Diamond and Carey (1986) have shown that judges for dog shows have more trouble distinguishing inverted dogs among dogs in the breed they judge with error rates similar to those for faces. For other dog breeds, as well as other objects, dog show judges score normally. Similar effects have also been shown for ranchers and the animals in their herds.

How and when do we learn this skill? Early studies indicated that our preference for faces develops sometime between two and four months. At this time, infants prefer to look at faces with their features arranged properly over empty face outlines or faces with their features rearranged.[18] In fact, all studies were consistent with this result, except one which showed infants as young as nine minutes preferring faces over other similar shapes.[19] At the time, most believed that those results were simply anomolous. However, Suzanne Dziurawiec and Hadyn Ellis have since replicated these results.[20] They too showed that infants as young as a few minutes old preferred to look at faces.

Mark Johnson and John Morton have now replicated Dziurawiec and Ellis's results and well as the results showing that one-month-old infants *lack* a preference for looking at faces.[21] What infants exhibit is a U-shaped learning curve. As Johnson and Morton point out, "it [is] difficult for theories which assume a single mechanism to account for developmental U-shaped curves. . . . It is difficult to see how to account for the pattern of data observed in terms of gradual increases in perceptual abilities or learning" (1991, pp. 36–37).

Ultimately, Johnson postulates the existence of four different mnemonic circuits.[22] Only two, though, need concern us here. There is a primitive processing loop available from birth which is sensitive to the visual structure of the human face. It allows the infant to track and orient toward faces; however, it cannot distinguish unique features among faces (a relatively simple visual-motor system, in other words). There is also another processing loop that allows infants to learn specific information about faces, as well as other things perhaps. This more sophisticated processor does not come fully "on-line" until two to four months after birth, as the influence of the primitive system declines. Presumably it learns most about faces because the more primitive system forces the infant to track human faces over almost anything else. The interaction of these two processors can account for the interesting learning curve for faces in individuals, as well as explain how adults can also learn to distinguish the features among other salient creatures.

We now have a variety of data pointing to two different mnemonic processors active in infant development: a set of fairly primitive visuo-motor S-R response patterns followed by the development of a more sophisticated processor that can learn the details of presented stimuli and then later respond to those details in different contexts. The early system is bound both by context and modality of stimuli presentation, while the later system can detach relevant information from its surrounding environment and supports cross-modal talk.

Notice that insofar as these two systems are defined and explicated entirely in terms of their causal roles (what inputs get mapped to what outputs via what intermediate steps), they are understood in straightforward traditional functional terms. (Presumably, as psychologists are better able to quantify their results, the resultant theory will be computational as well.) Moreover, as psychologists are interested in telling the developmental story of mnemonic processing in infants, their theory will be presented in terms of a causal/functional etiology. There is one level of analysis and explanation here, the level of "information processing," with the underlying "structures" that support the higher level regularities being of lesser importance.[23]

Not surprisingly, baby data are nortoriously difficult to collect and analyze, primarily because it is very difficult for infants to "tell" investigators what they are experiencing. As a result, only so much can be learned about the details of their mnemonic capacities from direct experimental testing. Once the basic framework is established, it is important to check these results against data from adult populations. Since we are not so limited in the tests we can run on adult subjects, tests run on this subject pool should be able to extend the framework from the infant literature by providing more information regarding what each system can do. That is, data from clinical and cognitive psychology should be able to refine developmental psychology conceptually by specifying entities belonging to the extensions of the predicates in the developmental theory, so that the ways in which the referents of these predicates are fixed now follow the new specifications (the second type of explanatory extension mentioned in chapter 5). It is to these studies I now turn.

The Distinction between Implicit and Explicit Memory

The same sort of memory limitations present in young infants also appear in amnesics. Perhaps infants and amnesics have similar mnemonic abilities, with both of their performances reflecting only more primitive "S-R" mnemonic loops. Infants then would be like adult amnesics in that neither can access their more sophicated memory processors; not yet developed in infants, the system (or access to it) would be damaged in amnesics.

In support this conjecture, Daniel Schacter and Morris Moscovitch (1984) report that amnesics perform exactly like infants in an AB type of search task. Amnesics continue to search for an object at its previously hidden location even though the new "hiding" place is in plain sight. Other evidence that amnesics function only with the more primitive "S-R" memory system intact includes the fact that they can learn skills (such as learning to complete a jig-saw puzzle or to do the Tower of Hanoi problem)[24] and exhibit classical conditioning effects,[25] though they cannot later report their training sessions or summarize what they supposedly learned. For example, H. M., a well-known amnesic, can learn to perform a variety of motor skills, all the while insisting that he could not remember events connected to previous trials, including trials that had taken place only minutes before.[26]

Interestingly enough, spared learning in amnesics is *not* confined to various visuo-motor tasks; many of the retained abilities are quite cognitive. For example, amnesics can learn to apply the Fibonacci rule, as well as other sequential patterns,[27] even though they all claim "unequivocally that they had never seen or done this task before" (Wood et al. 1982, p. 174). They can also learn to read mirror script, and they read normal sentences much faster a second time through.[28] Finally, amnesics can use the prior presentation of words when completing sentence fragments (e.g., adding an "LE" to "TAB__" when they were previously shown "TABLE" in a list of words). Indeed, their performance on this task is very similar to normal controls, except that the amnesics do not recognize the words in later recognition tasks, while the normals have no trouble explicitly recalling most of the words used in the tests.[29] Unlike infants then, amnesics' mnemonic abilities extend into more cognitive tasks. Though it is still fair to call their responses context-specific "S-R" behaviors, it is not quite accurate to speak only of learned or innate visuo-motor circuits. Nevertheless, the preserved functions in amnesics are strongly analogous to the tasks young infants can perform, and amnesics' deficits closely resemble what young infants cannot do.

A second sort of lesion patient relevant here are the visual agnosics, patients unable to recognize visually the class to which an object belongs.[30] Persons who exhibit this deficit have difficulty recognizing a variety of visually presented objects, though their individual deficits might be quite specific. As a particularly striking example, Antonio Damasio (1990) has reported a subject who has lost the ability to name vegetables and fruit. A specific sort of agnosia related to the discussion above is prosopagnosia, a deficit involved in the recognition of what should be familiar faces. Regardless, agnosics cannot name the objects whose memories they have apparently lost, nor can they non-verbally demonstrate that they know what the objects are by grouping them into semantic categories. Interestingly enough, though, they are able to recognize the objects in other modalities by touching them or by listening to their characteristic sounds or by hearing verbal descriptions. Prosopagnosics, for example, might recognize their loved ones if they were to hear their voices or if they were able to feel their faces.[31] Moreover, most agnosics do demonstrate some sort of implicit knowledge of the objects whose names they have lost. The galvanic skin response of prosopagnosics alters in response to familiar faces, even though the patients deny that they know whom they are viewing. (Amnesics too show similar reactions to faces they have recently met, but have already forgotten.)

Again, we are finding modality-specific response patterns and a dissociation between explicitly being able to recall an object versus exhibiting some sort of differential processing of stimuli. In this case, modality-specific processing occurs during attempted explicit retrieval of information. Given the framework outlined above, we should say that agnosias have lost their ability to make transmodal connections of information in explicit mnemonic processing, among other things. How exactly this might work and whether this is indeed the best description of an agnosia's deficits is discussed below.

Finally, I should mention the phenomena of dismorphopsia and blindsight. Patients with dismorphopsia cannot discriminate shapes very easily. For example, they would not be able to distinguish between a square and a rectangle. Nevertheless, these patients can locate the stimuli in their visual fields as well as navigate in their environment. Interestingly, these patients will anticipate the shapes of objects accurately in their hand movements if they are to pick them up or stroke them, while simultaneously reporting that they cannot distinguish what the objects look like.[32] In many ways, blindsight patients are similar to dismorphopics. These are patients who cannot report what they see in one area of their visual field (they are effectively blind there); however, they can make accurate discriminations of general object location, orientation, size, and texture if told to "guess" what is in their damaged area. They too anticipate the shape of objects in their hand and eye movements, even though they simultaneously report that they cannot see anything.[33] Rosaleen McCarthy takes these deficits to be evidence of spared visuo-motor pathways, but damaged semantic memories (or damaged access to semantic memory).[34]

Tying an infant's capacities to behavior exhibited by brain damaged adults is important for two reasons. First, the testing procedures used for the adult lesion subjects gives us a methodology by which we can compare normal adult performance with results from infant, amnesic, and agnosic tests simply by replicating the adult deficit tasks using normal adult subjects. This would then allow us to refine our original distinctions considerably since adult performace is quite nuanced and robust. Second, because we know quite a bit about the sort of brain lesions amnesics, agnosics, dismorphopsics, and patients with blindsight have sustained, we also have a way to connect our higher level mnemonic processors with lower level descriptions of neural processing. We can then use this information to develop other animal models in which we can study the processing pathways more invasively (and hence more completely). But before moving onto neurophysiology, let me just briefly mention some of the normal adult cognitive studies to show the range of empirical tests possible and what they show us about building interdisciplinary theories.[35]

Tulving, Schacter, and Stark (1982) gave a word completion task to normals, similar to the one mentioned above for amnesics. Subjects studied long lists of low-frequency words and were then given a yes/no recognition test and a fragment completion test one hour, one day, or one week later. In half the test conditions, the recognition test preceeded the completion test; in the other half, the completion test came first. They discovered that, as with amnesics, previous exposure to a word facilitates a subject's ability to complete a fragment of it. The magnitude of this priming effect (known as *implicit* priming) did not diminish over time; in contrast, recognition performance (or *explicit* priming) did decline severely over a week interval.

Similar results have been reported in perceptual identification tasks. Here, subjects attempt to identify a word presented during a brief (approximately 35 msec) exposure after having studied a word list that includes items to be repeated in the identification task. Facilitated identification occurs even after a twenty-four-hour delay between a single-study exposure and the identification task, but, as before, recognition memory declines significantly over the same period.[36] In addition, graphemic information is retained over long intervals in perceptual recognition. Indeed, implicit remembering can be tied to a particular episode, a particular modality, and a particular font, though not to a particular environment.

Altering the test conditions of this basic paradigm tells us much about the various and complimentary properties of the processing systems underlying implicit perceptual identification and explicit recall. For example, manipulations of the level of processing (brought about, e.g., by the instructions to examine a list of words for instances of the letter 'r' versus instructions to examine the list for concrete nouns) have no effect on the perceptual identification results, but they do substantially affect success in later recognition. Implicit priming does not transfer well across modalities, whereas recognition memory appears largely unaffected by changes in the modality of presentation from study to test sessions. Implicit primimg is insensitive to the amount of attention devoted to the task, whereas recognition is greatly affected by level of attention.[37]

Because priming is sensitive to some contextual factors but not others, the popular spreading activation model in cognitive psychology does not adequately capture priming phenomena.[38] Data tell us that the memory system(s) used in the more implicit priming tasks differs fundamentally from the ones tapped in the explicit recall tasks. To wit: the implicit memory system does not require explicit memory of the study episode. However, some sort of processing of the stimuli still must occur because the subject must already have at least some minimal representation of the stimuli before we see any sort of behavioral priming effect.[39] In addition, this preexisting representation is modality specific since changes in modality affect implicit priming. In contrast, the explicit memory system is probably not tied so closely to modality since explicit priming effects are not sensitive to modality changes. This system allows one to recall particular learning events and is sensitive to the length of time between study and test and to whether the subjects are asked to process the words in the list semantically, as well as to the number and spacing of repetitions among words.

This brief recitation of results does tell us some things about our memory systems that we did not know before. For example, from these experiments, it is clear that there probably is an episodic basis for the perceptual identification and repetition effects, which is very different from what the infant or clinical literature suggests. This hypothesis is bolstered by Jacoby and Dallas's (1981) observation that a single prior exposure to low frequency words increases perceptual recognition priming. Why would one additional exposure have such an effect? Perhaps, as they suggest, some early implicit system is in fact storing some contextual factors, thus implying that this memory system is a processing system faintly reminisent of a semantic memory built out of episodic traces. Nevertheless, these implicit systems need only retain fairly basic "structural" information of stimuli, and not its semantic character (since, among other things, new associations among words can lead to interference in performance in the second system, whereas the first system exhibits no such AB, AC interference effects for pairs of normatively unrelated words.)[40] Hence, these implicit systems must be more than a collection of isolated and independent facilitated input-output circuits because they feed into explicit memory and facilitate processing there, perhaps by increasing the activation, or by decreasing the activation threshold, for "structurally" similar representations. They are nonsemantic, though cognitive, and they operate automatically and independent of subject control.

Different evidence for the existence of an implicit processing system and its independence from explicit memory comes from unconscious priming data in normal adults. This is a different experimental paradigm for discovering the processing capacities of our memory systems and how they interact. Here we examine the difference between processing incoming stimuli above the threshold for conscious perception and below it in normal human adults. Once again, these results refine our theoretical models of our memory systems by increasing the list of processing attributes for each of the two systems.

It turns out that there is a significant difference in the way representations are primed when subjects consciously retain the prime versus when subjects receive the prime subliminally.[41] For example, researchers compare the effects of unmasked and masked polysemous primes on the processing of a word flashed immediately after the presentation of the prime amd semantically related to one of the prime's meanings.[42] They find that when unmasked, *PALM* facilitates processing *WRIST* only when it is preceded by the word *HAND*; when it is preceded by *TREE* it delays processing of *WRIST*. However, when *PALM* is masked, it facilitates processing *WRIST* regardless of what precedes it. These data are also consistent with the output of an early nonsemantic implicit system priming more than one item in explicit memory. Because subliminal priming data are so closely tied to the modality and graphemes of the stimuli, it is doubtful if the semantic aspects of the words play any large role in determining the output of the system.[43]

In contrast, our explicit memory only gives a single segmentation and semantic interpretation for each stimulus per unit time. That is, we are aware of only a single semantic hypothesis for each subitized data input—we explicitly entertain only one interpretation of some perceptual event at a time. A quick example of this phenomenon appears in figure 6.1. We can see the Necker cubes as both opening upward to the left or both downward to the right, but never opening in either direction at the same time. A second point the Necker cubes suggest is that in matching incoming stimuli with some semantic hypothesis, our explicit mnemonic system tries to account for as much of the data as possible with each semantic "guess." Even though the two cubes are two separate perceptual objects, we nonetheless perceive them as a single unit.

Anthony Marcel generalizes this observation and argues that what determines whether two logically separable events are in fact judged as a single unit is whether our semantic "schema" treats them as lying within the same parsed segment of its unitized description. We do find evidence for this sort of unitization in both the auditory and the visual domains.[44] These experiments indicate that we interpret incoming stimuli and we can only explicitly perceive things in virtue of our interpretation.

To summarize the results of these tests on normal adults: our implicit memory system need only be sensitive to the structure of the incoming stimuli; however, it can encompass more than one (nonsemantic) "interpretation" for each stimulus. On the other hand, the content or output of our explicit memory system seems to be the most economically fruitful semantic hypothesis possible at the time. Both of

Figure 6.1　*The Necker Cubes.*

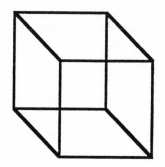 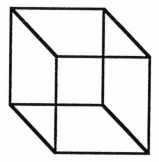

these facts can be used to extend the framework proposed in the infant literature: the visuo-motor S-R circuits are noncognitive in the sense that they only need record the basic structure of the relevant stimuli; the more sophisticated processor is semantic, though it can only give one semantic interpretation of stimuli at a time. These distinctions too fit with the evidence from lesion patients and help clear up the discrepancies between the clinical and the developmental literature. For example, the preserved "skills" in amnesics may be cognitive in the sense that they are not purely visuo-motor, yet they are not cognitive in the sense that they do not require semantic interpretations of events.

At the same time, though, we are receiving our first hint in the difficulty in putting together an interdisciplinary theory (and we still have yet to move beyond one level of analysis!). The early innate systems in infants are clearly not sensitive to details of the testing environment, while the implicit memory system in adults is. Are these still the same system? We really can't say. The answer to that question depends on what regularities developmental or cognitive psychologists take to be fundamental in building their theoretical characterizations. As discussed in chapter 3, there is no obvious response outside the perspective, and the biases, of either discipline.

Moreover, this difficulty is compounded by the fact that each of the different subdisciplines in psychology (developmental, clinical, and cognitive) use different vocabularies for describing their experimental results and conceptualizing the functional relations among stimuli, behavior, and other mental states. For example, developmental psychology speaks of visuo-motor S-R circuits and modality-independent retrieval systems. In contrast, clinical psychology refers to implicit procedural memory versus an explicit episodic memory. Finally, cognitive psychology posits an implicit structural memory (which is probably episodic) and an explicit semantic memory.[45] As a result, though each subdisciplines' abstract descriptions may resemble one another and, hence, may extend one another explanations, they do not *directly* support the theoretical predictions made by the others. Is the implicit procedural memory in amnesics just the structural memory in normal adults by a different name? The answer to this question again depends on how the scientists take these predicates to generalize. And that depends on which questions the scientists are trying to answer (cf., chapter 2).

Nevertheless, we can discern a general guiding framework among all these different approaches. From the data given thus far, we know that there is one memory system that automatically accesses information given certain inputs. It expresses its knowlege indirectly through differentially affecting behavioral responses to the same task, instead of through some overtly given verbal answer or meaningful gesture. A second memory system concerns more specific knowledge about surrounding circumstances and particular events. Though it too may differentially affect behavioral responses, memory in that system can be recalled in (more or less) explicit propositional form. This sort of guiding framework, which is not specific enough to make experimental predictions, yet still contrains how one thinks about mneumonic processing, forms one plank in building an interdisciplinary theory. How these general guiding frameworks are supposed to function will be fleshed out below.

However, even though we can only combine the theoretical descriptions of the event space into a general guiding framework, we should not thereby ignore, gloss over, or simplify the empirical data from various experiments used to support the descriptions. Instead, we should strive to describe the experimental protocols and their results in as neutral terms as possible (relative to the framework or any specific theoretical description). That is, we should simply list the tests and their results, much as I have done above. We can think of these descriptions as giving us (rather long-winded) *operational definitions* of the various phenomena that we can then use to make specific predictions about the results of other experiments. These descriptions will be unwieldy to say the least, but, insofar as we want to build an interdisciplinary theory, it is better to use these than any overarching description that already assumes some theoretical perspective or other.[46] Using these operational descriptions is one way to thereby minimize the influence of historical and sociological factors across disciplines. This facet too will be discussed in more detail below.

This ill fit among the different domains, even among the different subdisciplines within a single research area, also points to a danger in adopting a multidisciplinary perspective. One cannot simply borrow theoretical results wholesale from other fields without paying attention to the experimental procedures the investigators were using, the basic limitations of their subject pool, the data they actually got, their use of controls, and so on. For example, at first blush, it might look as though the research on implicit and explicit memory processing in normal adults provides unambiguous support for the distinction between the the two systems used by infants to recognize faces. Implict memory in

adults and the early face-recognizing system in infants are both automatic and sensitive only to basic structural features of stimuli, while
explicit memory in adults and the later face system in infants are both
subject initiated and sensitive to the details of the stimuli.[47] However, it
is also clear that the early face system in infants is innate, while the
implicit system in adults learns quite easily. Moreover, the early system
in infants can only track the gross structural features of faces, while the
implicit system in adults can distinguish quite sophisticated differences
among various inputs.

These difficulties in putting the perspective together are easily seen
once we put the answers that the psychologists give to their empirical
and theoretical questions into their proper contexts. Developmental
psychologists wanted to know why newborns preferred looking at faces,
while one month olds did not. They also wanted to know what features
two month olds could distinguish that newborns could not. Both of
these are etiological questions, asked of a subject over time. In contrast,
cognitive psychologists ask (traditional) systemic/functional questions
regarding the capacities of systems already in place. As a result, we don't
know whether the early face system in infants can learn new information (such as to distinguish more sophisticated features), since no one
is interested in that question (yet). But until we can answer these sorts
of questions, we can't know whether the innate system in infants later
underwrites implicit memory in adults.

The moral of this exercise is that care must be taken to include all
the pertinent details of the results (as given by the background context)
when constructing interdisciplinary theories. Simply relying on the
subdisciplines' own characterizations of the memory systems might
obscure important differences (though they might still provide useful
metaphors for designing future experiments or conceptualizing one's
own results). Already we can see that interdisciplinary theories are going
to be complicated and cluttered. They are going to require quite a lot of
information from all the domains involved. Nevertheless, a detailed
causal etiology will be the only way to capture all the data and their
implications.

The poor fit between all the subdisciplines also gives us reason to
search for answers and descriptions in different fields operating at different levels of analysis. As I argued in chapter 3, it is important to pay
attention to the constraints the surrounding levels of organization
engender. Indeed, if we have been describing the upper bound in a hierarchy of control, then the constraints should run both ways. Though

problems of multiple instantiability operate on all levels, the more we know about how brains actually process information across the different levels of description, the better our theories will be. Limitations on what we can test noninvasively and the questions we can ask of infant subjects, as do limitations on how many cells we can record from simultaneously in alert animals and the data we can analyze once gathered of nonhuman subjects, suggest that any hypothesis that remains on a single level of analysis will be severely underdetermined as a practical matter. Any hints or help we can receive from any level of analysis or organization should be welcome, principled philosophical arguments aside.

Let us now turn to what neurophysiology can tell us about dual processing systems of memory. There will be three sorts of evidence relevant to our dual memory hypothesis. First concerns the neuroanatomy and development of imprinting and other very early visual recognition systems in other mammals versus the more complex forms of recognition and memory that mature later; second will be postnatal development of mammalian cortex and what that can tell us about the developmental time course of our various processors; third is the relation between previously mapped processing pathways in human brain and the behavioral deficits exhibited as lesions occur in various places along the path.

Neural Evidence for the Dual Memory Hypothesis

Neurobiologists have had relative success in charting the neural sites for the early "automatic" visuo-motor memories in other (simpler) organisms. In general, they have found that such S-R learning only modifies preexisting circuitry such that additional inputs from other areas of the brain is not needed to initiate or maintain the learned (or innate) responses.[48] To take the example germane to our discussion, consider imprinting in chicks. Imprinting has been localized to the intermediate and medial part of the hyperstriatum ventrale (IMHV).[49] (See figure 6.2.) If the IMHV is oblated, or otherwise damaged, chicks lose the ability to learn the individual features of their conspecifics (their mothers, generally speaking), though they do not lose a predisposition to orient towards henlike stimuli.[50] (Chickens too seem to have more than one mnemonic system,[51] though all their memory systems are relatively primitive.) The phenomenon of imprinting in chicks then represents an early, learned, but automatically executed, visuo-motor circuit.[52]

Figure 6.2

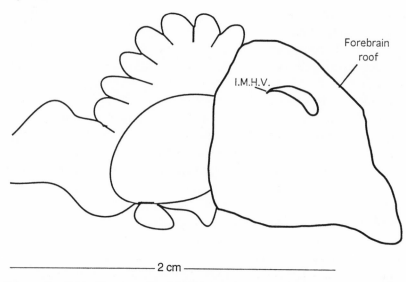

Schematic of the side view of a chick brain. I.M.H.V. refers to the intermediate and medial part of the hyperstriatum ventrale (adapted from Johnson and Morton 1991).

What changes occur in chicks' brains that correspond to such learning? The only change thus far uncovered is an increase in the average depth of the postsynaptic membrane by about 17 percent in the IMHV.[53] This change only occurs on the dendritic spines in the left hemisphere and indicates an increase in neurotransmitter receptor density there. So, as the chicks learn to recognize their mothers, the number of receptors in the left IMHV increases substantially, and nothing else much changes.[54] This fact will be important when we discuss the neurophysiology of semantic memory in a moment.) That the change is localized to only one area tells us that this sort of simple learning (a primitive visuo-motor, S-R circuit) only requires the sites that actually carry out the activity. A consequence of not requiring any sort of central processor to maintain these learned pathways is that these sorts of memories may be relatively diffused throughout large portions of the brain, with no single area dedicated to recalling these memories. Using only local changes in the various distributed circuits explains how these simple "memories" can be recalled quickly, automatically, and in parallel. Moreover, because the actual neural circuits responsible for the visuo-motor loop change as the stimuli and appropriate responses are learned, the learned behaviors, whatever they are, should occur whenever that circuit is triggered (disregarding any override mechanisms from above). This explains why there are few capacity limitations on automatic responses and why they are beyond intentional control.

The story behind our more complex semantic memory, however, looks very different. Larry Squire and Stuart Zola-Morgan have concluded that laying down the memories in this memory system requires the hippocampus and adjacent areas of cortex as a central instigator.[55] Their model is based on studying a variety of bilateral lesions in the medial temporal lobe in monkeys. It turns out that monkeys with the hippocampal formation removed bilaterally are severely impaired on memory tasks that required direct access to previous episodes, although they can still learn skills at normal levels. For example, hippocampal monkeys cannot perform delayed nonmatching-to-sample,[56] but these same monkeys can be trained in classical conditioning paradigms. In particular, they show normal performance in the incremental learning of skills and habits, including object and pattern discriminations.[57]

Later, Squire and Zola-Morgan discovered that damage to the amygdala did not affect semantic memory performance; instead, this memory was impaired when the cortical areas surrounding the amygdala were damaged. Indeed, memory is disrupted when only the perihinal and parahippocamal cortices are lesioned and the hippocampus and amygdala are spared. These investigations allowed them to map the major neural components of the controlled access memory system in monkeys (and presumably in humans as well). It consists in the hippocampal formation, including entorhinal cortex, and the adjacent perihinal and parahippocampal cortical areas. (See figure 6.3.)

Squire and Zola-Morgan hypothesize that the hippocampus indexes or summarizes explicit memories by conjoining sets of stimuli features distributed throughout neocortex. The medial temporal lobe system maintains a sketch of how the distributed set of respresentations fit together into a single coherent event. This sytem would thus be important for rapidly acquiring detailed information later be available for explicit recollection. (The medial temporal system's involvement in forming semantic memories is apparently only temporary; episodic memories that initially depended on an intact system were later unaffected by hippocampal lesions, suggesting that ultimately these memories too only require local interactions in neocortex.) Learning or retaining various motor or cognitive skills, as amnesics, young infants, and chicks can do, does not use this system. As a result, these sorts of condi-

Figure 6.3

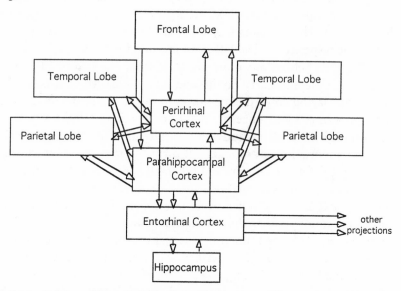

A diagram of the major pathways of the medial temporal lobe memory system. The frontal, temporal, and parietal lobes recriprocally project to the adjacent perirhinal and parahippocampal cortices, which then reciprocally project to the entorhinal cortex, a major source of projections to the hippocampus.

tioned responses are acquired at a slower pace (generally speaking) and are not stored in such rich detail.

"Long-term potentiation" (LTP) in the hippocampus is probably the mechanism responsible for first forming the semantic memories. For example, when rats learn new smells, LTP increases the strength of synaptic responses in the neuronal pathways involving the hippocampus and the sensory cortices. Indeed, the magnitude of LTP is correlated with speed of learning in rats.[58] Presumably, the more rats learn about a smell, the more the synaptic response is potentiated. As with imprinting, these changes are triggered by changes in the response components mediated by the NMDA synaptic receptors.[59] So, in adult mammals at least, when certain neuronal circuits in the medial temporal lobe system are triggered, LTP, in virtue of this activation, reinforces the circuits such that the organism learns and can later recall (reactivate?) them explicitly.

Thus far we have outlined the gross brain areas responsible for conditioned visuo-motor responses and explicit semantic memories and the underlying synaptic mechanisms reponsible for learning in general. Let us pause for a moment and analyze the type of neurophysiological explanations given here. On the one hand, they appear to exemplify classic systemic accounts of cognitive phenomena. That is, the inputs and outputs are described in nonfunctional terms, but with respect to the environmental impingements on the organism; the neuronal circuits are described in terms of the connections among the brain areas, and their firing patterns with respect to the connections and input stimuli. Moreover, we can fully expect that when all the neural reactions are completely documented and quantified, the explanation will be computational as well.

On the other hand, the explanations are multilevel with respect to both levels of description and level of analysis. Within single empirical models, we find descriptions of intentional motor behavior, of connections among fairly large-scale areas in the brain, as well as of chemical changes in the receptor sites for neurotransmitters. The causal etiology turns on analyses of both brain areas and receptor sites. Nevertheless, the theories are still functional because each of the decomposed component parts is defined in terms of its causal relation to other component parts. For example, Squire and Zola-Morgan's explication of semantic memory articulates the systematic correlations between some higher level event (correct mnemonic retrieval) with lower level descriptions of the relevant causal mechanisms. The connections among the processing components within each level, and across the levels, as well as the "input-output" function for the neural area define the attributes relevant to understanding the phenomenon. And like other systemic accounts, whether to consider some descriptions functional or structural all depends on the details of the descriptions. Whether to consider the description of LTP functional or structural depends on whether we are using the account in contrast to a description of changes in the connection strength among neural nets or of changes in the properties of the receptor sites.

However, both accounts differ from the classic understanding of functional analysis in at least one respect, for both explanations use models of specific systems from which we then draw some general morals about such systems as a whole. Indeed, the explanation of semantic memory uses more than one physical system (one for primates and one for rats) within a single theoretical account. Still, these different physical models are joined in a process analogous to functional decomposition, since one model acts as an account of the properties and functional composition of some component in the other. The idea of loosely conjoined models of different physical systems forms another plank in building interdisciplinary theories in cognitive science.

A second line of research that speaks to the dual memory system hypothesis in neuroscience are studies of cortical maturation. We know from the last chapter that infant brains change substantially during the first years of postnatal life. This change is not uniform though. Cortices develop from the inside out, as it were.[60] Actual brains are not massively interconnected. That is, unlike most connectionist models, each neuron in a brain is not effectively connected to every other neuron. Instead, human and primate cortices exhibit a layered structure, with the neurons in each layer densely interconnected but with each layer being rather sparsely connected to other layers. The layers closest to the center of the brain mature first, and the layers toward the skull mature later.

Neuroanatomical research has isolated at least two major visual pathways in humans,[61] each of which matures according to a different time course, given its location in the head. In crudest terms, we have a subcortical pathway for vision and at least one cortical one (though the subcortical path almost certainly has deep cortical projections and the cortical path passes through the lateral geniculate nucleus, a subcortical structure).[62] (See figure 6.4.) The subcortical pathway from the retina to the superior colliculus begins to mylinate prenatally and approximates mature form about three months after birth. The cortical pathway, on the other hand, only begins to mylinate at birth and both the lateral geniculate nucleus and the visual cortex itself continue to increase in volume for several months after birth. Only after this synaptic "exhuberance" has peaked and many connections subsequently have been pared away does this system appear to be up and running in infants.[63]

Presumably, the subcortical pathway would subserve the visuomotor S-R connections in infants, while the cortical paths would underwrite the more "cognitive" mnemonic functioning.[64] The subcortical pathway would allow newborns to orient towards things grossly structured like faces, while the cortical paths would support older infants' capacities to learn the details of individual faces and to respond preferentially to faces of people they know, as opposed to things that are merely configured roughly like faces. There is also a bit of single cell data that would support this contention, though not much. The earliest age at which researchers have discovered face-sensitive cells in monkey cortex is about six weeks,[65] which would fall in line with the developmental time course of their brains. (Of course, not finding any face-specific cells active

Figure 6.4

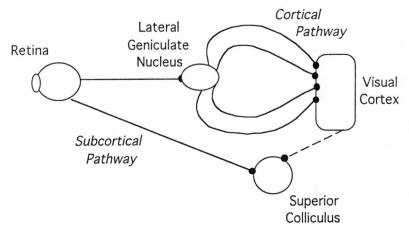

A schematic of the two major visual pathways: the subcortical pathway from the retina through the superior colliculus, and the cortical pathway from the retina through the lateral geniculate nucleus to the visual cortex

before six weeks in monkeys might only be our failure in measurement and not an indication of anything regarding brain maturity.)

The usual characterization of the two systems is that the subcortical pathway computes "where" things are and the cortical paths compute "what" the objects are. However, as Rosaleen McCarthey (1993) argues, damage along the cortical pathway can lead to impaired topographical processing for both places and routes. It is better to conceive of our cortical processors as creating "addressed representations," computations that require access to previously stored memories. In contrast, the subcortical route might be part of "assembled routines," "visuo-motor interactions . . . supported by the extraction of invariant properties of the input displays . . . and their direct coordination with somatic and vestibular/gravitational cues" (McCarthy 1993, p. 392). I am sympathetic to this distinction—surely what McCarthy is calling an addressed representation maps easily onto what I have been calling semantic memory—yet I worry that calling "assemblying routines" what our more primitive processors are doing is too intentional. The sorts of processing required for the simple recognition and S-R routines that newborms can perform can easily be performed using deformed matrices of neuronal grids between our visual and motor systems (essentially an elegant lookup chart),[66] so there need be little cognitive labor performed. Consequently, I shall continue to refer to the subcortical pathways as our visuo-motor S-R routines, though I stress that my view of these processors is in accord with McCarthy's.

Now we can use this anatomical information regarding our two visual processors to aid in our understanding of what has happened in the brain-damaged patients I discussed earlier. Like Squire and Zola-Morgan's monkeys, human amnesics suffer varying degrees of damage to their hippocampus and surrounding areas. H.M., the complete ante-riograde amnesic mentioned above, has lost both of his temporal lobes. Consequently, we must conclude that whatever mnemonic capacities he has left must be in virtue of systems that lie outside the medial-temporal lobe. It is important to stress that these results in no way suggest that H.M., or other amnesics, rely on subcortical systems to mediate their learning procedures or skills. In fact, they probably are using at least some corticostriatal connections.[67]

In contrast to amnesics, agnosics, dysmorphopsics, and patients with blindsight all have lost some area of cortex. Generally speaking, agnosics suffer from bilateral lesions in the ventral and mesial portions of the occipitotemporal visual areas; dysmorphophsics from damage to the magnocellular pathway, which runs from the retinal ganglion via the lateral geniculate nucleus to areas V1, V2, V3, and MT in visual cortex, and blindsight patients from lesions in V1. (See figure 6.5.) The assumption is that in losing these areas of cortex, subjects have lost areas in which the hippocampal-based mnemonic systems lays down new semantic memories, and the areas to which the cortical visual processors feed. The agnosics, for example, have lost the areas that contain memories of object

Figure 6.5

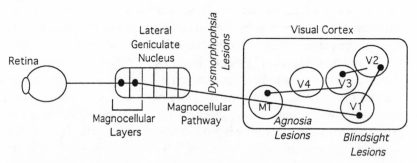

A diagram of the locations for various visual memonic lesions along the cortical visual pathway. Blindsight occurs with lesions to V1, the agnosias correspond to lesions in the occipitotemporal areas, and dysmorphophsia occurs with lesions along the magnocellular pathway.

names. (It is quite artificial to segregate mental functioning so much; agnosics also have impairments in basic visual processing.[68] Nevertheless, they have lost areas that *at least* contain object names.) Again, there is no evidence that these patients are relying on subcortical mechanisms to show the visual competencies they do. They could be using other cortical streams; however, these patients (unlike amnesics) have lost some corticostriatal connections as well, so it is more likely that subcortical processing plays a larger role in their preserved visuo-motor skills. Regardless, in each case, we have seen that severing some links in the cortical system results in distinct mnemonic deficits, while preserving those capacities associated with our subcortical system.

Having completed our tour of relevant neuroscience, we can see that any interdisciplinary theory that relies on these data will exemplify a hierarchy of control (cf., chapter 3), a hierarchy in which "control" runs downward. That is, the higher levels of organization set limits on what the lower levels can do. Explanations of such systems, however, are bidirectional, since the higher level is but one possible arrangment of lower level entities. That is, there is more than one way that a brain (or other storage device) could have visuo-motor and semantic memories. That it uses subcortical and cortical mechanisms is determined in part by higher level developmental feedback. This is a type of downward control. Conversely, there is more than one thing that the subcortical and cortical mechanisms could be doing. That they are used for memory processing allows for an "upward" looking explanation of the psychological events in terms of lower level neurophysiology.

Including evidence from neuroscience in the pool of relevant data for developing interdisciplinary theories to explain our memory systems only acts to expand what we already have—hypotheses we develop in considering all this information are based on only a bigger and better theory of the same phenomena (broadly construed). The real distinction between these sorts of models (i.e., a theory in cognitive science) and the ones in pychology or neuroscience proper is that the former are interdisciplinary while the latter are not. Indeed, the connections among different levels of description within a single discipline are of the same type as those among different levels of descriptions across more than one discipline.

Methodologically, the various individual models and explanations suggest variations on the psychological tests to give the different subjects. For example, the clinical neurology data suggest that one should try to develop an abstract version of a nonmatching-to-sample task for lesioned monkeys to determine how "cognitive" their deficits are. The developmental psychological data suggest that one should try to develop tasks for lesion patients that push on how well they can generalize newly learned skills in order to determine how much cortical processing is involved. The cognitive psychology literature suggests that one should develop habituation or conditioning tests of infants and young monkeys that determine how much these subjects can learn using only subcortical mechanisms.

A second advantage to using data from different disciplines is that we uncover different avenues of investigation and confirmation for analogous phenomena. For example, imprinting in chicks and facial recognition in infants both appear to be analogs of one another in some sense and each experimental paradigm can be used as weakly confirming evidence for the others. Knowing how chicks imprint gives us important clues regarding how newly born infants might track faces to the exclusion of other objects.

Nevertheless, it is similarity in methodology that ties these theoretical paradigms together. Developmental and cognitive psychologists, neurophysiologists, and clinical neurologists all use versions of the same basic task (matching-to-sample) in testing their hypotheses concerning memory processes. As a result, the vocabulary they use to describe their test results is quite similar. For example, all the experiments discussed above concern recognition and how to distinguish recognition from other sorts of mnemonic processes, and the results are discussed in those terms explicitly.

This middle level of description is more abstract than the pure observation sentences that describe particular phenomenal or behavioral events, since the middle level of description details what is common across several obervations. Yet this level is not quite as abstract as the descriptions in theoretical models, since no conclusions are drawn about the general properties of the causal mechanisms that entail the experimental results. Nevertheless, this middle level allows scientists from the different fields to converse with one another and to work together to come to some common understanding about how the memory systems function in higher mammals. The level of data interpretation and description links the diverse fields together.

As I have already discussed, the different fields currently disagree on what those results mean in terms of general principles from which to posit underlying causal mechanisms, even though they do agree on their descriptions of the experimental results. At the moment, the only links among disciplines are in virtue of the middle level descriptive models themselves, which function, at best, as analogs of one another.[69] Nevertheless, though the ties may seem rather tenuous, there are some fairly broad points that each of the accounts have in common—enough, I believe, to make the set including the different models a viable interdiscipinary theory.

The Theoretical Framework

We are able to exend our theory of dual memory systems with respect to properties investigated by neurophysiology but which, because of inherent limits on experimental methodology, are beyond the testing capabilities of developmental psychology or clinical neurology. As before, mutually reinforcing theoretical models come out of the different experimental paradigms such that they refine the definitions and descriptions contained in the general theory. Even though the individual models are of different organisms—chicks, monkeys, humans, and the like—we can combine these different models into one general account of dual mnemonic processing (in certain organisms) that contains principles true of all models.

I suggest that our understanding of our dual memory systems should be organized as follows. We have one sort of system that contains habits, skills, and classically conditioned "memories." This system is located either subcortically or among the corticostriatal connections of the brain. (I haven't really discussed this latter possibility in this chapter.) This system or systems actually appear to be little more than a collection of task-specific behavioral responses. That is, they do not store representations of particular events, but rather only learned responses to specific cues. However, it is not quite fair to call this memory system a "procedural" memory, for not all of the memories are embedded action responses; many of the learned "procedures" in adult humans are in fact quite cognitive.

Because there is evidence that these systems are actually epsiodic, though not necessarily semantic, I shall use the umbrella term *structural episodic (STE) memory* to refer to mnemonic processing of this general type. STE memories are modality specific and sensitive to things like font and graphemes but not to the environment or the context surrounding the stimuli. Furthermore, they are not sensitive to the type of processing the stimuli receive elsewhere (e.g., semantic versus phonetic), nor to the amount of attention focused on the task. STE memories are most likely formed through individually remembered episodes being laid on top of one another. Each mnemonic trace, once laid down, operates as a self-contained unit for pattern matching and hence does not depend on neighboring memories for input or support. Activated STE memories can then input to, or at least somehow affect, our semantic system(s).[70]

Our semantic memories form the basis for explicit recall. Although the larger hippocampal region and its connections to neocortex lay down these memories, the memories themselves are probably located only in the cortex (although the medial temporal region may have to maintain the cortical regions for several years before the memory is completely established there).[71] More specifically, this memory system is located in the diverse regions of the cortex that are responsible for analyzing and processing incoming sensory data. (For example, area TE in inferotemporal cortex may be the storehouse for visual memories.)[72]

Lynn Nadel has suggested that this system might have evolved to supplement the first system by storing the spatial contexts of incoming sensory information.[73] Now however, this system captures not just immediate physical surroundings, but all sorts of contextual information. Hence, we store both particular episodes and general "schemata" in this system. Because this system remembers specific events in terms of what these events mean to the individual subject, I shall refer to these memories as *semantic episodic (SEE) memory*.

In contrast to STE memories, SEE memories diminish rather rapidly over time, possibly through some consolidation procedure. They are sensitive to the level and type of processing a task demands as well as to the amount of attention devoted to any task. Moreover, these memories can be translated from one modality to another without loss of information. Though only single hypotheses about the meaning of the incoming stimuli are active at a time, the activated memories can show AB, AC interference, indicating not only that semantic ties among groups of data exist but also that they are not easily broken once formed. Nevertheless, SEE memories are not stable for a long period of time nor do they function independently of one another.

"Two-Part" Interdisciplinary Theories

Several points concerning how to build a theory from our recitation of data and the guiding frameword emerge. Any interdisciplinary theory in cognitive science will have two distinct parts. On the one hand, there will be more or less a laundry list of general principles governing the phenomena across several higher mammals (or whatever). These principles apply to all physical systems for which we have theoretical models of the phenomena; however, by their very nature, they are too general to use to make many specific predictions regarding any experimental procedure. On the other hand, the theory will also include the models of specific animal systems from which we derived the general principles. These models flesh out our general principles—we use them to make our principles concrete and to guide predictions for future experiments. However, these models are too specific to be applicable to all organisms that exhibit the phenomenon to be explained. Together, both elements comprise current interdisciplinary theories in cognitive science.

These two-part theories are analogous to the overlapping interlevel theories Kenneth Schaffner discusses as typifying biomedical research.[74] It will be helpful to compare my version of a two-part interdisciplinary theory with Schaffner's (1980, 1993) discussion of biomedical theories. In the end, though, I believe this view will need to be modified to encompass the sort of theories one finds emerging from cognitive science today.

Schaffner argues that biomedical theories are best understood as a series of "overlapping interlevel temporal models" (1980, p. 83). In their descriptions of explananda, these theories fall somewhere between biochemistry and evolutionary theory on a continuum of what Schaffner calls "levels of aggregation," criteria used to distinguish various organizational foci. One entity E1 has a higher level of aggregation than some other entity E2 if it contains E2 as some of its parts, and if E1 cannot be defined simply a sum of E2's, but requires additional organizing principles.

So, for example, we can explain retaining interpreted memories of stimuli as SEE memories in terms of the hippocampal-medial temporal lobe system of the brain, which is organized on the level of brain areas. Accounts specific to this level of analysis revolve around descriptions of how one area influences another, relying on such principles as signal-to-noise ratios and enhanced processing. However, changes in the hippocampal-medial temporal lobe system are supported by long-term potentiation via alterations in the NMDA receptors. Neurotransmitters and so forth of course operate at a different level of "aggregation," and accounts of these sorts of processes turn on things like molecular structure and the influx and efflux of ions, clearly different organizing principles. Still, both of these levels are included in a single theory, whose explanandum, SEE memories, are described in terms of yet another level of aggregation.

"Interlevel" in Schaffner's discussion just refers to entities within a particular theory that are grouped at different levels of aggregation. Any theory that acknowledges hierarchies of embedment, control, or constitution would count as an interlevel theory. I take it as obvious that the theoretical framework adumbrated here is a clear example of an interlevel theory.

Schaffner's theories are unveiled as related abstract descriptions of different entities undergoing some process or other. Taken together, these overlapping models constitute a theory. This picture again dovetails with our account of the animal models in a two-part interdisciplinary theory. In our case, each of the models worked out for specific animals concerns mnemonic processes in mammals, either as (part of) the SEE system, or as (part of) an STE system. We take the set of related models to comprise a single theory. The variations among organisms studied—the differences between hippocampal rats and amnesic adults, for example—are also part of the larger theory.

According to Schaffner, this variation within models in the same theory "smears out" the models and "makes them more a family of overlapping models, each of which may be . . . precise, but which as a collective theory is related by similarity" (1980, p. 85). Some features of the models are more robust and appear in (almost all) of the models that make up a particular theory. Others are more individual. Schaffner suggests that because of the "fuzzy" nature of biological theories, it would not be wise to try to axiomatize them for explanations based on mathematical deduction. Rather, what seems to occur is an *elaboration* by more detailed specification of aspects of one of the models, at usually a "lower" level of aggregation, in order to facilitate further investigation of particular phenomena.[75]

Elaborating aspects of models, usually at a lower level of aggregation, is again analogous to what I have described as how functional analysis works in a two-part interdisciplinary theory. In our case, each model explains some aspect of the computations involved in one of the memory systems for some animal. Explanation of each memory system as a whole is cobbled together from the different models, and in general, proceeds by exhibiting the dependency relations between some higher level phenomenon and the lower level causal mechanisms.

Nevertheless, the laundry list of general principles is part of the theory proper as well since, in actual practice, scientists rely on these principles to guide research questions and experimental models. They provide the broad theoretical framework that constrains empirical investigation and guides the functional decomposition (or the rational reconstruction of a functional analysis) of the phenomenon to be explained.

I believe the sort of two-part interdisciplinary theory that I have developed in this chapter will be typical of theories in cognitive science in general. As a true discipline still in the making, cognitive science is an amalgam of different disciplines, with each bringing incompatible research techniques and traditions to bear on a common set of interests. We have no reason to expect that the different domains will ultimately fuse into one; each could retain its autonomy as they address a set of central concerns, linked instead by a fuzzy set of entity attributes across a family of models and certain core framework principles. Taken together, the explications in neurophysiology, developmental psychological, clinical neurology, cognitive psychology, and neuropsychology for our different memory systems act as a blueprint for how theories in the fledgling science of cognitive science should go. We should see lots of fairly detailed etiological stories about learning and cognition connected by fuzzy extensions of concepts. Features in the explananda of these histories will overlap, but the path taken from explanans to explananda will not be the same. Instead, they share fundamental acceptance of the guiding framework, along with the general methodological strategies for investigation. And this acceptance binds together the bits of the diverse disciplines that make up the cognitive sciences, giving them a common framework and vocabulary by which to begin work together.

To conclude, I would like to compare my notion of a two-part interdisciplinary theory and Schaffner's overlapping interlevel biomedical theories with the semantic view. Highlighting the similarities and differences will bring out the features of a two-part interdisciplinary theory I believe are important. We can think of my view, like Schaffner's, as extensions of (though not identical to) the semantic conception of theories.

First let me highlight the aspects of the semantic view central for understanding interdisciplinary theories in cognitive science. (See also the discussion in the appendix.) According to the semantic view, a theory models the behavior of successive states in some physical system.

These physical systems are idealized version of systems in the world in which only a few chosen parameters operate. The theory describes what would happen in the actual world over time if the selected parameters were the only nonnegligible factors influencing some real system. (Often in fact systems are influenced by many variables that are not part of the theory.) Theories work by specifying models—versions of theories with the values of the parameters fixed—that in turn describe some particular physical system.

Three features of the semantic view are especially relevant for our discussions of two-part interdisicplinary theories: the way the semantic conception describes the temporal dimension of theories, the way it understands the scope of scientific laws, and the ways in which it claims theories can elaborate their models. Schaffner claims that biomedical theories are "temporal"; similarly, I have suggested that it is best to develop causal etiologies in cognitive science, which are nothing but descriptions of successive changes in the states in some physical system that culminate in the explanandum. A causal etiology, like Schaffner's temporal models, are clearly consistent with the semantic view of dynamic models.

How the semantic conception defines the scope of a law also dovetails with theories in the biological and cognitive sciences. As discussed in chapter 2, the semantic view holds that the scope of theories are classes of natural kinds. Here we assume a fairly weak notion of 'natural kind' as a set of objects defined in terms of common properties. We then use our theories to make universal statements about the set of possible objects falling under them. Biomedical theories are often restricted to particular species, which Suppe (1989) argues could be understood as natural kinds, since specie names denote natural attributes. I do not take most interdisplinary theories in cognitive science to be so restricted in scope; they might encompass all cognizers, or just mammals, or perhaps only humans and primates (though might just refer to our species). Regardless, these sets too are describable by proper lists of natural attributes.

Where the semantic view does diverge from Schaffner's understanding of biomedical theories and my conception of theories in cognitive science is in the treatment of the elaboration of models.[76] Schaffner points out that biomedical theories are often not axiomatized; instead, they are just given as sets of models that describe not only the "pure" types, but also variations and deviations due to mutations, and so forth. Though I have said nothing on this matter, it should be obvious that theories in cognitive science work in largely the same fashion. However, using models instead of axioms is fairly standard in science when the theories concern complex systems and the semantic view recognizes that point. Since it distinguishes theories from their linguistic formulations or diagrammatic specifications, a theory's mode of presentation is not terribly significant.

What I take Schaffner's point to be, however, is that the mutation variations presented in some models are an integral part of the theory itself and not just negligible parameters that may be abstracted over in some instances. In this case, there are no basic or "pure" models and then more complex elaborations of those models, as the semantic view holds. Instead there are overlapping models connected by fuzzy similarity relations, as Schaffner argues. Suppe suggests that if the overlapping models are considered "established by science," then they constitute "items of information" related by a deeper underlying unity (1989, pp. 273).[77] An account of this deeper unity would then be the actual theory—so even if there is no "pure" case today, the fact that the models are conjoined signals that a "pure" model should be forthcoming.

Though I cannot speak for Schaffner and biomedical theories, I do believe that Suppe would be mistaken about two-part interdisciplinary theories. The only real underling unity of the sort Suppe discusses in the theories of cognitive science could be the set of general principles spawned by the set of overlapping models. However, I have urged that these principles are not specific enough to function as an (interpreted) theory; rather, scientists work from the predictions based on the particular models. In practice, scientists focus on their individual models, which cannot be considered just elaborations of the general principles. If we force the principles to stand as supporting the models, instead of being derived from them, then we are not being true to science as it is actually done nor to hypotheses as they are actually conceived.

At this stage, general principles are more of a by-product of the models that help ensure a common language among the scientists; as such, they serve more as a practical link among the disciplines and their models than as their theoretical foundation. It all does depend on how we understand the guiding general principles though. Maybe, someday, the general principles will be formulated such that they can carry more weight; but then again, maybe not. We can engage in successful predictive science in the cognitive science just by developing and elaborating overlapping models. There is little motivation to make the general principles to be anything more than an added theoretical bonus and a practical communicative device.

Putting It All Together

Let us now summarize what an interdisciplinary theory in cognitive science should include. Since cognitive science encompasses different domains, any interdisciplinary theory may extend over several different levels of description and analysis. Nevertheless, the middle and lower levels of analysis would still count as a functional decomposition of higher level psychological theories. Insofar as we can consider theoretical models derived from such data as specifying the causal mechanisms of the higher level functional description in greater detail, then they are a straighforward functional analysis of the higher level description. So then, a model of our STE and SEE memories derived from animal lesions studies would serve as further analysis of the analogous models derived from reaction time studies in amnesics, perceptual identification studies in normals, and so on, since it can specify the psychological events with respect to neurophysiological processes and structures.

We use models from different domains to extend one another in order to overcome technological or theoretical limits. They are all then loosely tied together by virtue of a set of overarching general principles, which gives the scientists involved a common way of viewing their individual physical systems. These general principles can and do guide experimental research, but it is not quite accurate to say that they determine it. Instead, they inspire general investigative avenues within the contexts of specific models. For example, the general distinction between visuomotor circuits (or implicit memory) and explicit recall led Schacter and Moscovitch (1984) to connect research in amnesics with research involving infants. The infant literature then helped focus their understanding of the different mnemonic systems in normal adults. Ultimately, this has inspired Daniel Schacter to test normal adults using implicit and explicit paradigms for nonverbal stimuli.[78]

Aside from the general principles, different models are united into one theory in virtue of special middle level descriptions that give rise to a language scientists use in relating their data to their theoretical framework. Deciding that differential reaction times indicate priming effects in lexical decision tasks is one case in point. However, it is not a similarity in data interpretation per se that unites the models, since different domains have access to wildly different types of data (e.g., verbal reports versus single cell responses), but rather, how scientists analyze what that data means with respect to the general principles and other related empirical models lets the various specific models work together as one theory.

Nevertheless, we should not expect the different models to collapse into a single overarching account. We have no reason to expect or assume any version of reductionism. The beauty of cognitive science is that several independent and well-established investigative domains can (more or less) peacefully coexist, united in their quest to understand cognition from whatever perspective. To seek a reduction actively would be to wash out the complexities of biological phenomena and to gloss over our own limitations. It is far better to enjoy the rich multitude of perspectives and let the thousand flowers bloom in peace.

Chapter 7

Interdisciplinary Theories and Bridge Sciences: The Case of Event Related Potentials

> [We] must therefore always consider organisms as a whole and in detail at one and the same time, without ever losing sight of the peculiar conditions of all the special phenomena whose resultant is the individual.[1]

> A constant unifying theme is ... a viewpoint [that] takes both the practices and the results of the sciences seriously, as not to be analyzed away with neat logical distinctions but rather to be explicated in all their complexity and richness.... The use of heuristic techniques ..., the importance of taking organization quite seriously, and the crucial utility of thoerizing proceeding on many different and interacting levels are ... facets of this [viewpoint].... [It] is an attempt to make sense of significant scientific achievements without forcing them into a preconceived philosophical version of the procrustean bed.[2]

Cognitive science has amassed a plethora of data from anthropology, artificial intelligence programming, cognitive psychology, clinical neurology, developmental psychology, linguistics, neuropsychology, neurophysiology, sociology, and so on, all of which seem somehow relevant for building stories about cognitive processing in service of larger explanatory concerns. Sorting out the pertinent evidence is a big task and fitting it together into a coherent whole even bigger. Certainly what we are left with is nothing like the neat deductive-nomological theories we find in physics or mathematics. On the contrary, our investigation leaves us with lots of messy details lumped together from different levels of analysis, different theoretical frameworks, and different investigative questions. The connections at times seem tenuous at best. Is what we are left with really a solid interdisiplinary *theory*?

The previous chapter gave us a fairly complicated picture of how our memory systems work in broad outline (especially if we include the neurophysiology of the frontal lobe from chapter 5). In brief, I conjectured that the hippocampus and surrounding areas are responsible for laying down unitized memories into a long-term SEE store that are later explicitly accessible in something resembling declarative form. The memories themselves reside in distributed but perhaps modularized form throughout neocortex. Manipulating these memories (or any original percepts) in some fashion—including simply rehearsing them—requires processing mechanisms outside the neocortex. (For example, in normal adults, executive control over the memories resides in the frontal lobe-parietal cortex-limbic system circuit.) This system contrasts with the automatic system, which is little more than facilitated processing of familiar stimuli. Modality specific, though not specific to orientation, motion, or representational format, it cannot recall specific episodes but only the general cues needed to generate conditioned behavioral responses. It encompasses both perceptual and cognitive information, as well as more traditional motor skills. STE memories are located throughout cortex, as well as in the subcortical areas. They require no external processor to maintain or initiate the responses. Instead, they exist entirely as enhanced connections among previously existing processing circuits.

However, this story assumes the viability of linking disparate animal models together via a set of general principles. I have argued that a two-part interdisciplinary theory is required in order to explain cognitive phenomena. These theories are composed of general principles and a set of loosely linked models, which operate over several levels of description and analyses (with no single level privileged). Arranged properly, these models, tied together (in part) by the general principles, act as a functional decomposition of the relevant causal factors for the phenomenon to be explained by exhibiting systematic dependency relations between higher and lower level mechanisms.

In this chapter, I examine the argument that the general principles were drawn too hastily. We can understand Dennett and Kinsbourne (1992) as arguing (among other things) that experimental paradigms in psychology are too crude to allow us to tie psychological models to those in neuroscience successfully. Obviously, the only way an approach like this can succeed is if—apart from the epistemological and methodological concerns involving theory reduction—neurophysiological *properties* correspond in some way or another to psychological ones. As one might suspect, though, the problem of psychophysical identity within the cognitive sciences is not trivial. Indeed, the differential time courses between neuronal and psychological phenomena alone may be great enough to preclude any correspondence in actual practice. It may well be that the behavioral measures used in psychological experiments do not parse the phenomena finely enough for psychological-neuroscientific property translation.

In response to these concerns, I argue that a "bridge science"—in this particular instance, research involving evoked response potentials (ERPs)—is connected to both psychology and neuroscience such that it can link the two domains into a single explanatory framework, thus making room for truly interdisicplinary theories in the cognitive sciences.[3] In brief, a bridge science maintains the proper connections by adopting the background assumptions of both psychology and neuroscience (or whatever two sciences), and the important questions from one of those domains, while also maintaining its own contrast class and relevance relations distinct from either of them. In this way, a bridge science is a truly interdisciplinary field and, as such, can contribute significantly to both disciplines. But we should not understand this research program just as presenting us with a simple functional analysis of psychological phenomena nor as demonstrating systematic dependency relations among relevant causal mechanisms. Instead, it is a program in its own right—responding to its own concerns—that happens to be able to contribute to both psychology and neuroscience such that it also partially unites them.

The Challenge

Earlier I argued that Philip Kitcher's notion of explanatory extension helps us place divergent views about cognitive processes under a helpful rubric (chapter 5). The hope is that neuroscience will give us a way to identify cognitive processors without having to rely solely on verbal reports or behavioral reactions to perceived phenomena. Neurophysiology should give psychology some explanatory underpinnings on which to peg cognitive experiences. However, this rosy picture cannot be the entire story for interdisciplinary theories in the cognitive sciences. The messy connections of explanatory extension may not be strong enough to combine aspects of the two domains into a single theory or into a unified theoretical perspective. Moreover, the level of detail that each domain specifies may be incommensurable such that each can only provide hints that the other's approach is correct without allowing for the direct connections needed for a true interdisciplinary theory.

For example, some argue that implicit priming effects are just another instance of conditioned visuo-motor memory;[4] however, we do find instances of double dissociation between priming and skill learning. Heindel and his research group demonstrate that Alzheimer patients show impaired priming and normal motor skill learning, while Huntington's disease patients show normal priming effects but have trouble learning new motor skills.[5] In contrast, Daniel Schacter (1989b) argues that subliminal priming depends both on the activation of already established explicit memories in the SEE system and on new structural representations that can influence performance independently of conscious recall. But, on the other hand, in some cases it seems that priming also reflects the influence of new semantic representations on behavior even though these representations fail to gain access to explicit awareness.[6] There are (at least) two general suggestions for how implicit priming occurs. It either occurs as a type of automatic memory that then influences what is activated in semantic memory, thereby indirectly altering behavioral responses, or it acts apart from semantic memory, directly influencing behavior along with SEE representations. Which is the correct interpretation of data? When exactly does implicit priming occur?

Dennett and Kinsbourne (1992) intimate, among other things, that asking such questions is a nonstarter because the experimental paradigms are too crude to allow us to answer such queries. They note that psychological experiments are based on purely behavioral measures, using things such as mean reaction time and error distributions. These sorts of measures are simply too gross to decide the issue at hand since we have no way of parsing the processing stream into finer bits. They conclude that since there is no *psychologically* defined way to tell us which stages of processing occur prior to the activation of SEE memories and which occur during or after, deciding on the moment of activation of implicit priming itself would have to be arbitrary. Any distinction between the two falls apart under close scrutiny. (Stephan Harnad, on the other hand, understands the dilemma as an insoluble problem of measurement. Though he believes that there is no independent way of determining the precise timing of the actual events, he sees this "incommensurability as a methodological problem, not a metaphysical one" [1989].) In either case, my proposed theoretical framework for dual mnemonic systems is in trouble. Does the output of an early automatic system only influence the processing of later explicit memory, as I suggest it does, and so STE output is never actually perceived? Or does it operate alongside or after SEE memory activations, with its outputs rapidly forgotten? Our psychological window of investigation cannot tell us exactly what is perceived when.

In particular, we can easily apply this analysis to Marcel's subliminal priming experiments mentioned in the last chapter. If a stimulus is flashed briefly on the screen, followed a short time later by a "masking" stimulus, subjects will report only seeing the second stimulus. The usual account of this phenomena is that the second stimulus prevents the first from becoming processed in the SEE system. That is, it interferes with cognitive processing before subjects can become aware of the second stimulus. It is possible that subjects do indeed consciously experience the first stimulus but their memory of this experience is "blanked out" by the second stimulus, and we have no way of telling the differences between the two accounts as long as we are forced to rely on only verbal reports or other behaviors for data. As Dennett and Kinsbourne point out, both accounts are entirely adequate to the data. They are insinuating that we have no way to determine when various priming effects occur in a processing stream. Traditional cognitive psychology postulates a place in the head in which semantic memories become activated. This implies that we could define or locate all (or most) cognitive processing relative to this place. Dennett and Kinsbourne claim that this intuitively pleasing implication is false.

Dennett and Kinsbourne's point is important because perhaps we have found a psychological phenomenon that cannot be explained using purely psychological methods. This is more radical than the simple underdetermination of theory by evidence which holds that, as a practical matter, we can't collect all of the pertinent evidence; however, for each pair of possible interpretations, there is some evidence that can adjudicate between them. Dennett and Kinsbourne are claiming that there is no (psychological) evidence that could adjudicate the matter *at all*. The underdetermination is ubiquitous and cannot be overcome even counterfactually.

Dennett and Kinsbourne present psychological models of the mind as landing us in an empirically unresolvable difficulty, and as long as we are restricted to data from only one level of organization, the problem will remain. We are witnessing a potential problem in tying psychological phenomena to neurophysiological events, for if we cannot resolve the question of when each cognitive event occurs, relative to the other ones, then we have no way to link our psychological model to occurant neurophysiological processes. And if we cannot overcome this fundamental problem with measurement, then the possibility of useful explanatory extension—as well as the hope for truly interdisciplinary theories in cognitive science—remains in doubt, for we are losing all except the vaguest connections between psychological and neurophysiological descriptions.

ERPs

However, we do have one investigative path open to us that can tell us about the time course of psychological events with greater accuracy than most psychological experiments: that of using measurements of event related potentials (ERPs) to cognitive stimuli. Dennett and Kinsbourne accept verbal reports and other behaviors as indicators of psychological phenomena, but they do not argue that these reports are the only such indicators. There is no reason why we could not find other sorts of evidence that would tie the activations of our memory systems to the underlying neurophysiology, thereby providing a path to uncovering the actual time course of the mnemonic events. Indeed, as I shall indicate below, such evidence is already accruing.

Let me pause first though to explain how ERP recordings work in some detail. I do this not only to establish their legitimacy in investigating finer-grained temporal questions involving mental processes but also to underscore their interdisciplinary nature. This type of neuropsychological framework is exactly the right sort to use to conjoin psychology and neuroscience, and by spelling out the types of commitments and background assumptions one must make when interpreting averaged EEG waves, I illustrate why. I take ERP research to be a case study of a truly interdisciplinary science that functions to link disciplines. I then draw some morals concerning "bridge sciences" in general. These should be applicable to any strongly interdisciplinary domain, whether in the cognitive sciences or not.

(1) *ERP research assumes the descriptive categories of cognitive psychology.* Probably most functions defined in the psychological

domain are underwritten by the cooperative activity of a number of different anatomical systems. Nevertheless, in order to answer Dennett and Kinsbourne's concerns and to get an interdisciplinary theory off the ground, we have to sort out how (and indeed whether) the gross processes hypothesized by psychology map to underlying finer-grained brain organization. One road in to this enormous task is to find and measure physical variables related to the brain that we suspect can be mapped directly onto those processes and then later figure out how these variables are connected to lower level brain organization. ERP researchers, generally speaking, attempt to do just that. Typically they rely on the previously accepted categories of mental phenomena in cognitive psychology when analyzing their brain data. For example, they study "pattern recognition" and "stimulus classification," "detection" and "recognition," "phonetic processes," "selective attention," and "stimulus evaluation."[7] In this sense, ERP research not only borrows data from cognitive psychology but it actually assumes the general correctness of psychology's individuation of the event space. It looks to cognitive psychology for inspiration and collateral support, and it tries to build directly on the foundation that psychology has laid, answering some questions that psychologists assume to be important. Such strong and fundamental ties to psychology make ERP research a strongly interdisciplinary program.

We can also see its interdisciplinary nature in its use of electrical field theory. When studying the physical variables thought to be present in the ERP waves, we are confronted by the problems of definition (what counts as a component?) and measurement (how do we assign numerical values to properties of the components uncontaminated by other components and other confounding influences?). To solve these difficulties, ERP researchers rely on the theoretical and practical aid of electrical field theory. By incorporating the theory's hypotheses and problem-solving strategies into their own investigative domain and adopting them without substantial revision, the ERP program in neuropsychology again fits my understanding of a strongly interdisciplinary program.

(2) *ERP waveforms can be tied to (gross) anatomy and physiology.* In virtue of this strong dependence on psychology, I would say that ERP research in neuropsychology would allow for the sort of ties we need in order to develop a higher resolution of the psychological temporal scale.[8] However, given the nature of ERPs, tying ERP waveforms to specific neural activity is more difficult. Nevertheless, the surface waveforms do give us hints about the gross location of the relevant firing neurons; at least, we can generally decide the dominate hemisphere for

the cognitive task, as well as a rough time course of neurophysiological events. Work in pinning down the exact causal links between surface recordings and cortical activity is just beginning, and ERPs, along with PET scans and MRI's, can be used to triangulate onto the specific neural areas. In any event, ERP recordings can give us hints and suggest possibilities about the exact connection between psychological posits and neurophysiological hypotheses.

Just as in the more traditional psychological experiments, summed amplitude recordings of electric potentials on the scalp tell us little about the underlying neurophysiology. Because these potentials depend on the location of both the recording scalp electrodes and the active neurons, the recorded waves reflect the interaction of the location of the electrode with the spatial orientation of the source cells (and their temporal patterns of synaptic activation). Hence, the recorded waveforms are difficult to disentangle, both spatially and temporally, especially when we consider that EEGs reflect activities occurring at the same time in adjacent cortical regions. In addition, scalp recordings cannot tell us unambiguously the number, location, or orientation of the sources contributing to the surface potentials. Because surface EEG waves reflect only a statistical aggregate of the transmembrane currents of all active neurons at a particular time, each individual neuron's contribution is lost in the summation. We cannot even assume that the generators of the surface waves lie in brain structures directly beneath the region in which the EEG displays maximal amplitude. When the net orientation of the active tissues is not perpendicular to the surface of the head, amplitude maxima can occur in scalp regions far from the relevant neurons, including locations over the opposite hemisphere.

But even if we did know about the neurons that specifically contributed to a given surface EEG, and the relative magnitude of their contributions, the resulting waveform would still give us little insight into the computational procedures at the neuronal level. Consider, for example, the extracellular potentials generated by the lateral geniculate nucleus (LGN).[9] They reflect both LGN cells having on-center-off-surround receptive fields and those having off-center-on-surround receptive fields, as well as "X cells" having predominately sustained responses to visual stimulation and "Y cells" having predominately phasic responses. Because EEG waves recorded under such conditions cannot distinguish among the various types of cells, they can only indicate that *some* activity is occuring, not what that activity is. They cannot indicate the neural "operations" leading to the waveform.

Nevertheless, if the waveform recorded at the surface represents the sum of many fields generated by neurons functionally linked in some way, then the scalp distribution will reflect its spatial properties. In this way, we can still use surface potentials to index larger-scale functional properties, even though the actual relationship between the neural generators and their surface manifestation is not known. Hence, recorded EEG waves work as a gross tie to larger cognitive processes and to area activity. They can work to extend psychological hypotheses by providing a different sort indicator for psychological phenomena than those traditionally used in psychology proper and by giving additional clues about the neural equivalent of higher level information processes. These data then give scientists a way to operationalize their psychological definitions in terms of neurophysiological processes or structures, which could refine psychological conceptualizations of higher functions, such as the functional connections between the STE and the SEE systems. They could also help demonstrate the existence of some antecedently problematic hypothesis, such as particular explicit experiences being locatable at a point in time and space. For example, evoked potential studies in young infants show that orientation-selective mechanisms mature starting at around three weeks; however, infants are sensitive to black/white phase reversing from birth.[10] This sensitivity differential is seen even in infants born prematurely, who would have been exposed to more visual stimuli than full-term infants.[11] We can use these results to bolster the hypothesis that the early maturing subcortical pathways, presumably orientation insensitive, naturally operate prior to any one of several orientation-sensitive cortical mechanisms.[12]

In these ways, recorded EEG waves would bridge psychology and neuroscience, even though this neuropsychological approach is, strictly speaking, nonreductionistic. As far as the surface EEG waves are concerned, the relevant informational currency is the waveform itself, in particular, its latency and gross scalp distribution. Though we have no doubt that underlying individual neural activity causes this wave, we simply do not know enough about individual brain configurations such that tracing that particular causal story will help us understand the relation between higher level psychological phenomenon and its corresponding EEG wave pattern, nor would it help us understand the information processing capacities of the single cells themselves. For the moment, the only true level of analysis for ERP researchers is the surface waveform.

Surface waveforms provide a nice way to pursue our strategy of learning more about psychological information processing. ERP waves give us a way to study the activity of neurons taken together across cortical areas, and if we can isolate the components that reflect any particular processing system, we could say those components index the neuronal correlate of the higher level system. And if we can understand the space-time dynamics of the collection of neurons as a whole as reflected in the morphology and the latency of the waveform, then we might have a start in tying psychological phenomena to activated areas of neurons.

So then, ERP research that bridges psychology and neuroscience also functionally decomposes psychological phenomena in terms of neuropsychological components. However, ERP research operates with different organizing principles (at a different level of aggregation) than either psychology or neuroscience. Evoked potential experiments begin with the assumption that we can reduce neuropsychological signals to functions of voltage • time and then use the principles of electrical field theory to make generalizations about how to understand the recorded surface waveforms. None of this can be reduced or easily translated into psychological terms. In addition, the researchers interpret the waveforms themselves as indicators of psychological functions; they do not need to connect them explicitly to underlying physiology.

Nevertheless, even though ERP research has its own organizing principles, experimental paradigms, classic results, and central questions, it assumes psychological phenomena as the appropriate explananda and then it gives some evidence for neural localization. So, with ERP research, psychology is not merely snooping for answers in another investigative domain, but in a domain that has adopted psychology's basic theoretical framework as its own. And in doing so, any answers that it provides should count as legitimate responses to psychology's questions as well, for insofar as it adopts the same framework as psychology, it thereby assumes the appropriate contrast class, reference relations, and scientific audience. Hence, ERP research should be able to function as a true and well-grounded bridge between psychological theory and higher level neurophysiological descriptions.

The Timing of Priming

Let us now return to the question before us: whether subliminal or implicit priming occurs before explicit access to an item, so that we actually are aware of the stimulus faster, or whether priming actually occurs after awareness so that only our motor responses are affected. If we can answer this sort of question, we will learn something about the timing of our mnemonic processes, thereby providing additional support for the dual memory system framework. If we cannot answer this type of question, then Dennett and Kinsbourne are right, and we cannot have a truly interdisciplinary theory of the sort I propose.

Semantic priming has been studied using ERPs to visual and auditory stimuli. In general, when we compare the waveforms for semantically related pairs of words with semantically different word pairs, we find a difference in a late negative component that onsets at around 200 msec, peaks near 400 msec after the stimulus presentation, and is bigger over the right hemisphere than the left.[13] The waveform is generally referred to as the N400 wave. (See figure 7.1 for an example.) Study of this waveform under different probability conditions for semantic relatedness suggests that the N400 is sensitive to "the degree to which a word has been primed" (Kutas et al. 1984, p. 237). The more two words are *unrelated*, the *larger* the N400 waveform.

This type of paradigm has been repeated in the auditory domain, with similar results,[14] although the negativity had an earlier onset, a later peak latency, and a somewhat different scalp distribution. The N400 effect and the differences between the modalities for this effect are most clearly seen in ERP "difference waves," formed when the waveform for one experimental condition is subtracted from the other and the results plotted. (See figure 7.2.) The N400 has also been studied with respect to pseudowords and nonwords in an effort to understand with what *level* of processing (e.g., semantic, lexical, graphemic) it is correlated. We find an N400 wave for pseudowords (nonsense words that are

Figure 7.1 *The N400 Waveform*

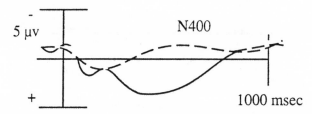

A schematic of grand mean target ERPs to semantically related words (solid line) and semantically unrelated words (dashed line) for the visual modality. Stimulus onset is the vertical bar.

still pronounceable and that follow standard English phonemic rules), but not for true nonwords (letter strings that are not pronounceable). Instead, the nonwords elicited a large positive component (a P3) during the period in which words and pseudowords produced the N400. (See figure 7.3.)

These results suggest that the N400 is specific to events that are members or potential members of a subject's language system.[15] It is possible that the N400 indexes some aspect of the lexical search process and that its amplitude and duration are a function of the extensiveness of the search. In this case, the N400 component may be smaller when the target is semantically related to the preceding prime because the search required for locating the target within a subject's lexicon is helped by the activation of the prime; it would then be larger with unprimed words because these words cannot facilitate the processing and so a more extensive search is required.

Figure 7.2 *The N400 Difference Wave*

A schematic of difference waves calculated by subtracting the ERPs for semantically related words from the ERPs for semantically unrelated words. Stimulus onset is the calibration bar.

Figure 7.3 *The P3 Effect*

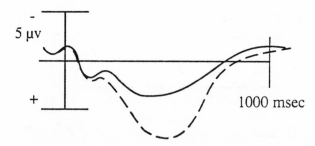

A schematic for grand mean target ERPs to identity primed pronounceable nonwords (solid line) and identity primed backwards nonwords (dashed line) in the visual modality. Stimulus onset is the calibration bar.

Related ERP measurements also indicate specialization for other domains. For example, Barrett and Rugg (1988, 1989) examine identity and semantic priming in faces. They found an early negative component similar to the N400 indexes primed versus unprimed faces. However, this waveform, an N250, is larger over the frontal and parietal regions, whereas the N400 is larger over the centro-posterior regions, and the N250 shows no hemispheric asymmetries, while the N400 is larger over the right hemisphere.[16] These results suggest that the N250 and the N400 are elicited by different brain systems even though they both can be primed by the previous context. When ERP results display different distributions (anterior versus posterior or right hemisphere versus left hemisphere), then they are generally taken to be generated by nonidentical neural systems. Indeed, nonidentical brain systems may carry out the processing and priming of words and faces, even though behaviorally the results are virtually indistinguishable.

ERP research is proving to be a useful methodology for teasing apart different processing systems in the brain—systems that we are able to identify functionally within cognitive psychology, even though behavioral results alone cannot easily separate them. This sort of investigation also indicates the relative time course of various cognitive events. For example, we can argue that the brain can recognize the semantic relatedness of two words after only 200–300 msec or so of processing. Though we may not be able to conclude conclusively when any specific processes occur, we certainly can compare the differential processing of two types of events and argue that one occurs before the other. For example, we know that the brain can recognize the semantic relatedness of spoken words faster than it can in the visual modality.

Researchers are now starting to gather data from ERP studies that suggest that accessing an implicit memory system gives rise to a qualitatively different kind of ERP wave than does accessing the memory system that apparently underwrites explicit conscious experience.[17] For example, Helen Neville and her colleagues investigated whether there are systems specialized for rapid linguistic analysis that are automatically accessed prior to consciousness and whether these systems are separate from our more general information stores. These domain-specific STE subsystems would stand in contrast to the more general SEE system that represents words, along with other types of knowledge about the world. However, if the general framework I sketched in the previous chapter for dual memory systems is correct, then these data cannot be the entire story, for I claim that the early STE system accesses and processes *non-*

word material. Fortunately, though, there is now evidence for implicit priming effects using completely novel visual stimuli.[18] Unfortunately, though, subjects showed implicit priming effects for the nonverbal stimuli in these studies only if the instructions for encoding forced them to form a structural description of the objects. (These results buttress Schacter et al.'s suggestion that implicit priming is due to a perceptual memory system specialized to represent an object's form.)

However, it could be that the reason the masked paradigms involving completely novel stimuli show no implicit priming effects is that the tasks simply use inputs too complicated for an early automatic system to encode rapidly. Masked priming effects for novel stimuli then should be seen immediately with simple input patterns. To test this hypothesis (as well as to try to characterize more fully the capabilities of these early systems) I have designed a series of experiments to compare the ERP waveforms in unmasked and masked priming conditions for simple five-line visual patterns.[19] Patterns consisted of five connected lines joining dots in a 3 x 3 dot matrix. Most of the patterns were variations of the patterns used in Musen and Treisman (1990) (with the exception that the dots of the matrix were not shown in this series of experiments). Patterns were sorted into three categories: *closed*, in which some part of the patterns formed an enclosed area; *continuous*, in which no portion of the patterns formed a closed area and in which the lines form a continuous shape; and *hatched*, in which patterns were neither closed nor continuous. Only closed and hatched patterns were used in these experiments in order to maintain consistent shape complexity. The targets were proceeded by primes either identical to, the mirror image of, in the same category as, or unrelated to the target. Figure 7.4 shows some examples.

Under the unmasked conditions, as one would expect, subjects were faster at deciding whether a shape is closed if that shape is preceded by a prime identical to, the mirror image of, or the same category as the target.[20] As illustrated in figure 7.5, there is a negative effect with identity and mirror priming similar to the negativity seen in the semantic paradigms discussed above.[21] These effects are followed by an amplitude and latency shift in the P3 component, similar to the effects of the nonword priming paradigm above (cf., figure 7.3).[22] (In the category priming condition, all we find is a modulation of the P3.) Figure 7.6 summarizes the ERP effects for the three measured epochs in the difference waves and it indicates a negative effect for both identity and mirror priming, as well as a P3 modulation in all three conditions.[23, 24] In sum-

Figure 7.4

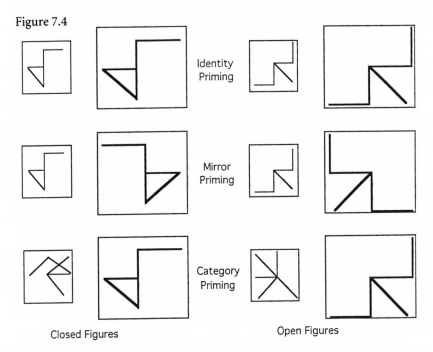

Identity Priming

Mirror Priming

Category Priming

Closed Figures   Open Figures

Examples of the novel visual stimuli priming conditions.

mary, the ERP results are fairly consistent with what one would expect given the priming data for words.

The reaction-time results in the masked condition are what one would expect as well. Schacter predicts that subjects who have no previous structural memory of some shape should show no priming effects and should not to be faster in deciding whether a target stimulus was closed. And there were no significant differences in the behavioral data.[25] However, the ERP data do not corroborate this hypothesis. Though there were considerable individual differences, I also found some significant masked priming effects in both the identity and mirror conditions when the subjects were averaged together, even though these effects were not reflected in reaction time.[26] With both identity and mirror priming, there was a priming-induced positivity onsetting at about 100 msec and continuing essentially for the duration of the recorded epoch.[27] (There were no significant changes however in the category priming condition.) (See figure 7.7.)

That there are effects at all suggests that the masked priming positivity with novel visual stimuli indexes something other than the specialized representation of words in a lexicon. However, because these

Figure 7.5 *ERP Waveforms for Unmasked Novel Visual Stimuli*

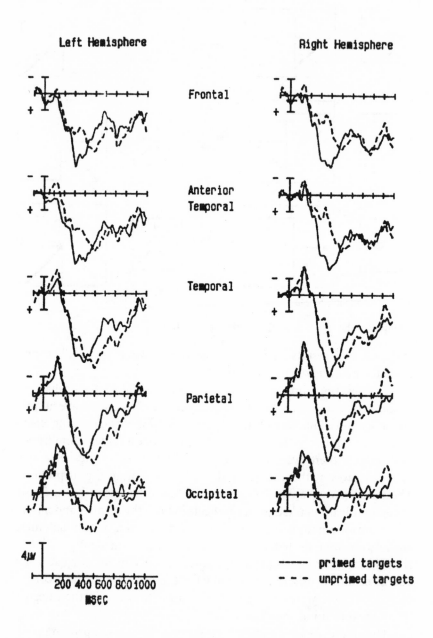

7.5A Grand mean target ERPs for identity primed versus not primed simple novel shapes. Time is in msec, each tic mark is 100 msec. Stimulus onset is the calibration bar.

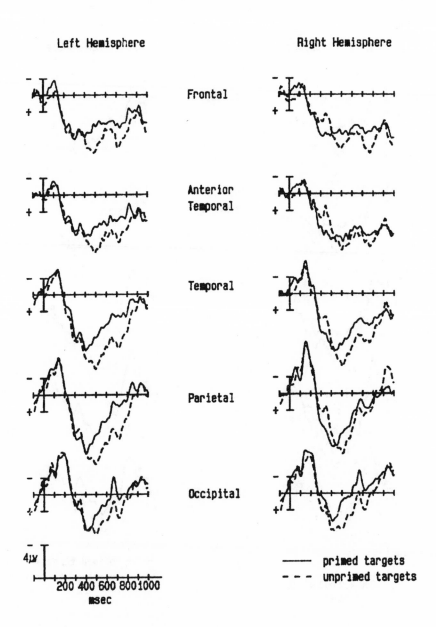

Left Hemisphere

Right Hemisphere

Frontal

Anterior
Temporal

Temporal

Parietal

Occipital

4 µV

200 400 600 800 1000
msec

——— primed targets
- - - unprimed targets

7.5B Grand mean target ERPs for mirror primed versus not primed simple novel shapes. Time is in msec, each tic mark is 100 msec. Stimulus onset is the calibration bar.

Figure 7.5 *(continued)*

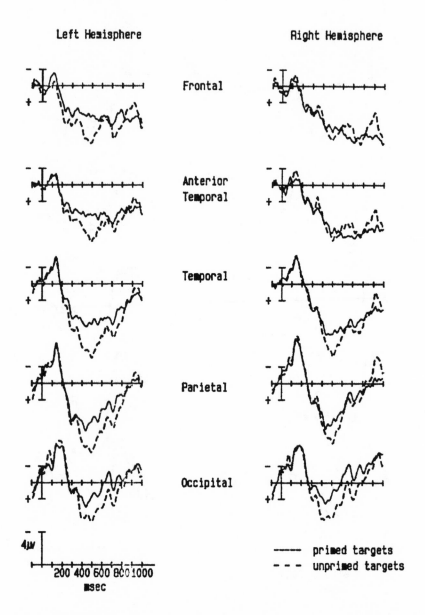

7.5C Grand mean target ERPs for category primed versus not primed simple novel shapes. Time is in msec, each tic mark is 100 msec. Stimulus onset is the calibration bar.

Figure 7.6 *Early, Middle, and Late Measures for Priming Effects Using Novel Visual Stimuli*

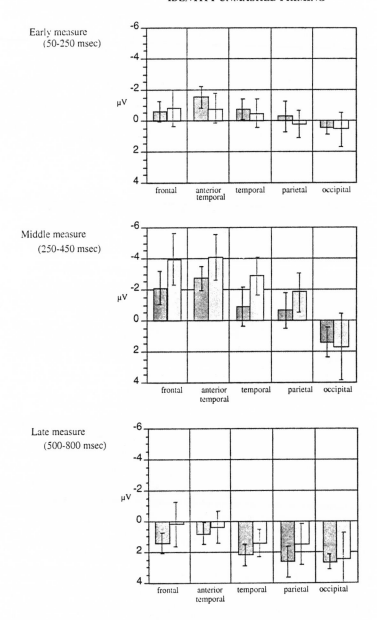

IDENTITY UNMASKED PRIMING

Early measure
(50-250 msec)

Middle measure
(250-450 msec)

Late measure
(500-800 msec)

Figure 7.6 *(continued)*

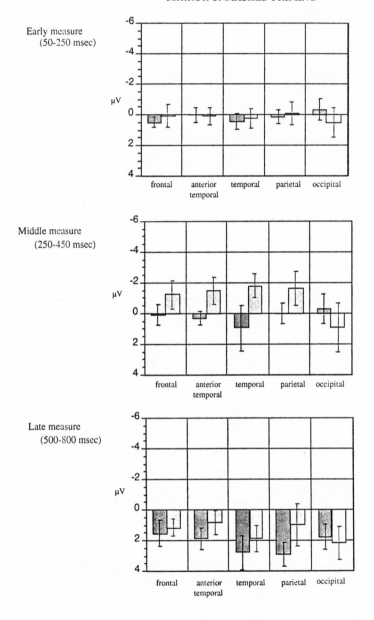

MIRROR UNMASKED PRIMING

CATEGORY UNMASKED PRIMING

Early measure (50-250 msec)

Middle measure (250-450 msec)

Late measure (500-800 msec)

left hemisphere

right hemisphere

These charts show no early effect in any priming condition, a negative effect for identity and mirror priming in the middle measures (the N400), and a late positive effect in all three conditions (the P3).

Figure 7.7 *ERP Waveforms for Masked Novel Visual Stimuli*

IDENTITY PRIMING

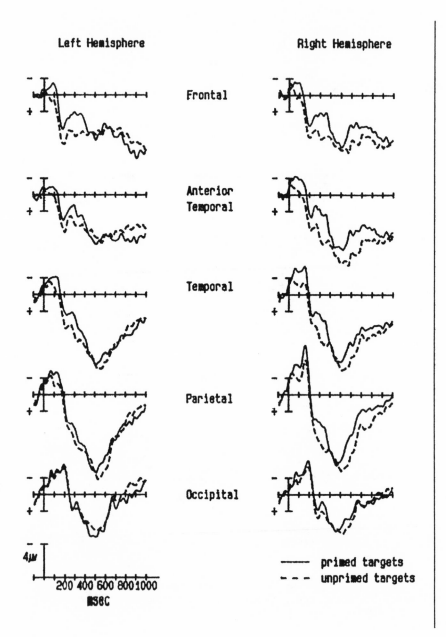

MIRROR PRIMING

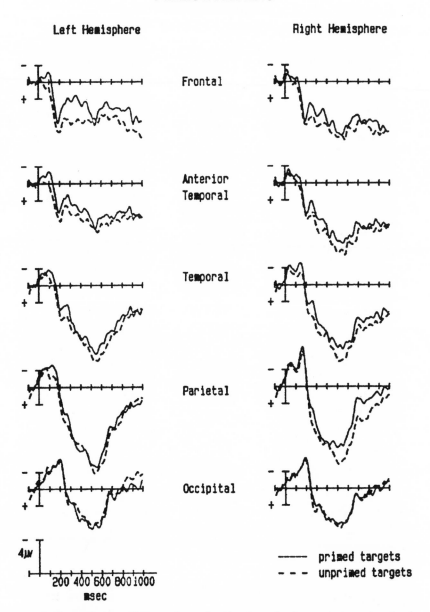

7.7A, B Shown here are ERP waveforms for identity and mirror priming using simple novel visual shapes. In both conditions, we find an enhanced positivity onsetting at approximately 100 msec and continuing essentially for the duration of the recorded epoch These effects are very different from the effects seen in the unmasked paradigm using the same stimuli.

Figure 7.7 *(continued)*

CATEGORY PRIMING

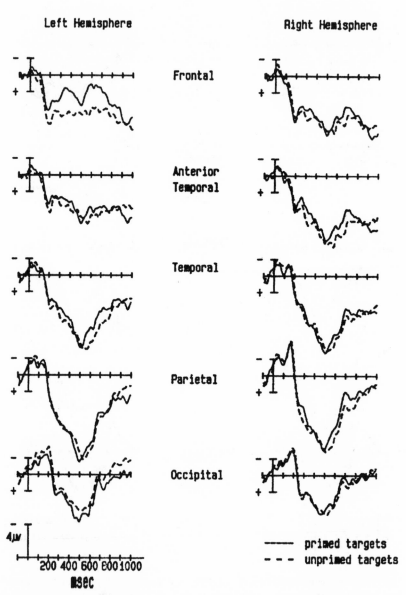

7.7C There are no ERP priming effects using the masked category primes.

effects are substantially different than those of semantic priming, a specialized early lexicon may still exist. These results only demonstrate that more than a lexicon operates prior to conscious processing. At the least, we are able to recognize simple nonsemantic visual information the same as or different from other stimuli prior to conscious access.

If we compare figures 7.6 and 7.8, it is clear that the masked priming effects are very different from the unmasked effects, again suggesting that masked and unmasked priming activate nonidentical systems. The system that underwrites masked priming seems to be activated automatically and accessed quite early in cognitive processing. Though it can perform rather sophisticated analyses (i.e., recognizing a stimulus as the same as or different from a previous stimulus), it is not capable of categorizing stimuli based on higher level distinctions, such as arbitrary category definitions. The conscious processing that supports unmasked priming, on the other hand, occurs later and appears to be sensitive to the more "abstract" properties of stimuli.[28] At least, it can be primed with information relative to the task at hand.

As we saw in the ERP semantic paradigms, the different timing and distribution of the unmasked and masked effects point to early and late processing systems that are consistent with the hypothesized STE and SEE memory systems. The systems have different processing capabilities, operate under different time frames, and use different nets of neurons. In the unmasked condition, we saw differential responses for both words and nonwords and for all three priming possibilities with novel visual stimuli. These effects began relatively late in the recorded epoch and were posteriorly distributed. In contrast, in the masked conditions, we only saw differential brain wave responses for repetition priming using meaningful words and for identity and mirror priming using completely novel visual shapes. These effects began earlier in the anterior portion of the brain. These data concerning the processing capacities of the two systems lend support to the hypothesis that the early system is more structural, while the later also includes "higher level" semantic analyses.

The fact that the behavioral data showed no masked priming effects only underscores the need for psychology to extend its theories via neuropsychological and neurophysiological data. While it shows that Dennett and Kinsbourne are quite right to argue that psychology alone may not be enough to answer all the questions we have about cognitive processing on the psychological level, we cannot thereby conclude that some psychological questions cannot be answered. ERPs can narrow the

Figure 7.8 *Early, Middle, and Late Measures for Masked Priming Using Novel Visual Stimuli*

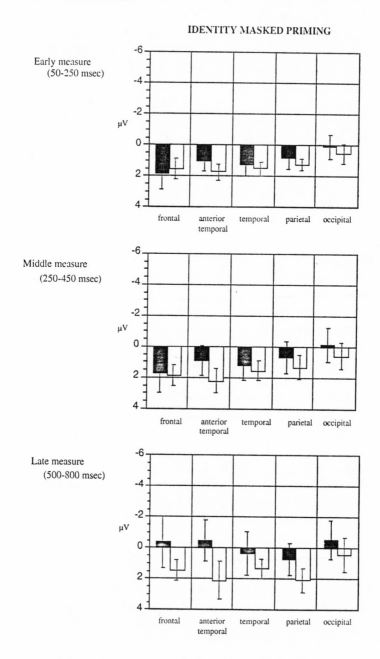

MIRROR MASKED PRIMING

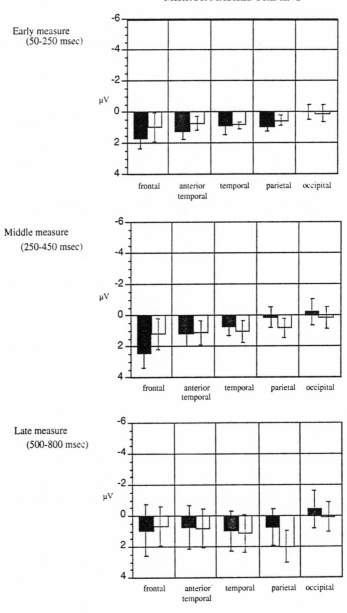

Early measure
(50-250 msec)

Middle measure
(250-450 msec)

Late measure
(500-800 msec)

Figure 7.8 *(continued)*

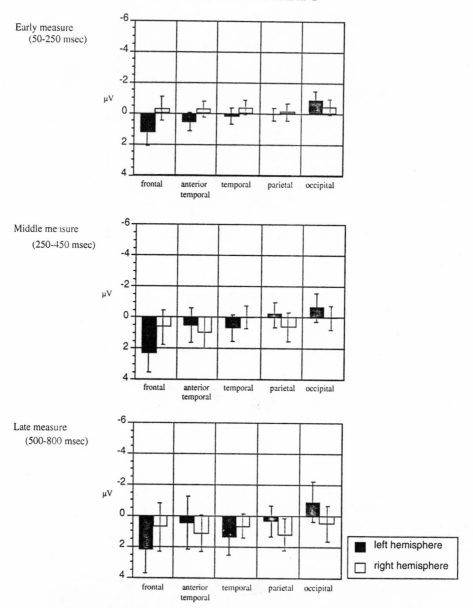

CATEGORY MASKED PRIMING

Early measure
(50-250 msec)

Middle measure
(250-450 msec)

Late measure
(500-800 msec)

■ left hemisphere
□ right hemisphere

These charts indicate that there is an early, middle, and late positive enhancement of the masked primed condition with both identity and mirror priming, but few effects with masked category priming. We can compare these effects with the early, middle, and late measures for the unmasked paradigm and see that masked and unmasked priming with novel visual shapes give rise to radically different effects across all conditions.

temporal window in which we have the power to distinguish various processes, and it can increase the resolution enough to determine whether the STE system is activated before the SEE system.

At the least, the two priming effects point out distinctly identifiable temporal processes within our mnemonic systems—Dennett and Kinsbourne are simply wrong when they claim that we cannot narrow our investigative window enough to distinguish when masked priming effects occur. There is some evidence that the effects occur (and STE memories are activated) before accessing an SEE memory. The hypothesis of a processing stream *from* activated STE memories *to* activated SEE memories remains plausible.

I conclude that results like these show how it is possible to parse psychological events finely enough in (neuro)psychological investigations to determine when particular psychological events do occur in the head. If we could align explicit recognition with some psychological event or (perhaps some other sort of neural process), then we should be able to articulate definitively when that event occurs in the processing stream (relative to other events) as long as that event can be correlated with an ERP waveform. Hence, we should be able to locate the timing of any particular (set of averaged) cognitive processes.

ERPs therefore occupy a rather unique position among the cognitive sciences. They work to extend the psychological theories by providing new sorts of evidence for psychological phenomena. At the same time, they also act to connect the more coarsely parsed psychological processes with the more finely defined underlying (gross) neurophysiolgy.

Bridge Sciences

We know that a straightforward and simple-minded function-to-structure reduction that helps justify a computational theory is impossible. As we saw in chapter 4, the important connections made between a theoretical model from one domain and data from another can come through a level of description that could be either functional or structural, depending on the amount of detail given. Moreover, the pragmatics of theory building entail that we cannot assume that because two theories are made over the same state space (or indeed over the same physical system), they will be able to be tied to one another. Connections among theoretical frameworks require more than shared subject matter; they require similar background assumptions brought about by some shared history, audience, or other such pragmatic aspect. The "bridge" between two domains somehow should include the defining assumptions of both.

I responded to these sorts of concerns by using the notion of a "bridge science" between psychology and neuroscience in order to maintain an nterdisciplinary framework for explaining cognitive processes. I concentrated on research using event related potentials, but other sorts of bridges in the cognitive sciences are possible, of course. For example, the rapidly burgeoning field of computational neuroscience effectively links computer science with neuroscience.[29] (Relevant to the discussion in the last two chapters, David Zipser has developed a neural network model of temporal activity during delayed matching-to-sample tasks,[30] and Ilya Rybak and his colleagues have built a neural network model of the "what" and "where" pathways in visual cortex.)[31] Even though higher level descriptions and analyses of the brain are not well developed for the most part, we can nonetheless still outline some general characteristics of the ERP bridge in cognitive science in order to clarify some of the conceptual foundations needed for any interdisciplinary science.

To serve as a bridge, ERP research shares theoretical assumptions with the domains it links. ERP research deliberately adopts many of cognitive psychology's questions and then ties its answers to gross physiology. Indeed, the experimental paradigm adopted by Neville and her colleagues for investigating the differences in masked and unmasked semantic processing is exactly the same as the one used by Forster and his colleagues in investigating the same events. (The only difference of course is that Neville recorded brain waves as well as reaction time.) Neville and other ERP investigators then use the framework provided by animal research and lesion studies to tie the recorded waveforms to different areas of the brain.

In addition, models of ERP data share aspects of both functional and structural descriptions. On the one hand, interpreting the averaged waves in terms of psychological processes gives us a higher level functional description of cognitive interactions based on data from the brain itself. On the other hand, the morphology and the latency of the waveforms provide an abstract structure for indicating the neural instantiation of cognition. And depending on to which domain we orient our theoretical discussion, these models can appear either purely functional or purely structural.

For example, if we define the psychological predicates operationally in terms of various wave component morphology or latency, then these descriptions are functional relative to the more detailed descriptions of the relevant neurophysiology. We define the predicates in terms of input stimuli, behavioral output, and intervening waveforms, and these descriptions are functional in comparison to anatomical descriptions of the neurons that cause the waveforms.

However, these same descriptions are also structural relative to coarser partitions in psychological state space that turn on data from behavioral experiments alone. The intervening waveforms would then be a crude indicator or representation of the underlying brain activity. Since averaged EEG waves can serve as both localization evidence and evidence for information processing theories of mind, it is difficult to talk about whether these sorts of descriptions are truly functional or structural.

Nevertheless, ERP descriptions (and other middle and lower levels of analysis) would still count as a functional decomposition of higher level psychological theories. Insofar as we can consider theoretical models derived from such data as specifying the causal mechanisms of the higher level functional description in greater detail, then they are a straightforward functional analysis of the higher level description. So then, a model of our STE and SEE memory systems derived from ERP data serves as further analysis of the analogous models derived from reaction time studies in amnesics, perceptual identification studies in normals, and so on, since it can specify the psychological events with higher temporal resolution.

However, even though it relies on psychology's contrast classes in formulating its central questions and psychological tasks for developing its own experimental paradigms, ERP research has its own theoretical framework as well. This framework, which borrows from eletrical field theory and the basic electrical properties of active neurons, allows scientists to interpret what they record from the scalp and then tie the recorded activity back to underlying brain areas. The recording techniques and the recorded waves give rise to new questions that have little to do with the original psychological queries. For example, much of the N400 discussion centers around how to interpret the waveforms (e.g., is it one effect or many?) before they are connected to psychologically defined events. In addition, ERP researchers—though they communicate their results to psychologists and neuroscientists—also form a unique audience for ERP data. For example, deciding whether the P3 has two components is a controversy peculiar to the ERP community, and even though the answer has implications for both psychology and neuroscience, only scientists actively involved in ERPs are carrying on the discussion.

So, though ERPs can link psychology and neuroscience in virtue of common assumptions, doing so would not constitute a reductive move in cognitive science. Since ERP research has its own organizing principles, central questions, audience, and interpretive concerns separate from those borrowed from psychology and neuroscience, neurophysiology, neuroanatomy, or cognitive psychology could never account for all the ERP results. Likewise, since it merely adopts psychological frameworks to verify neuroscientific conclusions, it would never be able to explain why the psychological framework is true in the first place. Instead, as part of a two-part interdisciplinary theory, it links the two domains through a common vocabulary, set of guiding principles, and shared framework assumptions.

However, there is a kind of practical limitation in science that assuming a common background cannot overcome. As this chapter suggests, technology not only shapes how we understand data but also limits the sorts of questions and answers we can develop about any physical system. Dennett and Kinsbourne argue that some questions simply cannot be answered even though they make eminent sense given the history and players of the domain. They believe that such limitations play an important role in how we can understand the phenomena we wish to explain. But regardless of whether one takes this more radical view or accepts merely that some problems of measurement are insoluble, the connection between data and model needs to be examined more carefully.

Patrick Suppes (1962) outlines three levels of models needed to relate empirical data to a theoretical model.[32] His idea is that the logical models of a theory may be too abstract to match empirical data precisely, so we should work our way though gradually more specified models until we have a model of empirical data that is a good analog of the truly theoretical model. His hierarchy of models allows us to go from possible outcomes of a particular experiment to answering whether those results can satisfy some theoretical model. But this hierarchy cannot help us understand which questions we can answer, given current limitations on technology.

Knowing which queries are feasible is theoretically important if our conception of the physical system turns on which questions are tenable.

We cannot simply create any model of the data we wish—we have to remain faithful to framework that spurred the experiment. Similarly, we cannot create any theoretical framework we wish, since frameworks depend on the sorts of questions we ask. Finally, simply adopting apparently relevant data in service of some theoretical goal cannot work. The models of the data and experiment must stand in a special relation to the theoretical model.

Here too is where bridge sciences are helpful, for they give us one way to connect data with theory conceptually. Because interdisciplinary programs tend to hop across different fields—and so the traditional boundaries of disciplines cannot prevent theoretical comingling—we need to pay particular attention to technological/methodological feasibility in these instances. Feasibility restricts the contrast class and determines some background context, which then ensures that the empirical results can be used to justify a particular theory in an interdisciplinary program. Bridge sciences tie data to models across disciplines in virtue of shared general principles and background assumptions that set the descriptive vocabulary of the physical system and help determine the physical system itself. However, since bridge sciences entail specific empirical models as well, they form more concrete ties than any set of general principles alone, which are too broad to support any particular model of the phenomenon.

We need to demark the pragmatic restrictions on which models can serve the same theory. Sharing the same contrast class and background assumptions is sufficient but not necessary—models only need be linked via some other model that shares fundamental assumptions with both the linked models. Moreover, what those fundamental assumptions are may depend on which questions we are technologically capable of answering. Hence, what counts as a successful explanation turns on pragmatic methodological restrictions as well as sociological factors. Explanations are answers to why-questions where the contrast class contains theoretically *and* technologically possible answers. Investigators still ask these elliptical questions against a background context, but that context includes the statements accepted by the interested scientific community as well as the methodologies used and accepted by the field.

APPENDIX

Cognitive Science and the Semantic View

Most of what I have written has been presented in terms of the semantic view of theories.[1] Here I briefly recapitulate the semantic view of theories and show how it applies to psychology. This appendix is fairly brief since details have already been presented elsewhere;[2] nevertheless, I thought it important to illustrate how the formal apparatus works for single discipline theories. (As discussed in chapters 6 and 7, I think this formalism breaks down for interdisciplinary theories of the sort found in cognitive science.) Let me emphasize, though, that I adopt the semantic view in this text not because I think it is inherently superior to the more traditional models (though I do)—indeed, everything that I claim can be translated into any view of theory you might have with greater or lesser ease—but, instead, because it highlights certain features of theories that are important for the discussions above.

Not surprisingly, there are many different versions of the semantic view, distinguishable by the type of mathematical system used to formalize theories.[3] In general, though, the semantic view holds theories to be abstract pictures of relations among variables. A picture with all of its parameters fixed is a model. Each theory has several (maybe indefinitely many) models, and we can think of a model as representing one of the possible worlds allowed by the theory. These models range in the amount of empirical or semantic content, from highly abstract, purely formal models to detailed sets of observed phenomena and their relations. What links the models together as a single theory is their common mathematical structure.[4]

Psychological theories are no exception either; they fit the mold of the semantic view of theories quite nicely.[5] To illustrate, let us take the particular example of Anne Treisman's feature-integration hypothesis.[6] She has developed a "spotlight" theory of attention that explains the serial processes of visual perception. Visual processing apparently occurs in two stages. First, features are extracted from the patterns of light that fall on the retina. This stage happens automatically for all incoming signals, and the different features (color, size, contrast, tilt, curvature, line ends, motion, and depth) are extracted and processed in parallel along different pathways in the brain. Only after these features have been analyzed separately does our brain combine them into objects and surroundings. This second stage of binding the primary components into units happens serially and only if attention is devoted to the task. The idea is that attention focuses on one location and combines only the features found at that spot. It then shifts to a different place and binds the features found there, and so on.

Visual processing begins by coding primitive features onto what Treisman calls metaphorically "a stack of maps." These maps preserve the spatial location of each feature, but this spatial information is not directly available for the later stages of processing. In these later stages, focused attention acts by using a "master map" of locations in which the location of discontinuities of the various features are recorded, but recorded without noting what the discontinuities are. Attention links this master map to the individual feature maps and selects all features that are present in one location. Finally, the results of the integration are entered into short-term memory or some other store for further processing.

The two basic points of her feature-integration hypothesis are:

(FI1) Preattentive processing, a relatively early stage in sensory processing, occurs in parallel, without attention, and automatically. It merely registers which features are present in the sensory field, though it may not register their locations.

(FI2) Focused attention, the next stage in sensory processing, requires attention, occurs serially, and with conscious subject involvement. It selects which features belong together as a unit via a master map of locations.

To simplify the presentation, I shall only use time and a master map of locations as the defining characteristics for the processes involved in feature integration. (In what follows I rely on set-theoretic notation, though what I say can be translated into just about any formulation you like.)

We can define the predicate, "is a model of feature-integration (FI)," as:[7]

x is a model of FI ($x \in M(\text{FI})$) iff

(1) $x = <S, F, O, L, T, \mathfrak{R}, P, A>$

(2) S is a finite, possibly empty set

(3) F is a finite, possibly empty set

(4) O is a finite, possibly empty set

(5) L is a singleton set

(6) T is a finite, ordered, nonempty set $<t_1, t_2, t_3, \ldots >$

(7) P: $\exists (t_i)(t_i$ and $S^* \rightarrow F^*$ where $S^* \subseteq S$ and $F^* \subseteq F)$

(8) A: $\forall o_i \in O^*$ where $O^* \subseteq O(F^\# \times L = o_i$ where $F^\# \subseteq F^*$ and $O^* \times T \rightarrow \mathfrak{R}^{+)}$

On the intended application of FI, S is the set of possible sensory input a subject could receive, F is the set of possible features present to the subject, O is set of the possible representation(s) of the final object (or objects), L is the master map of locations, T is the set of time instances, P is the preattentive processing relation from a proper subset of stimuli input to a set of features, and A is the focused attention processing relation from a proper subset of the set of features to the set of perceived objects.

Notice that this model also fits a version of the Shiffrin-Schneider distinction between controlled and automatic processing.[8] On this application of FI, S is the set of possible sensory input a subject could receive, F is the set of possible object/action memory schemas, O is set of the possible memories of objects, L is the attentional mechanism, T is the set of time instances, P is the automatic detection processing relation from a proper subset of stimuli input to a set of objects or action memory schemas, and A is the controlled search processing relation from a proper subset of the set of object or action schemas to the set of perceived object memories. In this simplified presentation, the same model represents two different hypotheses (that is, the structure of the two hypotheses are the same) and hence the two hypotheses are actually of the same theory.

This model can then be used to answer the following sorts of questions: Why did Mick see an orange carrot and a blue lake and not a blue carrot and an orange lake? (Why did o_1 occur at t_1 and o_2 occur at t_2, and not o_3 at t_1 and o_4 at t_2?); Why is Keith faster at recognizing the letter E presented among a display of numbers (after learning that as a target letter) than if it is presented among a display of other letters? (Why did

f_i, where $f_i \in F^*$, occur at t_i and o_1 occur at $t_j > t_i$?). The answer to the first is that a triangular shape and an orange color occurred at the same place on the master map of locations, while a circle and a blue color occurred at a different location. Hence, attentional processing would bind the triangle with the orange and the circle with the blue.[9] The answer to the second is that recognizing a letter among digits requires only automatic processing, while recognizing a particular letter among letters requires controlled processing. (This answer just falls out of the model itself.)

These two questions and their answers exemplify the types of problems involved in explaining visual processing; however, they are problems that concern two different psychological communities.[10] The first question contrasts seeing one particular arrangement of features with seeing a very different arrangement of the same features, while the second contrasts the speed of processing information across categories with the speed of processing information within a category. The contrast class of the first question (a different mix of the same features) simply would not arise for Shiffrin and Schneider because (for historical reasons that need not detain us here) their community was more interested in explaining the perceptual categories one uses than how object representations are constructed. Similarly, the contrast class of the second question would not occur in (this version of) Treisman's community because it concerns abstractions beyond the concatenation of features that she is interested in.

Notice too that this formalism does not fit exactly with proposed extensions of Treisman's theory. That is, the extending model is not isomorphic to the extended model. Isomorphism is a very general and rather vague constraint. How to cash this condition out is not yet clear; several different—and incommensurable—accounts exist.[11] However, since I am mainly concerned with similarity (another vague notion), this controversy should not affect my points. Here I appeal to your intuitions, for all I wish to claim is that extensions of theories have much of the same structure as the extended theories, enough that we would recognize the formalisms as similar, regardless of the metric used.

To take a particular example, Frances Crick has taken Treisman's model and used it as a stepping stone for his own neurophysiological model of attention.[12] He claims the attentional "spotlight" is controlled by the reticular complex and the perigeniculate nucleus of the thalamus. Rapid bursts of firing from a portion of the thalamic neurons correspond to the attentional process. These rapid bursts modify sensitive synapses (the Malsburg synapses) so that they then conjoin the various features coded by neighboring neurons. These "recoded" Malsburg synapses in effect produce transient cell assemblies that temporarily unite neurons at different levels of the processing hierarchy.[13]

In formalizing Crick's hypothesis, I shall simplify it somewhat. I have indicated the differences between this and Treisman's hypothesis in bold.

We can define the predicate, "is a neurophysiological model of attention (NPA)," as:

x is a model of NPA ($x \in M(\text{NPA})$) iff

(1) $x = <S, F, O, L, T, \mathbf{R}, \mathfrak{R}, P, A, \mathbf{N}>$

(2) S is a finite, possibly empty set

(3) F is a finite, possibly empty set

(4) O is a finite, possibly empty set

(5)   **L is finite, possibly empty set**

(6) T is a finite, ordered, nonempty set $<t_1, t_2, t_3, \ldots >$

(7) P: $\exists t_i (t_i$ and $S^* \to F^*$ where $S^* \subseteq S$ and $F^* \subseteq F)$

(8)   **N: $\exists (r_i, l_i,$ where $r_i \subseteq R$ and $l_i \subseteq L)(r_i \to l_i$ and $l_i \text{ x } T \to \mathfrak{R}^+)$**

(9) A: $\forall o_i \in O^*$ where $O^* \subseteq O(\mathbf{F^\#} \text{ x } \mathbf{l_i} = o_i$ where $F^\# \subseteq F^*$ and $O^* \text{ x } T \to \mathfrak{R}^+)$

On the intended application of NAP, S is the set of possible sensory input a subject could receive, F is the set of possible features present to the subject, **O is the set of the possible transient cell assemblies, L is the set of possible firing patterns across the Malsburg synapses, R is the set of possible bursting patterns across the reticular complex and the perigeniculate nucleus,** T is the set of time instances, P is the preattentive processing relation from a proper subset of stimuli input to a set of features, **N is the neurophysiological computational relation from a proper subset of thalamic bursting patterns to a proper subset of cell assemblies,** and A is the focused attention processing relation from a proper subset of the set of features to the set of perceived objects.

Though Crick works out his hypothesis in much greater detail, his point in this simplified version is still clear: He is attempting to provide psychology with a neurophysiological derivation for and a structural description of a rather troublesome term. (The neurophysiological suggestion adds formal structure to the notion of L through defining an additional function.) Treisman never actually defines what she means by "attention," and there are few good explanations in psychology. Instead, it is perhaps better to think of attention in psychology as a place holder for something to come. Into this relative vacuum steps neuro-physiology, which we can read as justifying (or trying to, at any rate) why it is reasonable for psychology to assume attentional processing without being ad hoc, for Crick models a process that psychology cur-rently uses in an explanans. Nevertheless, even though the explanans in psychology mentioning attention can be explained in part by referring to neurophysiological models, it does not follow that the *explanation* provided by psychology for visual processing would be improved if we replaced psychology's premises with Crick's model of attention. For what is relevant in explaining the neurophysiology of attention is not relevant in explaining the psychology of visual processing, in which statements concerning attention act as assumptions in Treisman's model.

Here though we do have two hypotheses that we can join together by virtue of a family resemblance in structure, forming a single "smeared out" interdisciplinary theory. It should be clear, though, that it would be difficult to construct a single basic formalism underlying both conjectures. Albeit helpful, the semantic view has reached its limits in the field of cognitive science.

NOTES

Chapter 1.
Cognitive Science Is Not Cognitive Psychology

1. von Eckhardt (1993), p. 337.

2. von Eckhardt (1993), p. 335.

3. Newell, Shaw, and Simon (1958); see also Newell and Simon (1972, 1976). Other roots for this position include competence-based linguistics (e.g., Chomsky 1964, 1965, 1972, 1975) and formal logic (e.g., Church 1936, Post 1936, Turing 1936).

4. See also Armstrong (1968), Lewis (1972), Putnam (1960).

5. See Amit (1989), Churchland and Sejnowski (1992), Gluck and Rumelhart (1990), Koch and Davis (1994), Nadel et al. (1989), Schwartz (1990), Touretsky (1991a, 1991b) for examples.

6. See Bechtel and Abrahamsen (1991), Clark (1990, 1993), McClelland and Rumelhart (1986), Rumelhart and McClelland (1986) for good introductions.

7. See, for example, von Eckardt (1993).

8. Osherson and Lasnik (1990); Osherson and Smith (1990); Osherson, Kosslyn, and Hollerback (1990); Posner (1989), Stillings et al. (1987).

9. See Churchland (1986) Churchland (1987) for discussion.

10. Cf., Kandel and Schwartz (1985), Shepherd (1979).

11. See also discussion in Middleton and Strick (1994).

12. See also Llinas (1986).

13. I return to this perspective in chapters 6 and 7.

14. This term is due to Patricia Kitcher.

15. This is a criticism I have of von Eckhart's otherwise masterful book.

16. See, e.g., von Eckardt (1993).

17. Culp and Kitcher (1989), Kitcher (1993).

Chapter 2.
The Dilemma of Mental Causality

1. Fodor (1990), p. 156.

2. Fodor (1987), p. xii.

3. Cf., LePore and Loewer (1987), p. 630.

4. It is my understanding that Putnam (1960, 1967) was the first to discuss realization in the distinction between computations and the mechanisms that implement the computations. See also Block (1980, 1990) Boyd (1980), Dennett (1978), Fodor (1974), Hellman and Thompson (1975), Kim (1989a), LePore and Loewer (1987, 1989), Pereboom and Kornblith (1991), Putnam (1975), and van Gulick (1992).

5. See Churchland (1981), Churchland (1986), Feyerabend (1963), Rorty (1965), Stich (1983).

6. Cf., Kim (1979) originally.

7. Examples include theories of cognitive dissonance (e.g., Festinger 1957), interpersonal distancing (e.g., Kaplan and Markus-Kaplan 1981), infant development (e.g., Piaget 1954), emotion and stress (e.g., Mandler 1984) along with theories concerning more purely "cognitive" phenomena like memory (e.g., Schacter 1985a), linguistic capacities (e.g., Langacker 1984), and reasoning (e.g., Kahneman, Slovic, and Tversky 1982).

8. For example, Churchland (1981) Churchland (1986), Shapiro (1994), Stich (forthcoming), Stich and Laurence (forthcoming) vs. Dretske (1988), Fodor (1989), Schiffer (1982), Searle (1983).

9. See, e.g., Broad (1925), Campbell (1970), Feigl (1970), Goldman (1969), Honderich (1988), Kim (1979, 1989b, 1990), Macdonald and Macdonald (1986), Malcolm (1982), Schiffer (1989), Sosa (1984).

10. Chapter 1, Fodor (1981), Putnam (1967); see also Davidson (1993).

11. This point is elaborated on in chapter 4. See also Fodor (1974), Putnam (1973), Wimsatt (1976).

12. Mackie (1979), Skillen (1984).

13. Cf., Achenstein (1977), Anscombe (1975), Dretske (1988), Honderich (1983), Searle (1983), Sosa (1984).

14. When musing about multiple realization, it is tempting to think that it entails some asymmetric relation between mind and brain (see Fodor 1987, 1989; Jackson and Pettit 1990; Yablo 1992). But it does not do so obviously. Mul-

tiple realization does not say that for any P, M could have occurred without it. For example, no M can occur without being spatially extended. But perhaps multiple realization means that for all M, and for all P that determine M, it is possible that c has M but not P (Yablo 1992). But this too has to be wrong, since M must necessitate *some* P that necessitates M in return, since M is identical to some P. That is just what materialism requires. While it is true that the levels of physical properties supervene on one another, mental properties must exist as one of the higher levels. (See also Davidson 1980, Feigl 1970, Smart 1963, 1980.)

15. Though see Chalmers (forthcoming), van Gulick (1993) for a contrary position.

16. See also Fodor (1989), Jackson and Pettit (1990), Kim (1993b), McLaughlin (1989).

17. Kim (1983; 1989a, 1989b; 1992a, 1993a, 1993b); see also Block (1990), Field (1980), Fodor (1981), LePore and Loewer (1989), Segal and Sober (1991), Smart (1963).

18. It might appear that multiple realizability rules out this sort of move, since it entails that a true reduction of M is not possible. Our principles of causal realization are not strong enough to allow for lower level causal generalizations of higher level phenomena. Nevertheless, argues Kim in response, we still have "instance reduction" and that is enough to diminish the mental (1992, p. 11). Causal realization tells us that M cannot be a natural kind, suitable for use in proper scientific theories. Consider a simpler and better known case. "Jade" does not refer to a natural kind because jade is either jadeite or nephrite. (We understand the claim that S is made of either R or Q in terms of some sort of nomic unity in "R v Q;" otherwise we could make that claim for any Q whatever. That is, the disjunctive property "R v Q" has to be the sort of thing that science could use, although how to define that unity is beyond the scope of this work (though see Armstrong 1989, Lewis 1983, Owens 1989, Quine 1969, Seager 1991 for discussion). Jade supervenes on its microstructure; the microstructure determines the macroproperty of being jade; and the microstructure is what is important in explanation. "Jade" turns out to be just a rough and ready concept we use in everyday communication. Perhaps mental states could work in the same way. "M" could refer to just the disjunction of the P's that instantiate it. In this case, M would not be a natural kind. The best we could have is a series of local reductions, with no overarching theory of mind possible. When asked what all the instances of M have in common such that they are multiply instantiated, Kim's answer is merely that those instances fall under the concept M and that is all.

19. Humphries (1992) also points out that this raises the question of what it means to be distinct. If the properties are distinct, then we can have only

physics, but if they are not distinct, the differences among the sciences can only be an illusion.

20. See Fodor (1989), Humphries (1992), and van Gulick (1993) for different arguments to the same conclusion.

21. Fodor (1989) seems to make this mistake also. He writes: "Mental events cause behavior in virtue of physical mechanisms" (p. 76).

22. It is also clear that many levels of description across the more broadly defined domains overlap to a certain extent. For example, the description of the influx and efflux of ions through a semipermeable membrane fall easily under neurophysiology as well as biochemistry. Likewise, some "biological" descriptions exist at the same level as some psychological descriptions. See also chapters 2 and 4.

23. See also Churchland (1986), Fodor (1974), Kim (1993b), Oppenheim and Putnam (1958) for similar views.

24. Or perhaps causal closure only occurs at the most basic level (cf. Baker 1993). As long as one is a materialist, exactly how to define causal closure is orthogonal to the arguments presented here. All I need is the assumption of materialism and that each particular event is connected to multiple causal relations.

25. This view of causality has been discussed rather extensively in Sober (1984); see also Jackson and Pettit (1990).

26. I borrow this term from Sober (1984), see his pp. 186–187 for discussion and elaboration.

27. See in particular Fodor (1974), Kitcher (1984), Suppe (1989).

28. Winfree and Strogatz (1983).

29. Segal (1965).

30. Yorke and Li (1975).

31. See also van Gulick (1993).

32. Suppe (1989). What counts as a natural kind has not reached a consensus in philosophy. For our purposes, we can think of natural kinds as set of objects that are defined in terms of attributes possessed without using proper names. In any event, science refers to natural kinds in its theories and laws.

33. On reflection, admitting the possibility of causal overdetermination seems almost trivial. Suppose a three-ton rock is lifted by a backhoe. Clearly there is some causal connection between the movement of the backhoe and the movement of the rock, and this connection exists because of some property of

the backhoe in virtue of which it acted as a causal agent. What is this property? Is it that the backhoe exerted an upward force greater than three tons? Is it that the backhoe exerted an upward force of 3.21 tons? Is it that the backhoe exerted an upward force greater than the downward force of the rock? As Fodor remarks, "it may be that [c] ... has many—even many, many—properties in virtue of which it is capable of being the cause of [e] ... , and it need not be obvious which one of these properties is the one in virtue of which it actually *is* the cause of [e]. ... At least, I can assure you, it need not be obvious to me" (1989, p. 64). (See also Heil and Mele 1991.)

34. This view is also expressed by van Gulick (1993).

35. Audi goes on to argue that moral properties are importantly different from mental ones and that only properties that nomically supervene (as opposed to conceptually supervene) can enter into causal relations. A discussion of this point falls outside the scope of this project, though see section 2.4 for related considerations. See also Fodor (1987), Jackson and Pettit (1990) for more examples.

36. See especially Fodor (1974), Hardcastle (1992), Kitcher (1984), Putnam (1973).

37. This example of Freud's analysis comes from one of Freud's case studies (1953). Dora was a young woman who exhibited signs of depression and hysteria. In the course of therapy, she explained that her father's friend, Herr K., had made unwanted sexual advances toward her, even while she was attracted to him. There was also some suggestion that she had been molested by her father, though Freud did not follow up on the hints. In fact, Dora terminated her analysis after only three months, so many questions regarding her case are left unanswered. For a modern, computational interpretation of Freudian psychoanalysis, see Oatley (1993).

38. For example, Kim (1983, 1992a, 1992b), LePore and Loewer (1987, 1989). See also Davidson (1993), Honderich (1983), Kim (1993a), Macdonald and Macdonald (1986), McLaughlin (1989), Sosa (1993), Stoutland (1980), van Gulick (1993) for discussion.

39. I take it that this alleged difference is similar to what van Gulick has in mind when he claims that the properties referred to in the special sciences act by "selective activation" of the lower level physical powers (1993, p. 252). Van Gulick sees a (further) difference between the special and the "hard" sciences: he also claims that the special sciences pick out the "boundary" conditions for the laws of physics (p. 250). I am not sure what he intends here.

40. See also Hardcastle (1992), van Fraassen (1980) for discussion.

41. I take some of the following examples from Suppe (1989).

42. See the appendix for a more rigorous treatment of theories and their interpretations using Treisman's hypotheses as illustrative examples.

43. See also Bogen and Woodward (1988). Though Bogen and Woodward argue for a point similar to mine, they use different terminology. What I am calling "phenomena," they call "observation," and what I call "data sets," they refer to as "phenomena."

44. See especially chapters 5 and 6.

45. LePore and Loewer (1989) also rely on a similar move, which I find equally implausible for similar reasons, though see section 3 for more discussion.

46. See also Dennett (1991), van Gulick (1993).

47. For a discussion of this issue, see Dennett (1991), Hardcastle (1991), Nelkin (forthcoming); though see Cartwright (1979) for an opposing view.

48. This again is just another expression of multiple realizability.

49. See Freud (1953), Jamner et al. (1988) for relevant data; Berliner and Loftus (1992), Ceci and Loftus (1994), Loftus (1993, 1994). Thompson et al. (1992) for related discussions.

50. Grünbaum (1984).

51. Dennett entertains a similar view. He writes: "If one finds a predictive pattern . . . one has ipso facto discovered a causal power—a difference in the world that makes a subsequent difference testable by standard empirical methods of variable manipulations" (1991, pp. 43–44n22).

52. See Cartwright (1979), Eells (1988), Hardcastle (1991), Heslow (1976), Otte (1985) for more rigorous presentations of probabilistic notions of causality.

53. See, e.g., Cartwright (1979), Hardcastle (1991), Salmon (1971), Wimsatt (1984b).

54. For simplicity's sake, I shall use the neutral term N when discussing the screening-off relation. However, one could rewrite all my formulations in terms of M^* and P^* and I believe that similar arguments should still go through.

55. Wimsatt (1984b) loosens this notion for actual scientific practice. He argues that we should actually perform a cost-benefit analysis so that we would say that M "effectively" screens off P if the addition of variable P to our explanation improves our understanding of e only slightly and that P is expensive information to procure. In practice, determining whether some variable screens off another is partially a pragmatic decision. This loosening of the relation is most important when considering which levels of organization to priv-

ilege which level is the most appropriate will (in part) be determined by which is anticipated to give us the most bang for the buck, as it were. In any model of phenomenon to be explained, we should only include the parts and their relations that make a significant difference in output. Not all causal influences are created equal and some will be left aside in any reasonable explanation.

56. See also Salmon (1971), p. 55.

57. Brandon (1982), as discussed in Lloyd (1988).

58. I take it that this is in accord with what Jackson and Pettit (1990) and Yablo (1992) suggest (although the manner in which they conceive of this problem differs fundamentally from me). Interestingly enough, this is exactly what LePore and Loewer (1987) deny. Obviously, I disagree.

59. Jackson and Pettit (1990) miss this point in their "realization" hypotheses, as does Yablo (1992) in his discussion of causal explanation.

60. This point is discussed more extensively in chapter 3.

61. See Kitcher (1993) for discussion of these points.

62. See Hempel (1966), Kitcher (1989), Railton (1981), and especially van Fraassen (1980).

63. See also Culp and Kitcher (1989).

64 . See, e.g., Kitcher (1984, 1993), Railton (1981), van Fraassen (1980, 1990).

65. That is, I agree as long as we understand individual choice as (at least in large part) governed by historical, contextual issues.

66. Indeed, Jim Klagge raised this question (personal communication).

67. It is a separate question whether these properties are actually truth conducive. I leave that one aside.

68. Even if the norm in science were sets of equally good incompatible models, then the best one could argue would be that the criteria we use to differentiate true models from false is inadequate.

69. See also Fodor (1987), Owens (1987), Schiffer (1982).

Chapter 3.
Hierarchies in the Brain

1. Hull (1980), pp. 316–317.

2. This possibility was suggested to me by Tom Kerner.

3. I must stress how much this position is pure bias today. For example, it is becoming clear that the glia cells in the brain, which constitute over one third of the brain's mass, perform computational functions similar to those of neurons. However, their role in cognition is quite unknown and research in this area is quite stunted. For discussion, see Travis (1994).

4. This picture is complicated when temporal aspects are taken into account (see also the discussion in chapter 7). Behavioral and cognitive events might require only 200 msec to become active, but most of the techniques involved in recording at the higher level are sensitive to only about 5–10 msec (Leslie Kay, personal communication).

5. Cf., Churchland and Sejnowski (1992), Gluck and Rumelhart (1990).

6. For example, Burge (1986), Fodor (1981), Fodor and LePore (1991), Putnam (1973, 1975), Stich (1983).

7. See, e.g., Broadbeck (1968).

8. Sober (1984).

9. Elliot Sober however suggests that the disagreement is illusory because each side understands and uses "sum" slightly differently.

10. Individualists maintain this position partially because they attach lesser importance to the more distant environmental events—how to parse the event space of cognition is a matter up for dispute.

11. Sober (1984).

12. Kitcher (1985) makes this point as well.

13. See, e.g., Alexander (1920), Morgan (1923).

14. In the social sciences and in evolutionary biology, the debate also seems to run along the vertical axis.

15. Though see Wimsatt (forthcoming) for further discussion on the metaphysical dimension.

16. See Fuster (1980), Goldman-Rakic (1987) for excellent summaries. See also discussion in chapter 5.

17. Goldman (1971), Goldman and Rosvold (1970), Goldman et al. (1971), Goldman-Rakic (1987), Gross and Weiskrantz (1964), Mishkin (1957).

18. Fuster (1973); see also Kubota and Niki (1971).

19. Fuster and Alexander (1971), Kojima and Goldman-Rakic (1982, 1984).

20. Reduction is the topic of chapter 5.

21. See, for example, Lehky and Sejnowski (1988).

22. It is still an ongoing debate whether patients with severed corpus callosa have two separate streams of consciousness as a result, or whether consciousness is localized in only one hemisphere (Gazzaniga 1985; Gazzaniga and LeDoux 1978; Gazzaniga et al. 1979, 1987; Sperry 1965, 1977, 1985; Marks 1981; Natsoulas 1987).

23. Traditionally, neuroscientists have looked to split-brain patients to answer this question. However, how to understand the individual verbal reports and nonlinguistic behavior of split-brain patients is far from clear. Moreover, if we look at the corpus callosum developmentally, we have little reason to assume it is in the business of transferring semantic information from one hemisphere to the other (Cyander et al. 1981, Innocenti 1986, Nahm 1989)—as those who tie consciousness to language and argue that both hemisphere are aware must—so whether the callosum alone is severed may have little bearing on qualitative experience.

24. This method of investigation would seem especially fruitful because subcortical or other extraneous influences between the hemispheres could not confound the data (as they would with simple split-brain patients).

25. Bishop (1983, 1988), Hacaen (1976), St. James-Roberts (1981).

26. See also Grene (1987, 1988), Mayr (1982).

27. Dawkins (1976), Eldredge and Salthe (1984), Grene (1987, 1988), Mayr (1982), Pattee (1969, 1973).

28. Mayr (1982); see also Eldredge (1985), Eldredge and Salthe (1984), Grene (1987, 1988) for discussion.

29. Grene (1987, 1988); see also Dawkins (1976), Pattee (1969, 1973).

30. Notice that as a hierarchy of classification, a hierarchy of embedment could really be either constitutive or aggregational (except for the fact that there seem to be no emergent properties [Grene 1988, p. 6]).

31. Grene (1988).

32. See Putnam (1973) for examples of how this might work in psychology.

33. This example is discussed in Eldredge (1985), Grene (1988).

34. Groves (1983), Kandel and Schwartz (1985), Penney and Young (1983), Shepherd (1979), Wilson et al. (1983), Wilson and Groves (1980).

35. Heiligenberg (1987, 1988, 1991), Heiligenberg and Rose (1985).

36. Even in developmental neuroscience, triggering cause explanations are given of the ontogeny of particular organisms.

37. See also Bechtel and Richardson (1993), Bogen and Woodward (1988), Hardcastle (1993b, forthcoming) for additional discussion.

38. Chapter 7 discusses this point in more detail.

39. Bechtel and Richardson (1993).

40. Cf., Kandel and Schwartz (1985), pp. 531–532.

41. See, e.g., Cartwright (1980, 1983), Sober and Lewontin (1984).

42. Grene (1987), Eldredge (1985), Sereno (1990).

43. See also Wimsatt (1984b).

44. Williams (1966, 1985, 1992).

45. For example, Lloyd (1988), Mayo and Gilinsky (1987), Wimsatt (1984a).

46. Latour (1979).

47. Hutchins (1980).

48. I take it that this fact is well documented and well discussed in the philosophical literature, so I shall not dwell on it here.

49. Schneider and Shiffrin (1977), Shiffrin and Schneider (1977).

50. Treisman (1986), Treisman and Galade (1980), Treisman and Schmidt (1982).

51. Forster (1981), Forster and Davis (1984).

52. See also the appendix for a more detailed treament of these theories.

Chapter 4.
Computationalism and Functional Analysis:
A Pragmatic Approach

1. Kripke (1981), p. 28.

2. Searle (1992), p. 212.

3. This section owes a lot to the work of Oron Shagrir.

4. See, for example, Cummins (1975, 1983, 1989), Cummins and Schwarz (1992), Haugeland (1978, 1981a, 1981b, 1985).

5. Other identities with recursion followed: e.g., Markov's theory of algorithms (1951), Post's theory of normal systems (1943). Each of these added to the credibility of Church's original suggestion. Though there can be no formal proof of Church's thesis (primarily because of the vagueness of any intuitive notions), it is regarded as sound.

6. Cf., Beeson (1985). The question remains, of course, whether physical systems can compute nonrecursive functions—Pour-El and Richards (1981) suggest that they can—and insofar as the question is unanswered, there is an uncomfortable split between the Church-Turing thesis and physical systems.

7. See discussion in the previous two chapters concerning how to interpret and generalize defined physical systems.

8. See also Kripke (1981), Searle (1992), Stabler (1987).

9. I get this example from Stabler (1987).

10. See also Hardcastle (1992) for related discussion.

11. Cf. Salmon (1971), van Fraassen (1980).

12. Cf. Hempel (1966), Kitcher (1989), Railton (1981), van Fraassen (1980).

13. Cf. Kitcher and Salmon (1987), Lloyd and Anderson (1993).

14. Although the Turing thesis assumes digital computation, and its extension to physical systems assumes the approximation of digital computation, there is no real reason to restrict our notion of computation in this way. Many systems are described as sets of dynamical functions, and I see no reason why we might not want to claim that some systems compute these analog functions. Nothing in the definitions I have elaborated here rules out these sorts of computations.

15. This approach borrows heavily from Cummins's discussion of step satisfaction; see also Demopoulos (1987).

16. These criteria on based on distinctions drawn by Shagrir (1991).

17. See Hardcastle (1992). Cartwright (1979) on the other hand holds that scientific laws literally partition the world for us; all we have to do to understand causal relationships in the world is to understand the laws underlying them.

18. Block (1980), Cummins (1975, 1983, 1989); see also Dennett (1971), Fodor (1965, 1968a, 1968b).

19. Cf., Marr (1977, 1982), Newell and Simon (1976), Pylyshyn (1984), Putnam (1960, 1973), Simon (1969).

20. I note that the motivation for philosophy is slightly different. That is discussed below.

21. For example, Wimsatt (1976), Wright (1974).

22. Bechtel (1986), Cummins (1975), Dennett (1975), Lycan (1981, 1987), Sober (1993); for a detailed discussion of the types of teleological functional explanations, see Shaffner (1993), chapter 8.

23. Compare, for example, Fodor (1981), Pylyshyn (1984), Stich (1983), with Cummins (1975), Dennett (1971), Haugeland (1978, 1985), Lycan (1987).

24. See also Burge (1992).

25. Notice that this motivation differs from psychology's proper. See discussion above.

26. See, e.g., Boyd (1980), Davidson (1970), Hellman and Thompson (1977), Kim (1979).

27. Armstrong (1968), Lewis (1972), Putnam (1960)

28. See, for example, Armstrong (1970, 1977), Lewis (1969, 1970, 1972), Smart (1959, 1971).

29. For example, Fodor (1975), Haugeland (1978, 1985), Mandler (1985), Newell and Simon (1976), Putnam (1973), Pylyshyn (1984), Stich (1983).

30. See also Putnam (1973, 1975).

31. See also Newell and Simon (1976) and occasionally Pylyshyn (1984).

32. See also Marr (1982).

33. See Pylyshyn (1984) for a clear and fairly recent example of this metaphor.

34. See also chapter 5 for more discussion of this point.

35. Churchland (1986), Lycan (1987).

Chapter 5.
Reductionism in the Cognitive Sciences

1. Fodor (1974), p. 113.

2. Fodor (1983), p. 135.

3. Dennett (1981), Fodor (1974, 1978), Putnam (1973).

4. Three possible exceptions are Bechtel (1983), Churchland (1986), and Fodor (1974).

5. See also Nagel (1949), Quine (1964), Woodger (1952).

6. Richardson (1979) quite rightly states that Nagel himself did not require the biconditional relationship that I outline here. In fact, Nagel explicitly denied it: "The linkage between A [a reduced term] and B [a reducing term] is not necessarily biconditional in form, and may for example be only a one-way relationship" (1961, p. 335n). Although Richardson's exegetical point is well taken, I maintain that the reductionist tradition assumes (rightly or wrongly) biconditional links (cf., Kemeny and Oppenheim 1967; Schaffner 1967, 1976; Brandt and Kim 1967; Kitcher 1980).

7. For a more complete discussion, see Schaffner (1967).

8. See especially the discussion in chapter 2 above.

9. Pettigrew and Konishi (1976); this example comes from Hatfield (1988), p. 736.

10. Cf., Churchland (1984, 1986), Enç (1983), Richardson (1982).

11. As Richardson (1982) urges, this position seems historically correct, too. Nagel asserts that we should view correspondence rules as "asserting that the occurrences of the states of affairs signified by a certain theoretical expression 'B' in the primary [reducing] science is a *sufficient* (or a necessary and sufficient) condition for the state of affairs designated" (1961, p. 354).

12. See also Richardson (1979).

13. See also Fodor and Pylyshyn (1988), Putnam (1973), and Pylyshyn (1980, 1984).

14. Cf. Marr (1982).

15. See also Strongman (1987) for a good summary of Mandler's theory.

16. Advances have made linking the effects of benzodiazepines on the $GABA_A$ receptors to emotional anxiety. Most of the neuropharmacological and neurophysiological research ties the anxiety to classically conditioned aversive behavioral responses in rats or rabbits (e.g., inhibited lever pressing). While the ties between anxiolytics and the suppression of a conditioned emotional response is well documented, very little is known about the neural sites required for the behavioral effects; most especially, more information is needed in defining the interaction of the BZ/GABA complex and monoamine nueorns in the limbic system. (See Iversen 1985 for discussion; though also see Haefely et al. 1983.)

17. Schachter (1964, 1965), Schachter and Singer (1962). Although there has been controversy surrounding the interpretations given by Schachter and

Singer, the data themselves still stand. At the least, Schachter and Singer demonstrate that emotion is influenced by cognitive appraisal. The extent of that influence appears to be great, although not exactly known.

18. See also Kitcher (1980) for another argument to the same conclusion.

19. We find a different type of solution in Rosenberg's (1985) use of the relation of supervenience. However, the relation is agnostic about the different sorts of properties each level may have and so is a fairly minimalist account of the relationship among different domains of inquiry. A richer story, if possible, is preferable.

20. We can also see this approach reflected in Culp and Kitcher (1989), even though they explicitly deny that they are discussing theories.

21. An antecedently problematic presupposition is some hypothesis that the accepted background of the extended theory conjoined with the the theory itself imply, but for which we also find reasonable arguments from other premises that it is false.

22. See, e.g., Bechtel (1982, 1983), Churchland (1986), Churchland and Sejnowski (1992).

23. J. M. Mandler (1984).

24. Asmead and Perlmutter (1980).

25. See Fuster (1980), Goldman-Rakic (1987) for excellent summaries.

26. See, for example, Butters et al. (1972), Harlow et al. (1952), Meyer et al. (1951), Passingham (1975), Pribram et al. (1952), Rosvold et al. (1961).

27. Goldman (1971), Goldman and Rosvold (1970), Goldman et al. (1971), Gross and Weiskrantz (1964), Mishkin (1957).

28. Fuster (1973); see also Kubota and Niki (1971).

29. Fuster and Alexander (1971), Kojima and Goldman-Rakic (1982, 1984).

30. Goldman-Rakic et al. (1983).

31. Bachevalier and Mishkin (1984).

32. This hypothesis is discussed in detail in the next chapter.

33. It was originally thought that motion is a primitive visual building block as well, but we now know that the visual system extracts a three-dimensional object first from shading cues and then uses that image to perceive motion. (See Ramachandran 1988 for a summary.)

34. Some have expressed doubts that results like these could ever alter the ways in which the referents of the predicates are fixed since simulations are not

plausible neural instantiations. However, work is already underway to test this new hypothesis using single cell recordings of the visual cortex in monkeys. Undertaking this project directly resulted from Ramachandran's psychophysical data and Sejnowski's and Lehky's simulation (M. Sereno, personal communication). The bottom line is that these sorts of simulations *do* have a significant effect on the direction of neuroscience.

35. Cf., Kitcher (1984).

36. See Hatfield (1988, Pylyshyn (1980).

37. I believe that Burton (1993) conflates these two.

38. Though see Hardcastle (1991).

Chapter 6.
The Dual Memory Hypothesis
and the Structure of Interdisciplinary Theories

1. Johnson and Morton (1991), p. 1, italics theirs.

2. Pettit (1994), p. 162.

3. Duhem (1914), pp. 70–71.

4. I should note that though I recite data from others, the interdisciplinary theory I develop is my own. Hence, any flaws are not the responsibility of those whose data I use.

5. Anderson and Bower (1973), Collins and Loftus (1975), Keele (1973), LaBerge (1973a, 1973b, 1975), LaBerge and Samuels (1974), Posner and Snyder (1975a, 1975b), Schneidner and Shiffrin (1977), Shiffrin (1975), Shiffrin and Geisler (1973), Shiffrin and Schneidner (1977), Turvey (1974); see also discussion of this theory in the appendix.

6. Schneider and Shiffrin (1977), Shiffrin and Schneider (1977); see also the discussion of their research in the appendix.

7. For review, see Fagen and Rovee-Collier (1982).

8. Papousek (1969).

9. Piaget (1954); see also Gratch (1976).

10. Corter et al. (1980), Zucker (1982).

11. Cohen et al. (1977), Fagan (1971), McCall et al. (1977), J. Mandler (1984).

12. Gottfried et al. (1977, 1979), Mackay-Soroka et al. (1982), Rolfe and Day (1981), Rose et al. (1978, 1979).

13. Cornell (1975), Dirks and Gibson (1977), Fagan (1979), Moscovitch (1984), chapter 3.

14. Year-old infants are largely unaffected by crossmodal, intermodel, or intramodel testing.

15. Meltzoff and Moore (1983, 1989). Indeed, neonatal lip imitations have been shown in infants as young as a minute old (Reissland 1989).

16. See also Brewer (1993), Jeannarod (forthcoming), Meltzoff (1993) for further discussion and relevant data.

17. For discussion of these points, see Johnson and Morton (1991). I should also mention that their book provides an excellent example of an interdisciplinary theory, exhibiting all the earmarks I shall discuss in this chapter.

18. Kagan et al. (1966) Fantz (1966), Fantz and Nevis (1967), Mauerer and Barrera (1981), Sigman and Darmalee (1974), Wilcox (1968) as outlined in Johnson and Morton (1991).

19. Goren et al. (1975).

20. See discussion in Ellis (1989).

21. See Johnson and Morton (1991).

22. Johnson (1990a, 1990b).

23. I stress that these are features of the *theory*, and do not necessarily represent the interests of the researchers. Indeed, Johnson and Morton (1991) make heavy use of lower level data in supporting their higher level theory. More on how this works below. For now, I just want to get clear on the general design of the higher level theory.

24. Brooks and Baddeley (1976), Cohen (1984).

25. Brooks and Baddeley (1976), Graf et al. (1984), Moscovitch (1982), Parkin (1982), Schacter and Graf (1986), Shimamura (1986), Squire and Cohen (1984), Weiskrantz (1984), Wood et al. (1982).

26. Corkin (1965, 1968), Milner et al. (1968); in addition, Weiskrantz and Warrington (1979) report that two severely amnesic patients could not recognize the conditioning apparatus they had been trained on several times, even though the conditioned responses of the patients were near normal.

27. Nissan and Bullemer (1987).

28. Cohen and Squire (1980), Moscovitch (1982).

29. Warrington and Weiskranz (1970, 1974), Graf et al. (1984), Jacoby and Witherspoon (1982).

30. See Farah (1990), especially chapter 4, for discussion.

31. Damasio et al. (1990); see also the discussion in Farah (1990).

32. Efron (1968), Milner et al. (1991); see also McCarthy (1993).

33. Barinaga (1992), Cowey and Stoerig (1991, 1992), Critchley (1979), Fendrich et al. (1992), Pernin and Jeannerod (1975), Ptito et al. (1991), Weiskrantz (1988, 1992), Weiskrantz et al. (1974); see also Humphreys et al. (1992).

34. McCarthey (1993).

35. These results are covered in more detail in my forthcoming work (Hardcastle, forthcoming). Here I only attempt to give the flavor of these experiments.

36. Jacoby and Dallas (1981) report that the number and spacing of repetitions affect the perceptual identification task and the recognition task in a similar fashion (though the priming effect on lexical decision tasks does not decrease with increasing time lags between the first and second presentation of the word in normal subjects [Scarborough et al. 1977; Scarborough et al. 1979]). Subjects are better at both tasks when exposed to multiple instances of the stimuli.

37. Jacoby and Dallas (1981); see also Hinzman et al. (1972), Morton (1979).

38. Cf., Jacoby and Dallas (1981).

39. Graf and Schacter (1989).

40. Graf and Schacter (1987).

41. Marcel (1980, 1983a, 1983b); see also Fowler et al. (1981), Kemp-Wheeler and Hill (1988), Tipper (1985).

42. Marcel (1983b); see also Fowler et al. (1981), Kemp-Wheeler and Hill (1988), Mandler (forthcoming), and Marcel (1983a).

43. Marcel (1983a, 1983b) offers a different interpretation of these data.

44. Bregman and Rudnicky (1975), Dember and Purcell (1967), Kristofferson et al. (1975), Jacobson (1973), Taylor and Chabot (1978).

45. This last distinction is mine (cf., Hardcastle forthcoming), though others make similar divisions. See especially Schacter (1985a, 1990), Schacter and McGlynn (1989), Schacter et al. (1990).

46. Another way of putting the same point is in terms of empirical versus theoretical models using the semantic view of theories (cf., Suppes 1967). Here I am proposing to differentiate the two sharply. Indeed, I hold that the biases

inherent in the theoretical model need not appear in, or even constrain, the empirical models, though presumably the empirical model has biases of its own, especially regarding the treatment of error; see Mayo (forthcoming).

47. That is, the structure of the theoretical models correspond.

48. Cf., Davis et al. (1982), Groves and Thompson (1970), Tischler and Davis (1983).

49. Bateson et al. (1972), Horn (1981, 1985), Horn et al. (1973, 1979), Kohsaka et al. (1979), Maier and Scheich (1983), McCabe et al. (1982).

50. Johnson and Horn (1973).

51. Details of how the systems interact can be found in Johnson and Morton (1991).

52. Johnson and Morton (1991) use ethological evidence to argue that the social structure of animals determines in part whether imprinting phenomena will be learned or innate. To keep this chapter from simply getting too unwieldy, I shall be ignoring the contraints from above. I do not mean to suggest, however, that there aren't any. Indeed, if Johnson and Morton are correct, then sociological factors will go far in explaining why our learning systems are configured the way they are.

53. Horn et al. (1985).

54. Fagg and Matus (1984); McCabe and Horn (1988).

55. See Squire and Zola-Morgan (1991) for an excellent review. See also Bachlevier and Mishkin (1984), and Eichenbaum et al. (forthcoming).

56. Malamut et al. (1984), Zola-Morgan and Squire (1984).

57. Mahut and Moss (1984), Malamut et al., (1984), Zola-Morgan and Squire (1984).

58. Barnes (1979), Squire (1987).

59. Bliss and Lomo (1973), Lynch and Baudry (1984), Lynch and Granger (1992), Swanson et al. (1982).

60. Johnson (1990a), Marin-Paddila (1990), Rabinowicz (1979); see also Atkinson (1993), Conel (1939–1967).

61. I am simplifying matters here somewhat, for the cortical "pathway" looks to be several different streams, each of which processes a different aspect of the visual field. For our purposes, however, I shall generalize over these different streams and speak of "the" cortical pathway.

62. Atkinson (1984, 1993), Braddick and Atkinson (1988), Bronson (1974), Felleman and Van Essen (1991), Johnson (1990a, 1990b), Maunsell

and Newsome (1987), Mauerer and Lewis (1979), Schneider (1969), Zeki and Shipp (1988).

63. Conel (1939–1967), Garey and de Courten (1983), Goldman-Rakic (1987), Huttenlocher (1993), Huttenlocher et al. (1982), Leuba and Garey (1987), Yakovlev and Lecours (1967); see also Johnson (1990a) for more details and additional citations.

64. See also Atkinson (1984), Braddick and Atkinson (1988).

65. Rodman and Gross (1989), as reported in Johnson and Morton (1991).

66. See discussion in Churchland (1986, 1989), Pellinoiz and Llinas (1985).

67. Bachlevier and Mishkin (1984).

68. See Farah (1990) for discussion.

69. Schaffner (1993), chapter 6, makes this same point.

70. See also Lynch and Granger (1992) for a different version of serial mnemonic processes.

71. Cf., Squire (1987).

72. Mishkin (1982); see also Squire (1992).

73. Nadel (1987); see also Reber (1992).

74. See also Darden and Maull (1977), Maull (1977), Wimsatt (1976).

75. We can understand the attributes of the entities in these models that form "smeared out" interlevel theories in the following way. (The following is my way of characterizing Schaffner's account; however, I believe that it is consistent with his view.) We can define a group of entities E in terms of a set F of properties $f_1, f_2, \ldots, f_n$. Each entity has some probability of falling under each property such that each entity has a probability approaching one that it will possess several of the properties in F. Moreover, each f has a high probability of being possessed by a large number of entities in E. So no f is necessary for membership in E, though some f may be sufficient for membership. Nevertheless, it should be possible to consider E to be a class constituting the extension of some concept $[C]$, defined in terms of the properties in F.

76. I note that this is my point and that Schaffner offers a different (and more congenial) treatment of the relationship between the semantic view and biomedical theories in his (1993).

77. See also Shapere (1974).

78. Schacter et al. (1991).

Chapter 7.
Interdisciplinary Theories and Bridge Sciences:
The Case of Evoked Response Potentials

1. Bernard (1957) [1865], p. 91.

2. Schaffner (1993), pp. 515–516.

3. Abrahamsen (1987) develops a similar idea.

4. See Cohen (1984), Squire (1987), Squire and Cohen (1984).

5. Heindel et al. (1988).

6. Schacter et al. (1988). Even repetition priming itself is not a unitary phenomena. We find a double dissociation between two types of priming among patients with temporal-parietal lesions, who show priming effects for stimuli that is repeated within a short time but no priming effects if the repeated item occurs more than 5 stimuli presentations later, and patients with dorsolateral prefrontal lesions, who show the opposite effects (Kersteen-Tucker and Knight 1989).

7. McCarthy and Donchin (1981), Parasuraman and Beatty (1980), Picton et al. (1978), Ritter et al. (1982), Wood (1975); I take these examples from Allison et al. (1986).

8. Of course, exactly how psychological processes map onto the components of ERP waveforms and the nature of that mapping is not known. ERP researchers often conclude that some component "reflects" or "indexes" some psychological processes, but how strongly that we are to understand that tie is far from clear. Moreover, even if we do conclude that some ERP measure x reflects some psychological process y, we cannot go backward and conclude that therefore x can be used as a measure of process y.

9. I get this example from Allison et al. (1986).

10. Braddick et al. (1986, 1989).

11. Atkinson et al. (1990).

12. See also discussion in Atkinson (1993), Johnson and Morton (1991).

13. Bentin et al. (1985), Holcomb (1988), Holcomb and Neville (1991), Rugg (1985).

14. Holcomb and Neville (1991), McCallum et al. (1984).

15. Holcomb and Neville (1991), see also Kutas and Van Petten (1988).

16. Knaudt (1990).

17. Neville et al. (1989), Paller (1990), Paller and Kutas (1992).

18. Gabrielli et al. (1990), Haist et al. (1991), Musen (1989), Musen and Squire (1991), Musen and Treisman (1990), Schacter et al. (1991).

19. Hardcastle (1993b).

20. Average response time to identity primed shapes (532.54 msec; s.e. = 27.09 msec), mirror priming (reaction time: 493.44 msec; s.e. = 29.87 msec), and category priming (reaction time: 562.52; s.e. = 26.49) was significantly faster than the unprimed targets (mean reaction time: 581.59 msec; s.e. = 22.42 msec) ($t(9) = -5.6$; $p < .001$, $t(9) = -7.3$; $p < .001$; $t(9) = -1.8$; $p < .001$, respectively). Though the mean reaction time for mirror priming is less than the reaction time for identity priming, the difference was not significant ($t(9) = 1.6$).

21. These results call into question previous suggestions that the general N400 effect is specific to linguistic or semantic events (e.g., Kutas and Van Petten 1988, Holcomb and Neville 1991, Rugg and Doyle 1992).

22. However, these P3 effects were not the same across the various priming variables. As can be seen in figure 7.6A, there is a main effect for latency in the identity primed condition (main effect of priming condition: $F(1, 9) = 13.67$, $p < .005$), with the primed peak occuring on the order of 120 msec earlier. In addition, the amplitude of the identity primed P3 waveform was larger frontally and smaller posteriorly than the amplitude of the unprimed waveform (priming condition x electrode site effect: $F(4, 36) = 4.76$, $p < .04$).

The P3 component in the mirror primed condition was also significantly different from the unprimed component. Here, however, the amplitude of the mirror primed P3 was less than the amplitude of the unprimed component at all electrode sites (main effect of priming condition: $F(1, 9) = 10.42$, $p < .01$). Surprisingly, there were no latency effects in the unmasked mirror priming condition.

As is clear in figure 7.6C, there is a significant main effect for amplitude in the category priming condition (main effect for priming condition: $F(1, 9) = 11.69$, $p < .008$). Indeed, the mean amplitude for the analyzed epoch was significantly less with category priming than with no priming (main effect for priming condition: $F(1, 9) = 6.63$, $p < .03$). There was also a significant effect for latency (main effect of category priming x electrode site: $F(4, 36) = 4.62$, $p < .006$), with the primed P3 peaking earlier than the unprimed one in the bilateral posterior regions.

23. The most prominent feature in the identity priming difference wave, and a component also found in the right hemisphere of the mirror priming difference wave (though absent in the category priming difference wave), is a large negativity peaking at about 375 msec, with a duration ranging from 100–300 msec. This "N375" is followed by a longer positivity, onsetting at approx-

imately 450 msec and continuing for several hundred msec. (This positivity is present in the difference waves for all priming conditions.)

The N375 effect has significantly greater amplitude under the identity priming condition than with mirror priming (main effect of amplitude: $F(1, 9)$ = 12.55, p <.006; main effect for mean amplitude: $F(1, 9)$ = 4.78, p <.06). In the mirror priming difference waves, the peak amplitude of the N375 is greater over the right hemisphere and absent at the occipital sites (effect of priming condition x electrode sites: $F(4, 36)$ = 7.32, p < 006).

In contrast to the N375, there were no significant differences in the size between the identity priming difference wave and the mirror priming difference wave for the positivity reflecting latency or amplitude shifts in the P3. The positive effect in the category priming difference wave has a different morphology. It onsets earlier and lasting longer, reflecting the different sort of P3 attenuation seen with category priming. Nonetheless, the general distribution of the P3 effect is the same.

24. Helen Neville has suggested that there might only be a shift in latency in the P3, which would account for the N400-like effects (Neville, personal communication).

25. Average response time to identity primed targets (543.6 msec; s.e. = 22.19 msec), mirror primed targets (532.3; s.e = 25.29), and category primed targets (554.27 msec; s.e. = 21.54) were not significantly faster than the unprimed targets (538.89 msec; s.e. = 18.64 msec).

26. An enhanced positivity began bilaterally over the N1 waveform in both the identity and mirror primed conditions (mean amplitude main effect of identity priming condition: $F(1, 9)$ = 7.60, p <.02; of mirror priming condition: $F(1, 9)$ = 6.14, p <.04). This effect induced a longer latency in both the priming conditions (peak latency main effect for identity priming condition: $F(1, 9)$ = 12.77, p <.005; of mirror priming condition: $F(1, 9)$ = 23.24, p <.0009) and a greater peak amplitude in the identity priming condition (mean effect of condition: $F(1, 9)$ = 12.52, p <.006). There were no significant effects with category priming other than an increase in latency in the primed condition (main effect of condition: $F(1, 9)$ = 18.18, p <.002).

The bilateral positivity continues through the P2 in both the identity and mirror priming conditions (main effect for mean amplitude for identity priming condition: $F(1, 9)$ = 9.62, p <.01; for mirror priming condition: $F(1, 9)$ = 47.03, p <.0001). The amplitude of the P2 is less in the identity primed condition over both hemispheres (main effect for peak amplitude: $F(1, 9)$ = 6.76, p <.03) and over the right hemisphere in the mirror priming condition (peak amplitude condition x hemisphere effect: $F(1, 9)$ = 5.31, p <.05).

As can be seen in figure 7.7, the morphology and distribution of the components across the two priming conditions in the difference waves are very similar, though the effects of mirror priming are smaller. An enhanced positivity begins approximately 50 msec after target presentation, continues for about 300–400 msec, begins again between 400 and 500 msec and continues for about 200–250 msec. The effects are globally distributed and are not significantly different between hemispheres or across electrode sites. The only significant difference between the set of difference waves for the two priming conditions is a difference in the amplitude of the middle measure (250–400 msec), with identity priming being more positive than mirror priming (main effect of priming condition: $F(1, 9) = 8.26$, $p < .02$).

27. Masked identity priming effects begin between 50 and 100 msec and continued to remain significantly different from the unprimed condition until 150 to 200 msec (amplitude main effect for 50–100 msec: $F(1, 9) = 11.99$, $p < .007$; for 100–150 msec: $F(1, 9) = 5.48$, $p < .04$; for 150–200 msec: $F(1, 9) = 6.18$, $p < .03$). A significant difference in amplitude again returned between 250 and 300 msec ($F(1, 9) = 6.37$, $p < .03$).

Amplitude differences began in the masked mirror priming condition between 100 and 150 msec and continued through 250 to 300 msec (100–150 msec: $F(1, 9) = 8.79$, $p < .02$; 150–200 msec: $F(1, 9) = 9.59$, $p < .01$; 200–250 msec: $F(1, 9) = 22.85$, $p < .001$; 250–300 msec = 10.68, $p < .01$).

There were no significant differences in amplitude sustained over 100 msec with masked category priming.

28. These data from using completely novel, nonverbal stimuli also suggest that priming is not a phenomenon that requires previously established memories.

29. See Arbib (1989), Churchland and Sejnowski (1992), Gluck and Rumelhart (1990) for discussion.

30. Zipser (1991); see also McAuley and Stampfli (1993), Anton et al. (1991), Granger and Lynch (1991), Gluck and Granger (1993), Leow and Miikkulainen (1992), O'Reilly and McClelland (1992), Sirosh and Miikkulainen (1992) for other neural models of episodic memory.

31. Rybak et al. (1993).

32. See also Lloyd (1988).

Appendix

1. The semantic view was developed by Beth (1949), Sneed (1971), Suppe (1974, 1989), Suppes (1956, 1962), and van Fraasseen (1970, 1980).

2. See especially Beatty (1981), Bickle (1993), Giere (1980, 1984), Lloyd (1984, 1988), Suppe (1989), Thompson (1983, 1989).

3. Suppes (1956, 1967), Sneed (1971), Stegmüller (1976) use set theory (see also Giere (1980, 1984) for a generalization of this approach); Lloyd (1988), Suppe (1974, 1989), van Fraassen (1970, 1980) rely on state spaces; Balzer et al. (1987) prefers set theory in conjunction with category theory; and Giere (1988) attempts a computational version.

4. Cf., Giere (1988), Suppe (1974, 1989), Suppes (1956, 1967), van Fraassen (1980, 1989). One should note that "model" here refers to a structure or set of relations. It is not an interpretation function; instead, it refers to the objects themselves that interpretation functions quantify over.

5. See Bickle (1993).

6. Treisman (1986), Treisman and Gelade (1980).

7. I also used this example in Hardcastle (1995).

8. Schneider and Shiffrin (1977), Shiffrin and Schneider (1977).

9. Of course, it is possible for our feature-integration systems to make mistakes, and how and why this occurs is quite interesting. However, taking this fact into consideration would complicate the model beyond what I need for my point. Suffice it to say that I am not giving Treisman's entire story here.

10. Treisman's feature-integration hypothesis does account for other similar "pop-out" effects; however, they turn on the number of features processed (i.e., whether the map of locations is needed for an answer) instead of a hierarchy of semantic categorization.

11. See Bickle (1993), Mormann (1988), Rott (1987) for an overview.

12. Crick (1984).

13. I should point out that recent research his shown that thalamic neurons do not quite have the property Crick needs in order to get his hypothesis to work. Still, a modified version of his hypothesis might be possible.

REFERENCES

Abrahamsen, A. A. (1987) "Bridging Boundaries versus Breaking Boundaries: Psycholinguistics in Perspective." *Synthese* 72: 355–388.

Achenstein, P. (1977) "The Causal Relation." *Midwest Studies in Philosophy* 4: 368.

Alexander, S. (1920) *Space, Time, and Deity.* 2 vols. London: Macmillan.

Allison, T., Wood, C. C., and McCarthy, G. (1986) "The Central Nervous System." *Physiological Systems and Their Assessment*, pp. 5–25.

Amit, D. J. (1989) *Modeling Brain Function.* Cambridge, MA: Cambridge University Press.

Anderson, J., and Bower, G. (1973) *Human Associative Memory.* Washington, DC: Winston.

Anscombe, E. (1975). "Causality and Extensionality." In E. Sosa (ed.), *Causation and Conditionals.* New York: Oxford.

Anton, P. S., Lynch, G., and Granger, R. (1991). "Computation of Frequency-to-Spatial Transform by Olfactory Bulb Glomeri." *Biological Cybernetics* 65: 407–414.

Arbib, M. A. (1989) *The Metaphorical Brain 2: Neural Networks and Beyond.* Wiley-Interscience.

Armstrong, D. (1989) *Universals.* Boulder, CO: Westview Press.

Armstrong, D. M. (1968) *A Materialist Theory of Mind.* London: Routledge and Kegan Paul.

Armstrong, D. M. (1970) "The Nature of Mind." In C. V. Borst (ed.), *The Mind/Brain Identity Theory.* London: Macmillan.

Armstrong, D. M. (1977) "The Causal Theory of the Mind." *Neue Heft für Philosophie* 11: 82–95.

Asmead, D., and Perlmutter, M. (1980) "Infant Memory in Everyday Life." In M. Perlmutter (ed.), *New Directions for Child Development: Children's Memory*, vol. 10. San Francisco: Jossey-Bass.

Atkinson, J. (1984) "Human Visual Development over the First Six Months of Life: A Review and a Hypothesis." *Human Neurobiology* 3: 61–74.

Atkinson, J. (1993) "A Neurobiological Approach to the Development of 'Where' and 'What' Systems for Spatial Representation in the Human

Infant." In N. Eilan, R. McCarthy, and B. Brewer (eds.), *Spatial Representation: Problems in Philosophy and Psychology.* Cambridge, MA: Basil Blackwell, pp. 325–339.

Atkinson, J., Braddick, O. J., Anker, S., Hood, B., Wattam-Bell, J., Weeks, F. Rennie, J., and Coughtry, H. (1990) "Visual Development in the VLBW Infant." *Transactions of the IVth European Conference on Developmental Psychology,* University of Stirling, p. 193.

Audi, R. (1993) "Mental Causation: Sustaining and Dynamic." In J. Heil and A. Mele (eds.), *Mental Causation.* Oxford: Clarendon Press, pp. 53–76.

Bachevalier, J., and Mishkin, M. (1984) "An Early and a Late Developing System for Learning and Retention in Infant Monkeys." *Behavioral Neuroscience* 298: 770–778.

Baker, L. R. (1993) "Metaphysics and Mental Causation." In J. Heil and A. Mele (eds.), *Mental Causation.* Oxford: Clarendon Press, pp. 77–96.

Balzer, W., Moulines, C. U., and Sneed, J. D. (1987) *An Architectonic for Science.* Dordrecht: Reidel.

Barinaga, M. (1992) "Unraveling the Dark Paradox of Blind Sight." *Science* 258: 1438–1439.

Barnes, C. A. (1979) "Memory Deficits Associated with Senescence: A Behavioral and Neurophysiological Study in the Rat." *Journal of Comparative Physiological Psychology* 93: 74–104.

Barrett, S. E., and Rugg, M. D. (1989) "Event-Related Potentials and the Semantic Matching of Faces." *Electroencephalography and Clinical Neurophysiology* 60: 343–355.

Barrett, S. E., Rugg, M. D., and Perrett, D. I. (1988) "Event-Related Potentials and the Matching of Familiar and Unfamiliar Faces." *Neuropsychologia* 26: 105–117.

Bateson, P. P. G., Horn, G., and Rose, S. P. R. (1972) "Effects of Early Experience on Regional Incorporation of Precursors into RNA and Protein in the Chick Brain." *Brain Research* 84: 207–220.

Beatty, J. (1981) "What is Wrong with the Received View?" In P. Asquith and R. Giere (eds.), *PSA 1980,* vol. 2. East Lansing, MI: Philosophy of Science Association, pp. 397–439.

Bechtel, W. (1982) "Two Common Errors in Explaining Biological and Psychological Phenomena." *Philosophy of Science* 49: 549–574.

Bechtel, W. (1983) "A Bridge Between Cognitive Science and Neuroscience: The Functional Architecture of Mind." *Philosophical Studies* 44: 319–330.

Bechtel, W. (1986) "Teleological Functional Analysis and the Hierarchical Organization of Nature." In N. Rescher (ed.), *Current Issues in Teleology*. Lanham, MD: University Press of America, pp. 26–48.

Bechtel, W., and Abrahamsen, A. (1991) *Connectionism and the Mind: An Introduction to Parallel Processing Networks*. Cambridge, MA: Basil Blackwell.

Bechtel, W., and Richardson, R. C. (1993) *Discovering Complexity: Decomposition and Localization as Strategies in Scientific Research*. Princeton, NJ: Princeton University Press.

Beeson, M. J. (1985) *Foundations of Constructive Mathematics*. Berlin: Springer.

Bentin, S., McCarthy, G., and Wood, C. C. (1985) "Event-Related Potentials Associated with Semantic Processing." *Electroencephalography and Linear Neurophysiology* 60: 343–355.

Berliner, L., and Loftus, E. F. (1992) "Sexual Abuse Accusations: Desperately Seeking Reconciliation." *Journal of Interpersonal Violence* 7: 570–578.

Bernard, C. (1957/1865) *An Introduction to the Study of Experimental Medicine*. Trans. H. C. Green. New York: Dover.

Beth, E. (1949) "Towards an Up-to-Date Philosophy of the Natural Sciences." *Methods* 1: 178–185.

Bickle, J. (1993) "Connectionism, Eliminativism, and the Semantic View of Theories." *Erkenntnis* 39: 359–382.

Bishop, D. V. M. (1983) "Linguistic Impairment After Left Hemidecortication for Infantile Hemiplegia? A Reappraisal." *Quarterly Journal of Experimental Psychology* 35A: 199–207.

Bishop, D. V. M. (1988) "Can the Right Hemisphere Mediate Language as Well as the Left? A Critical Review of Recent Research." *Cognitive Neuropsychology* 5: 353–367.

Bliss, T. V. P., and Lomo, T. (1973) "Long-Lasting Potentiation of Synaptic Transmission in the Dentate Area of the Anesthetized Rabbit Following Stimulation for the Perforant Path." *Journal of Physiology* 232: 331–356.

Block, N. (1980) "Introduction: What is Functionalism?" In N. Block (ed.), *Readings in the Philosophy of Psychology*, vol. 1. Cambridge, MA: Harvard University Press, pp. 178–189.

Block, N. (1990) "Can the Mind Change the World?" In G. Boolos (ed.), *Meaning and Method: Essays in Honor of Hilary Putnam*. Cambridge: Cambridge University Press, pp. 137–170.

Bogen, J., and Woodward, J. (1988) "Saving the Phenomena." *Philosophical Review* XCVII: 303–352.

Boyd, R. (1980) "Materialism without Reductionism: What Physicalism Does Not Entail." In N. Block (ed.), *Readings in the Philosophy of Psychology*, vol. 1. Cambridge, MA: Harvard University Press, pp. 67–106.

Braddick, O. J., and Atkinson, J. (1988) "Sensory Selectivity Attentional Control and Cross-Channel Integration in Early Visual Development." In A. Yonas (ed.), *20th Minnesota Symposium on Child Psychology*. Hillsdale, NJ: Lawrence Earlbaum.

Braddick, O. J., Atkinson, J., Wattam-Bell, J., and Hood, B. (1989) "Characteristics of Orientation-Selective Mechanisms in Early Infancy." *Investigative Opthamology and Visual Science* (suppl.) 30: 313.

Braddick, O. J., Wattam-Bell, J., and Atkinson, J. (1986) "Orientation-Specific Cortical Responses Develop in Early Infancy." *Nature* 320: 617–619.

Brandon, R. N. (1982) "The Levels of Selection." *PSA 1982*, vol. 1. East Lansing, MI: Philosophy of Science Association, pp. 315–323.

Brandt, R., and Kim, J. (1967) "The Logic of the Identity Theory." *Journal of Philosophy* 64: 515–537.

Bregman, A., and Rudnicky, A. (1975) "Auditory Segregation: Stream or Streams?" *Journal of Experimental Psychology: Human Perception and Peformance* 1: 263–267.

Brewer, B. (1993) "The Integration of Spatial Vision and Action." In N. Eilan, R. McCarthy, and B. Brewer (eds.), *Spatial Representation: Problems in Philosophy and Psychology*. Cambridge, MA: Basil Blackwell, pp. 294–316.

Broad, C. D. (1925) *Mind and Its Place in Nature*. London: Routledge and Kegan Paul.

Broadbeck, M. (ed.) (1968) *Readings in the Philosophy of the Social Sciences*. New York: Macmillan.

Bronson, G. W. (1974) "The Postnatal Growth of Visual Capacity." *Child Development* 45: 873–890.

Brooks, D. N., and Baddeley, D. (1976) "What Can Amnesics Learn?" *Neuropsychologia* 14: 111–122.

Burge, T. (1986) "Individualism and Psychology." *The Philosophical Review* CV: 3–45.

Burge, T. (1992) 'The Philosophy of Language and Mind: 1950-1990." *The Philosophical Review* 101: 3-56.

Burton, R. G. (1993) "Reduction, Elimination, and Strategic Interdependence." In R. G. Burton (ed.), *Natural and Artificial Minds*. Albany: State University of New York Press, pp. 231–243.

Butters, N., Pandya, D. N., Stein, D., and Rosen, J. (1972) "A Search for the Spatial Engram Within the Frontal Lobes of Monkeys." *Acta Neurobiologica* 32: 305–329.

Campbell, K. (1970) *Mind and Body*. New York: Macmillan.

Cartwright, N. (1979) "Causal Laws and Effective Strategies." *Nous* 13: 419–437.

Cartwright, N (1980) "Do the Laws of Nature State the Facts?" *Pacific Philosophical Quarterly* 61: 75–84.

Cartwright, N (1983) *How the Laws of Physics Lie*. Oxford: Clarendon Press.

Ceci, S. J., and Loftus, E. F. (1994) "'Memory Work': A Royal Road to False Memories." *Applied Cognitive Psychology* 8: 351.

Chalmers, D. J. (forthcoming) *Toward a Theory of Consciousness*. Cambridge, MA: The MIT Press.

Chomsky, N. (1964) *Current Issues in Linguistic Theory*. The Hague: Mouton.

Chomsky, N. (1965) *Aspects of the Theory of Syntax*. Cambridge, MA: MIT Press.

Chomsky, N. (1972) *Language and Mind, Enlarged Edition*. San Francisco: Harcourt Brace Jovanovitch.

Chomsky, N. (1975) *Reflections on Language*. New York: Random House.

Church, A. (1936) "An Unsolvable Problem of Elementary Number Theory." *American Journal of Mathematics* 58: 534–363.

Churchland, P. M. (1981) "Eliminative Materialism and the Propositional Attitudes." *Journal of Philosophy* 78: 67–90.

Churchland, P. M. (1984) "Observables and the Super-Empirical Virtues." In P. M. Churchland (ed.) *The Image of Science*. Princeton, NJ: Princeton University Press.

Churchland, P. M. (1989) *A Neurocomputational Perspective: The Nature of Mind and the Structure of Science*. Cambridge, MA: MIT Press.

Churchland, P. S. (1986) *Neurophilosophy: Toward a Unified Science of the Mind/Brain*. Cambridge, MA: MIT Press.

Churchland, P. S. (1987) "Epistemology in the Age of Neuroscience." *Journal of Philosophy* 544–553.

Churchland, P. S. and Sejnowski, T. (1992) *The Computational Brain*. Cambridge, MA: MIT Press.

Clark, A. (1990) *Microcognition: Philosophy, Cognitive Science, and Parallel Distributed Processing*. Cambridge, MA: MIT Press.

Clark, A. (1993) *Associative Engines: Connectionism, Concepts, and Representational Change.* Cambridge, MA: MIT Press.

Cohen, L.B., DeLoache, J. S., and Pearl, R. (1977) "An Examination of Interference Effects in Infants' Memory for Faces." *Child Development* 48: 88-96.

Cohen, N. J. (1984) "Preserved Learning Capacity in Amnesia: Evidence for Multiple Memory Systems." In L. R. Squire and N. Butters (eds.), *Neuropsychology of Memory.* New York: Guilford Press, pp. 83–103.

Cohen, N. J., and Squire, L. (1980) "Preserved Learning and Retention Pattern-Analyzing Skill in Amnesia: Dissociation of 'Knowing How' and 'Knowing That'." *Science* 210: 207–209.

Collins, A., and Loftus, E. (1975) "A Spreading-Activation Theory of Semantic Processing" *Psychological Review* 82: 407–428.

Conel, J. L. (1939–1967) *The Postnatal Development of the Human Cortex,* vols. 1–8. Cambridge, MA: Harvard University Press.

Corkin, S. (1965) "Tactually Guided Maze Learning in Man: Effects of Unilateral Cortical Excisions and Bilateral Hippocampal Lesions." *Neuropsychologia* 3: 339–351.

Corkin, S. (1968) "Acquisition of Motor Skill After Bilateral Medial Temporal-Lobe Damage." *Neuropsychologia* 6: 255–265.

Cornell, E. H. (1975) "Infants' Visual Attention to Pattern Arrangement and Orientation." *Child Development* 46: 229–232.

Corter, C. M., Zucker, K. J., and Galligan, R. F. (1980) "Patterns in the Infants' Search for Mother During Brief Separation." *Developmental Psychology* 16: 62–69.

Cowey, A., and Stoerig, P. (1991) "The Neurobiology of Blindsight." *Trends in Neuroscience* 14: 140.

Cowey, A., and Stoerig, P. (1992) "Reflections on Blindsight." In A. D. Milner and M. D. Rugg (eds.), *The Neuropsychology of Consciousness.* New York: Academic, pp. 11–37.

Critchley, M. (1979) *The Divine Banquet of the Brain.* New York: Raven Press.

Culp, S., and Kitcher, P. S. (1989) "Theory Structure and Theory Change in Contemporary Molecular Biology." *British Journal for the Philosophy of Science* 40: 459–483.

Cummins, R. (1975) "Functional Analysis." *Journal of Philosophy* 72: 741–765.

Cummins, R. (1983) *The Nature of Psychological Explanation.* Cambridge, MA: MIT Press.

Cummins, R. (1989) *Meaning and Mental Representation.* Cambridge, MA: MIT Press.

Cummins, R., and Schwarz, G. (1992) "Connectionism, Computation, and Cognition." In T. Horgan, and J. Tienson (eds.), *Connectionism and the Philosophy of Mind.* Boston: Kluwer.

Cynader, M., Lepore F., and Guillemot, J. P (1981) "Interhemispheric Competition During Postnatal Development." *Nature* 290: 139–140.

Damasio, A. R. (1990) "Category-Related Recognition Defects as a Clue to the Neural Substrates of Knowledge." *Trends in Neuroscience* 13: 95–98.

Damasio, A. R., Tranel, D., and Damasio, H. (1990) "Face Agnosia and the Neural Substrates of Memory." *Annual Review of Neuroscience* 13: 89–109.

Darden, L., and Maull, N. (1977) "Interfield Theories." *Philosophy of Science* 44: 43–64.

Davidson, D. (1980) *Essays on Actions and Events.* Oxford: Clarendon.

Davidson, D. (1993) "Thinking Causes." In J. Heil and A. Mele (eds.), *Mental Causation.* Oxford: Clarendon, pp. 3–18.

Davis, M., Gendelman, D. S., Tischler, M. D., and Kehne, J. H. (1982) "A Primary Acoustic Startle Circuit: Lesion and Stimulation Studies." *Journal of Neuroscience* 2: 791–805.

Dawkins, R. (1976) "Hierarchical Organization, A Candidate Principle for Ethology." In P. P. G. Bateson and R. A. Hinde (eds.), *Growing Points in Ethology.* Cambridge: Cambridge University Press.

Dember, W., and Purcell, D. (1967) "Recovery of Masked Visual Targets by Inhibition of the Masking Stimulus." *Science* 157: 1335–1336.

Demopoulos, W. (1987) "On Some Fundamental Distinctions of Computationalism." *Synthese* 70: 79–96.

Dennett, D. C. (1971) "Intentional Systems." *The Journal of Philosophy* 68: 87–106.

Dennett, D. C. (1975) "Why the Law of Effect Won't Go Away." *Journal for the Theory of Social Behavior* 5: 169–187.

Dennett, D. C. (1978) "Current Issues in the Philosophy of Mind." *American Philosophical Quarterly* 15: 249–261.

Dennett, D. C. (1981) "Three Kinds of Intentional Psychology." Reprinted in D. C. Dennett (1987), pp. 43–68.

Dennett, D. C. (1987) *The Intentional Stance.* Cambridge, MA: MIT Press.

Dennett, D. C. (1991) "Real Patterns." *Journal of Philosophy* 88: 27–51.

Dennett, D. C., and Kinsbourne, M. (1992) "Time and the Observer: The Where and When of Consciousness in the Brain." *Brain and Behavioral Sciences* 15: 183–200.

Diamond, A., and Carey, S. (1986) "Why Faces Are and Are Not Special: An Effect of Expertise." *Journal of Experimental Psychology: General* 115: 107–117.

Dirks, J., and Gibson, E. J. (1977) "Infants' Perception of Similarity between Live People and Their Photographs." *Child Development* 48: 124–130.

Dretske, F. (1988) *Explaining Behavior: Reasons in a World of Causes.* Cambridge, MA: MIT Press.

Duhem, P. (1914) *Aim and Structure of Physical Theory.* 2d ed. Trans. P. P. Weiner. New York: Atheneum.

Eells, E. (1988) "Probabilistic Causal Laws." In B. Skyrms and W. L. Harper (eds.), *Causation, Chance, and Credence,* vol. 1. New York: Reidel, pp. 109–133.

Efron, R. (1968) "What is Perception?" *Boston Studies in the Philosophy of Science.* New York: Humanities, pp. 137–173.

Eichenbaum, H., Otto, T., and Cohen, N. J. (forthcoming) "Two Component Functions of the Hippocampal Memory System." *Behavioral and Brain Science.*

Eldredge, N. (1985) *Unfinished Synthesis: Biological Hierarchies and Modern Evolutionary Thought.* New York: Oxford University Press.

Eldredge, N., and Salthe, S. N (1984) "Hierarchy and Evolution." In R. Dawkins and M. Ridley (eds.), *Oxford Surveys of Evolutionary Biology.* New York: Oxford University Press, pp. 184–208.

Ellis, H. D., and Young, A. W. (1989) "Are Faces Special?" In A. W. Young and H. D. Ellis (eds.), *Handbook of Research on Face Processing.* Amsterdam: North-Holland Press.

Enç, B. (1983) "In Defense of the Identity Theory." *Journal of Philosophy* 80: 279–298.

Fagan, J. F. (1971) "Infants' Recognition Memory for a Series of Visual Stimuli." *Journal of Experimental Child Psychology* 11: 244–250.

Fagan, J. F. (1979) "The Origins of Facial Pattern Recognition." In M. Bornstein and W. Kessen (eds.), *Psychological Development From Infancy.* Hillsdale, NJ: Erlbaum.

Fagan, J. F., and Rovee-Collier, C. K. (1982) "A Conditioning Analysis of Infant Memory." In R. L. Issacson and N. Spear (eds.), *The Expression of Knowledge.* New York: Plenum.

Fagg, G. E., and Matus, A. (1984) "Selective Assocation of N-Methyl D-Aspartate and Quiqualate Types of L-Glutamate Receptor with Post-Synaptic Densities." *Proceedings of the National Academy of Science, USA* 81: 6876–6880.

Farah, M. (1990) *Visual Agnosia: Disorders of Object Recognition and What They Tell Us about Normal Vision.* Cambridge, MA: MIT Press.

Feigl, H. (1970) "Mind-Body, Not a Pseudo-Problem." In C. V. Borst (ed.), *The Mind-Brain Identity Theory.* New York: St. Martin's, pp. 33–41.

Felleman, D. J., and Van Essen, D. C. (1991) "Distributed Hierarchical Processing in the Primate Cerebral Cortex." *Cerebral Cortex* 1: 1–47.

Fendrich, R., Wessinger, C. M., and Gazzaniga, M. S. (1992) "Residual Vision in a Scotoma: Implication for Blindsight." *Science* 258: 1489–1491.

Festinger, L. (1957) *A Theory of Cognitive Dissonance.* Stanford, CA: Stanford University Press.

Feyerabend, Paul (1963) "Mental Events and the Brain." *Journal of Philosophy* 60: 295–296

Field, H. (1980) "Mental Representation." In N. Block (ed.), *Readings in the Philosophy of Psychology,* vol. 2. Cambridge, MA: Harvard University Press, pp. 78–114.

Fodor, J. A. (1965) "Explanations in Psychology." In M. Black (ed.), *Philosophy in America.* London: Routledge and Kegan Paul.

Fodor, J. A. (1968a) "The Appeal to Tacit Knowledge in Psychological Explanation." *Journal of Philosophy* 65: 627–640.

Fodor, J. A. (1968b) *Psychological Explanation.* New York: Random House.

Fodor, J. A. (1974) "Special Sciences." *Synthese* 28: 77-115. Reprinted in J. A. Fodor (1983), pp. 127-145.

Fodor, J. A. (1978) "Computation and Reduction." In W. Savage (ed.), *Minnesota Studies in the Philosophy of Science: Perception and Cognition,* vol. 9. Minneapolis: University of Minnesota Press, reprinted in J. A. Fodor (1983), pp. 146–174.

Fodor, J. A. (1981) *Representations: Philosophical Essays on the Foundations of Cognitive Science.* Cambridge, MA: MIT Press.

Fodor, J. A. (1983) *The Modularity of Mind.* Cambridge, MA: MIT Press.

Fodor, J. A. (1987) *Psychosemantics.* Cambridge, MA: MIT Press.

Fodor, J. A. (1989) "Making the Mind Matter More." *Philosophical Topics* 17: 59–80.

Fodor, J. A. (1990) *A Theory of Content.* Cambridge, MA: MIT Press.

Fodor, J. A., and LePore, E. (1991) *Holism.* Cambridge, MA: Blackwell.

Fodor, J. A., and Pylyshyn, Z. (1988) "Connectionism and Cognitive Architecture: A Critical Analysis." *Cognition* 28: 3–71.

Forster, K. I. (1981) "Priming and the Effects of Sentence and Lexical Contexts on Naming Time: Evidence for Autonomous Lexical Processing." *The Quarterly Journal of Experimental Psychology* 33A: 465–495.

Forster, K. I., and Davis, C. (1984) "Repetition Priming and Frequency Attenuation in Lexical Access." *Journal of Experimental Psychology: Learning, Memory, and Cognition* 10: 680–698.

Forster, K. I., Davis, C., Schoknech, C., and Carter, R. (1987) "Masked Priming with Graphemically Related Forms: Repetition or Partial Activation?" *The Quarterly Journal of Experimental Psychology* 39A: 211–251.

Fowler, C. A., Wolford, G., and Slade, R. (1981) "Lexical Access with and without Awareness." *Journal of Experimental Psychology: General* 110: 341–362.

Freud, S. (1953) "Fragment of an Analysis of a Case of Hysteria ('Dora')." In J. Strachey (ed. and trans.), *Standard Edition of the Complete Psychological Works of Sigmund Freud*, vol. 12. London: Hogarth Press, pp. 107–120.

Fuster, G. M., and Alexander, G. E. (1971) "Neuron Activity Related to Short-Term Memory." *Science* 173: 652–694.

Fuster, J. M. (1973) "Unit Activity in Prefrontal Cortex during Delayed-Response Performance: Neuronal Correlates of Transient Memory." *Journal of Neurophysiology* 36: 61–78.

Fuster, J. M. (1980) *The Prefrontal Cortex: Anatomy, Physiology, and Neuropsychology of the Frontal Lobe.* New York: Raven Press.

Gabrielli, J. D. E., Milberg, W., Keane, M. M, and Corkin, S. (1990) "Intact Priming of Patterns Despite Impaired Memory." *Neuropsychologia* 28: 417–427.

Garey, L., and de Courten, C. (1983) "Structural Development of the Lateral Geniculate Nucleus and Visual Cortex in Monkey and Man." *Behavioral Brain Research* 10: 3–15.

Gazzaniga, M. S. (1985) *The Social Brain.* New York: Basic Books.

Gazzaniga, M. S., and LeDoux, J. E (1978) *The Integrated Mind.* New York: Plenum.

Gazzaniga, M. S., Holtzman, J. D., and Smylie, C. S (1987) "Speech without Conscious Awareness." *Neurology* 37: 682–685.

Gazzaniga, M. S., LeDoux, J. E., Volpe, V. T., and Smylie, C. S (1979) "Plasticity in Speech Organization Following Commissurotomy." *Brain* 102: 805–815.

Giere, R. (1980) "Causal Systems and Statistical Hypothesis." In L. Cohen and M. Hesse (eds.), *Applications of Inductive Logic.* Oxford: Oxford University Press, pp. 251–270.

Giere, R. (1984) *Understanding Scienctific Reasoning.* 2d ed. New York: Holt, Reinhart, and Winston.

Giere, R. (1988) *Explaining Science.* Chicago: University of Chicago Press.

Gluck, M. A., and Granger, R. (1993) "Computational Models of the Neural Bases of Learning and Memory." *Annual Review of Neuroscience* 16: 667–706.

Gluck, M. A., and Rumelhart, D. E. (eds.) (1990) *Neuroscience and Connectionist Theory.* Hillsdale, NJ: Erlbaum.

Gödel, K. (1931) "Über Formal Unentscheidbare Sätze der Principia Mathematica und Verwandter Systeme, I." *Monatshefte für Mathematik und Physik* 3: 173–198.

Gödel, K. (1934) Lectures on *On Undecidable Propositions of Formal Mathematical Systems.* Notes by S. C. Kleene and J. B. Rosser. Printed with corrections and postscript in M. Davis (ed.) (1965), *The Undecidable.* New York: Raven, pp. 39–74.

Godfrey-Smith, P. (1992) "Additivity and the Units of Selection." *PSA 1992,* vol. 1. East Lansing, MI: Philosophy of Science Association, pp. 315–328.

Goldman, A. (1969) "The Compatibility of Mechanism and Purpose." *Philosophical Review* 78: 468–482.

Goldman, P. S. (1971) "Functional Development of the Prefrontal Cortex within the Dorsolateral Prefrontal Cortex in Early Life and the Problem of Neuronal Plasticity." *Experimental Neurology* 32: 366–387.

Goldman, P. S., and Rosvold, H. E (1970) "Localization of Function within the Dorsolateral Prefrontal Cortex of the Rhesus Monkey." *Experimental Neurology* 29: 207–304.

Goldman, P. S., Rosvold, H. E., Vest, B., and Galkin, T. W. (1971) "Analysis of the Delayed Alternation Deficit Produced by Dorsolateral Prefrontal Lesions in the Rhesus Monkey." *Journal of Comparative Physiological Psychology* 77: 212–220.

Goldman-Rakic, P. S. (1987) "Circuitry of Primate Prefrontal Cortex and the Regulation of Behavior by Representational Knowledge." In F. Plum and V. Mountcastle (eds.), *Handbook of Physiology—The Nervous System,* vol. 5. Bethesda, MD: American Physiological Society, pp. 373–417.

Goldman-Rakic, P., Isseroff, I., Schwarz, M., and Bugbee, N. (1983) "The Neurobiology of Cognitive Development," in F. Plum and V. Mountcastle (eds.), *The Handbook of Child Development.* Bethesda, MD: American Physiological Society, pp. 282-331.

Goodman, N. (1979) *Fact, Fiction, and Forecast.* Cambrige, MA: Harvard University Press.

Goren, C. C., Sarty, M., and Wu, P. Y. K. (1975) "Visual Following and Pattern Discrimination of Face-Like Stimuli by Newborn Infants." *Pediatrics* 56: 544–549.

Gottfried, A. W., Rose, S. A., and Bridger, W. H. (1977) "Cross-Modal Transfer in Human Infants." *Child Development* 48: 118–123.

Gottfried, A. W., Rose, S. A., and Bridger, W. H. (1979) "Effects of Visual, Haptic, and Manipulatory Experiences on Infants' Visual Recognition Memory of Objects." *Developmental Psychology* 14: 305–312.

Graf, P., and Schacter, D. (1987) "Selective Effects of Interference on Implicit and Explicit Memory for New Associations." *Journal of Experimental Psychology: Learning, Memory, and Cognition* 12: 45–53.

Graf, P., and Schacter, D. (1989) "Unitization and Grouping Mediate Dissociations in Memory for New Associations." *Journal of Experimental Psychology: Learning, Memory, and Cognition* 15: 930–940.

Graf, P., Squire, L. R., and Mandler, G. (1984) "The Information That Amnesic Patients Do Not Forget." *Journal of Experimental Psychology: Learning, Memory, and Cognition* 10: 164–178.

Granger, R., and Lych, G. (1991) "Higher Olfactory Processes: Perceptual Learning and Memory." *Current Opinion in Neurobiology* 1: 209–214.

Gratch, G. (1976) "On Levels of Awareness of Objects in Infants and Students Thereof." *Merrill-Palmer Quarterly* 22: 157–176.

Grene, M. (1987) "Hierarchies in Biology." *American Scientist* 75: 504–510.

Grene, M. (1988) "Hierarchies and Behavior." In G. Greenberg and E. Tobach (eds.), *Evolution of Social Behavior and Integrative Levels.* Hillsdale, NJ: Erlbaum, pp. 3–17.

Gross, C. G., and Weiskrantz, L. (1964) "Some Changes in Behavior Produced by Lateral Frontal Lesions in the Macaque." In J. M. Warren and K. Akert (eds.), *The Frontal Granular Cortex and Behavior.* New York: McGraw-Hill, pp. 74–101.

Groves, P. M. (1983) "A Theory of the Functional Organization of the Neostriatum and the Neostriatal Control of Voluntary Movement." *Brain Research Reviews* 5: 109–132.

Groves, P. M., and Thompson, R. F. (1970) "Habituation: A Dual Process Theory." *Psychology Review* 77: 419–450.

Grümbaum, A. (1984) *The Foundations of Psychoanalysis: A Philosophical Critique.* Berkeley: University of California Press.

Hacaen, H. (1976) "Acquired Aphasia in Children and the Ontogenesis of Hemispheric Functional Specialization." *Brain and Language* 3: 114–134.

Haefely, W., Polc, P., Pieri, L., Schaffner, R., and Laurent, J. P. (1983) "Neuropharmacology and Benzodiazepines: Synaptic Mechanisms and Neural Basis of Action." In E. Costa (ed.), *The Benzodiazepines: From Molecular Biology to Clinical Practice.* New York: Raven, pp. 21–66.

Haist, F., Musen, G., and Squire, L. R. (1991) "Intact Priming of Words and Nonwords in Amnesia." *Psychobiology* 19: 275–285.

Hardcastle, V. G. (1991) "Partitions, Probabilistic Causal Laws, and Simpson's Paradox." *Synthese* 86: 209–228.

Hardcastle, V. G. (1992) "Reduction, Explanatory Extension, and the Mind/Brain Sciences." *Philosophy of Science* 59: 408–428.

Hardcastle, V. G. (1993a) "The Naturalists versus the Skeptics, The Debate over a Scientific Understanding of Consciousness." *Journal of Mind and Behavior* 14: 27–50.

Hardcastle, V. G. (1993b) "An ERP Analysis of Priming Using Novel Visual Stimuli." unpublished ms.

Hardcastle, V. G. (1995) "Philosophy of Psychology Meets the Semantic View." In D. Hull et al. (eds.), *PSA 1994*, vol. 2. East Lansing, MI: Philosophy of Science Association, forthcoming.

Hardcastle, V. G. (forthcoming) *Locating Consciousness.* Amsterdam: John Benjamins.

Harlow, H. F., Davis, R. T., Settlage, P. H., and Meyer, D. R. (1952) "Analysis of Frontal and Posterier Association Syndromes in Brain Damaged Monkeys." *Journal of Comparative Physiological Psychology* 45: 419–429.

Harnad, S. (1989) "Editorial Commentary." *Brain and Behavioral Sciences* 12: 183.

Hatfield, G. (1988) "Neuro-philosophy Meets Psychology: Reduction, Autonomy, and Physiological Constraints." *Cognitive Neuropsychology* 5: 723–746.

Haugeland, J. (1978) "The Nature and Plausibility of Cognitivism." *The Brain and Behavioral Sciences* 1: 215–226.

Haugeland, J. (1981a) "Analog and Analog." *Philosophical Topics* 12: 213–225.

Haugeland, J. (1981b) "Semantic Engines." In J. Haugeland (ed.), *Mind Design.* Cambridge, MA: MIT Press, pp. 1–34.

Haugeland, J. (1985) *Artificial Intelligence.* Cambridge, MA: MIT Press.

Heil, J., and Mele, A. (1991) "Mental Causes." *American Philosophical Quarterly* 28: 61–71.

Heiligenberg, W. (1987) "Central Processing of Sensory Information in Electric Fish." *Journal of Comparative Physiology* A 161: 621–631.

Heiligenberg, W. (1988) "Electrosensory Maps Form a Substrate for the Distributed and Parallel Control of Behavioral Responses in Weakly Electric Fish." *Brain and Behavioral Evolution* 31: 6–16.

Heiligenberg, W. (1991) *Neural Nets in Electric Fish.* Cambridge, MA: MIT Press.

Heiligenberg, W., and Rose, G. (1985) "Neural Correlates of the Jamming Avoidance Response (JAR) in the Weakly Electric Fish *Eigenmannia.*" *Trends in Neuroscience* 8: 442–449.

Heindel, W. C., Butters, M. N., and Salmon, D. P. (1988) "Impaired Learning of a Motor Skill in Patients with Huntington's Disease." *Behavioral Neuroscience* 102: 141–147.

Hellman, G., and Thompson, F. W. (1975) "Physicalism: Ontology, Determination, Reduction." *Journal of Philosophy* 72: 551–564.

Hellman, G., and Thompson, F. W. (1977) "Psychicalist Materialism." *Nous* 11: 309–345.

Hempel, C. G. (1966) *Philosophy of Natural Science.* Englewood Cliffs, NJ: Prentice Hall.

Heslow, G. (1976) "Discussion: Two Notes on the Probabilistic Approach to Causality." *Philosophy of Science* 43: 290–292.

Hintzman, D. L., Block, R. A., and Inskeep, N. R. (1972) "Memory for Mode of Input." *Journal of Verbal Learning and Verbal Behavior* 11: 741–749.

Holcomb, P. J. (1988) "Automatic and Attentional Processing: An Event-Related Brain Potential Analysis of Semantic Priming." *Brain and Langauge* 35: 66–85.

Holcomb, P. J., and Neville, H. J. (1991) "Auditory and Visual Semantic Priming in Lexical Decision: A Comparison Using Event-Related Potentials." *Language and Cognitive Processes* 5: 281–312.

Honderich, T. (1983) "The Argument for Anomalous Monism." *Analysis* 42: 59–64.

Honderich, T. (1988) *Mind and Brain: A Theory of Determinism.* Oxford: Oxford University Press.

Horgan, T. (1989) "Mental Quasation." *Philosophical Perspectives* 3: 47–76.

Horn, G. (1981) "Neural Mechanisms in Learning: An Analysis of Imprinting in the Domestic Chick." *Proceedings of the Royal Society of London,* Series B 213: 101–137.

Horn, G. (1985) *Memory, Imprinting, and the Brain.* Oxford: Clarendon.

Horn, G., Bradley, P., and McCabe, B. J. (1985) "Changes in the Structure of

Synapses Associated with Learning." *Journal of Neuroscience* 5: 3161–3168.

Horn, G., Rose, S. P. R., and Bateson, P. P. G. (1973) "Monocular Imprinting and Regional Incorporation of Tritated Uracil into Brains of Intact and 'Split-Brain' Chicks." *Brain Research* 56: 227–237.

Horn, G., McCabe, B. J., and Bateson, P. P. G. (1979) "An Autoradiographic Study of the Chick Brain after Imprinting." *Brain Research* 168: 361–373.

Hubel, D., and Weisel, T. (1977) "The Functional Architecture of Macaque Monkey Visual Cortex." *Proceedings for the Royal Society of London, Series B* 198: 1–59.

Hull, D. (1980) "Individuality and Selection." *Annual Review of Ecology and Systematics* 11: 311–312.

Humphreys, G. W., Troscianko, T., Riddoch, M. J., Boucart, M., Donnelly, N., and Harding, G. F. A. (1992) "Covert Processing in Different Visual Recognition Systems." In A. D. Milner and M. D. Rugg (eds.), *The Neuropsychology of Consciousness.* New York: Academic, pp. 36–68.

Humphries, P. (1992) "On 'Mental Causation' and Emergent Properties." ms.

Hutchins, E. (1980) *Culture and Inference: A Trobriand Case Study.* Cambridge, MA: Harvard University Press.

Huttenlocher, P. R. (1993) "Morphometric Study of Human Cerebral Development." In M. H. Johnson (ed.), *Brain Development and Cognition.* Cambridge, MA: Basil Blackwell, pp. 112–124.

Huttenlocher, P. R., de Courten, C., Garey, L. G., and van der Loos, H. (1982) "Synaptogenesis in Human Visual Cortex—Evidence for Synapse Elimination during Normal Development." *Neuroscience Letters* 33: 247–252.

Innocenti, G. M (1986) "General Organization of Callosal Connections." In E. G. Jones, and A. Peters, (eds.), *Cerebral Cortex,* vol. 5. New York: Plenum.

Iversen, S. D. (ed.) (1985) *Psychopharmacology: Recent Advances and Future Prospects.* New York: Oxford University Press.

Jackson, F., and Pettit, P. (1990) "Causation in the Philosophy of Mind." *Philosophy and Phenomenological Research* 1(suppl.): 195–214.

Jacobson, J. (1973) "Effects of Association on Masking and Reading Latency." *Canadian Journal of Psychology* 27: 58–69.

Jacoby, L. L., and Dallas, M. (1981) "On the Relationship between Autobiographical Memory and Perceptual Learning." *Journal of Experimental Psychology: General* 13: 456–463.

Jacoby, L. L., and Witherspoon, D. (1982) "Remembering without Awareness." *Canadian Journal of Psychology* 36: 300–324.

Jamner, L. D., Schwartz, G. F., and Leigh, H. (1988) "The Relation between Repressive and Defensive Coping Styles and Monocyte, Eosinophie, and Serum Glucose Levels: Support for the Opinid Peptide Hypothesis of Repression." *Psychosomatic Medicine* 50: 567–575.

Johnson, M. H. (1990a) "Cortical Maturation and the Development of Visual Attention in Early Infancy." *Journal of Cognitive Neuroscience* 2: 81–95.

Johnson, M. H. (1990b) "Cortical Maturation and Perceptual Development." In H. Block and B. Bertenthal (eds.), *Sensory Motor Organization and Development in Infancy and Early Childhood*. Dordrecht: Kluwer Academic Publishers.

Johnson, M. H., and Morton, J. (1991) *Biology and Cognitive Development: The Case of Face Recognition*. Cambridge, MA: Basil Blackwell.

Kahneman, D., Slovic, P., and Tversky, A. (eds.) (1982) *Judgment under Uncertainty: Heuristics and Biases*. Cambridge: Cambridge University Press.

Kandel, E., and Schwartz, E. (1985) *Principles of Neural Science*. Hillsdale, NJ: Elvesier.

Kaplan, K., and Markus-Kaplan, M. (1981) "Toward Operationalizing the Self in Relationship: A Bidemsional Taxonomy of Reciprocal, Compensatory, and Noncontingent Distancing Patterns." ms, as discussed in S. Rakover (1990) *Metapsychology*, New York: Paragon House.

Keele, S. (1973) *Attention and Human Performance*. Pacific Palisades, CA: Goodyear.

Kemeny, J. G., and Oppenheim, P. (1967) "On Reduction." In B. Brody (ed.), *Readings in the Philosophy of Science*. Englewood Cliffs, NJ: Prentice Hall, pp. 307–318.

Kemp-Wheeler, S. M., and Hill, A. B. (1988) "Semantic Priming without Awareness: Some Methodological Considerations and Replications." *The Quarterly Journal of Experimental Psychology* 40A: 671–692.

Kersteen-Tucker, Z. A., and Knight, R. T. (1989) "Cortical Lesions Dissociate Short- and Long-Term Components of Repetition Priming." *Society of Neuroscience Abstracts* 15: 245.

Kim, J. (1979) "Causality, Identity, and Supervenience in the Mind-Body Problem." *Midwest Studies in Philosophy* 4: 31–49.

Kim, J. (1983) "Supervenience and Supervenient Causation." *Southern Journal of Philosophy* 22 (suppl.): 54.

Kim, J. (1989a) "Mechanism, Purpose, and Explanatory Exclusion." *Philosophical Perspectives* 3: 77–108.

Kim, J. (1989b) "The Myth of Nonreductive Materialism." *Proceedings and Addresses of the American Philosophical Association* 63: 31–47.

Kim, J. (1990) "Explanatory Exclusion and the Problem of Mental Causation." In E. Villaneuva (ed.), *Information, Semantics, and Epistemology*. Oxford: Blackwell, pp. 36–56.

Kim, J. (1992a) "'Downward Causation' in Emergence and Nonreductive Physicalism." In A. Beckerman, H. Flohr, and J. Kim (eds.), *Emergence or Reduction? Essays on the Prospects of Nonreductive Physicalism*. New York: Walter de Gruyter, pp. 119–138.

Kim, J. (1992b) "Multiple Realization and the Metaphysics of Reduction." *Philosophy and Phenomenological Research* LII: 1–26.

Kim, J. (1993a) "Can Supervenience and 'Non-Strict Laws' Save Anomolous Monism?" In J. Heil and A. Mele (eds.), *Mental Causation*. Oxford: Clarendon, pp. 19–26.

Kim, J. (1993b) "The Non-Reductivist's Troubles with Mental Causation." In J. Heil and A. Mele (eds.), *Mental Causation*. Oxford: Clarendon, pp. 189–210.

Kitcher, P. S. (1984) "1953 and All That. A Tale of Two Sciences." *The Philosophical Review* XCIII: 335–373.

Kitcher, P. S. (1989) "Explanatory Unification and the Causal Structure of the World." In P. S. Kitcher and W. Salmon (eds.), *Scientific Explanation: Minnesota Studies in the Philosophy of Science*, vol. 13. Minneapolis: University of Minnesota Press.

Kitcher, P. S. (1993) *The Advancement of Science: Science without Legend, Objectivity without Illusions*. New York: Oxford University Press.

Kitcher, P. S., and Salmon, W. (1987) "Van Fraassen on Explanation." *Journal of Philosophy* 84: 315–330.

Kitcher, P. W. (1980) "How to Reduce a Functional Psychology?" *Philosophy of Science* 47: 134–140.

Kitcher, P. W. (1985) "Narrow Taxonomy and Wide Functionalism." *Philosophy of Science* 52: 1.

Knaudt, P. (1990) "ERPs Elicited by Upright and Inverted Faces Presented in Primed and Unprimed Conditions," unpublished ms.

Koch, C., and Davis, J. L. (eds.) (1994) *Large-Scale Neuronal Theories of the Brain*. Cambridge, MA: MIT Press.

Kohaska, S., Takamatsu, K., Aoki, E., and Tsukada, Y. (1979) "Metabolic Mapping of the Chick Brain after Imprinting Using [14C] 2-Deoxyglucose Technique." *Brain Research* 172: 539–544.

Kojima, S., and Goldman-Rakic, P. S. (1982) "Delayed-Related Activity of Prefrontal Cortical Neurons in Rhesus Monkeys Performing Delayed Response." *Brain Research* 248: 43–93.

Kojima, S., and Goldman-Rakic, P. S. (1984) "Functional Analysis of Spatially Discriminative Neurons in Prefrontal Cortex of Rhesus Monkey." *Brain Research* 291: 229–240.

Kripke, S. (1981) *Wittgenstein on Rules and Private Language.* New York: Oxford University Press.

Kristofferson, A., Galloway, J., and Hanson, R. (1975) "Complete Recovery of a Masked Visual Target." *Bulletin of the Psychonomic Society* 13: 5–6.

Kubota, K. and Niki, H. (1971) "Prefrontal Cortical Unit Activity and Delayed Alternation Performance in Monkeys." *Journal of Neurophysiology* 34: 337–347.

Kutas, M., and Van Petten, C. (1988) "Event-Related Potential Studies of Language." In P. K. Ackles, J. R. Jennings, and M. G. H. Coles (eds.), *Advances in Physiology* 3. Greenwich, CT: JAI Press.

Kutas, M., Lindamood, T., and Hillyard, S. A. (1984) "Word Expectancy and Event-Related Brain Potentials during Sentence Processing." In S. Kornblum and J. Requin (eds.), *Preparatory States and Processes.* Hillsdale, NJ: Erlbaum.

LaBerge, D. (1973a) "Attention and the Measurement of Perceptual Learning." *Memory and Cognition* 1: 268–276.

LaBerge, D. (1973b) "Identification of the Time to Switch Attention: A Test of a Serial and Parallel Model of Attention." In S. Kownblum (ed.), *Attention and Performance* IV. New York: Academic.

LaBerge, D. (1975) "Acquisition of Automatic Processing in Perceptual and Associative Learning." In P. M. A. Rabbitt and S. Dornic (eds.), *Attention and Performance* V. New York: Academic.

LaBerge, D., and Samuals, S. (1974) "Toward a Theory of Automatic Information Processing Reading." *Cognitive Psychology* 6: 293–323.

Langacker, R. W. (1984) *Foundations of Cognitive Grammar.* Palo Alto, CA: Stanford University Press.

Latour, B. (1979) *Laboratory Life: The Social Construction of Scientific Facts.* Beverly Hills, CA: Sage.

Lehky, S. R., and Sejnowski, T. J. (1988) "Network Model of Shape-from-Shading, Neural Function Arises from Both Receptive and Projective Fields." *Nature* 333: 452–454.

Leow, W. K., and Miikkulainen, R. (1992) "Representing Visual Schemas in Neural Networks for Object Recognition." Technical Report AI92–190, University of Texas, Austin.

LePore, E., and Loewer, B. (1987) "Mind Matters." *Journal of Philosophy* 84: 630–642.

LePore, E., and Loewer, B. (1989) "More on Making the Mind Matter." *Philosophical Topics* 17: 175–191.

Leuba, G., and Garey, L. J. (1982) "A Morphometric Developmental Study of Dendrites in the Lateral Genigulate of the Monkey." *Neuroscience* 7 (suppl.): 131.

Lewis, D. (1969) "Review of *Art, Mind and Religion.*" *Journal of Philosophy* 66: 23–35.

Lewis, D. (1970) "How to Define Theoretical Terms." *Journal of Philosophy* 67: 427–444.

Lewis, D. (1972) "Psychophysical and Theoretical Identification." *Australasian Journal of Philosophy* 50: 249–258.

Lewis, D. (1983) "New Work for a Theory of Universals." *Australasian Journal of Philosophy* 61: 347–377.

Llinas, R. (1986) "'Mindness' as a Functional State of the Brain." In C. Blakemore and S. Greenfield (eds.), *Mind Matters.* Oxford: Basil Blackwell.

Lloyd, E. A. (1984) "A Semantic Approach to the Stucture of Population Genetics." *Philosophy of Science* 51: 242–264.

Lloyd, E. A. (1988) *The Structure and Confirmation of Evolutionary Theory.* New York: Greenwood.

Lloyd, E. A., and Anderson, C. G. (1993) "Empiricism, Objectivity, and Explanation." ms.

Loftus, E. F. (1993) "The Reality of Repressed Memories." *American Psychologist* 48: 518–537.

Loftus, E. F. (1994) "The Repressed Memory Controversy." *American Psychologist* 49: 443–445.

Lycan, W. G. (1981) "Form, Function, and Feel." *Journal of Philosophy* 78.

Lycan, W. G. (1987) *Consciousness.* Cambridge, MA: MIT Press.

Lynch, G., and Baudry, M. (1984) "The Biochemistry of Memory: A New and Specific Hypothesis." *Science* 224: 1057-1063.

Lynch, G., and Granger, R. (1992) "Variations in Synaptic Plasticity and Types of Memory in Corticohippocampal Networks." *Journal of Cognitive Neuroscience* 4: 189–199.

Macdonald, C., and Macdonald, G. (1986) "Mental Causes and Explanation of Action." *Philosophical Quarterly* 36: 145–158.

Mackay-Soroka, S., Trehub, S. E., Bull, D. H., and Corter, C. M. (1982) "Effects of Encoding and Retrieval Conditions on Infants' Recognition Memory." *Child Development* 53: 815–818.

Mackie, J. L. (1979) "Mind, Brain, and Causation." *Midwest Studies in Philosophy* 6: 19–29.

Mahut, H., and Moss, M. (1984) "Consolidation of Memory: The Hippocampus Revisited." In L. R. Squires and N. Butters (eds.), *The Neuropsychology of Memory*, New York: Guilford Press, pp. 297-315.

Maier, V., and Scheich, H. (1983) "Acoustic Imprinting Leads to Differential 2-Deoxy-D-Glucose Uptake in the Chick Forebrain." *Proceedings of the National Academy of Science, USA* 80: 3860–3864.

Malamut, B. L., Saunders, R. C., and Mishkin, M. (1984) "Monkeys with Combined Amygdalo-Hippocampal Lesions Succeed in Object Discrimination Learning Despite 24-Hour Intertrial Intervals." *Behavioral Neuroscience* 98: 759–769.

Malcolm, N. (1982) "The Conceivability of Mechanism." In G. Watson (ed.), *Free Will.* Oxford: Oxford University Press, pp. 127–149.

Mandler, G. (1984) *Mind and Body: The Psychology of Emotion and Stress.* New York: W. W. Norton.

Mandler, G. (1985) *Cognitive Psychology: An Essay in Cognitive Science.* Hillsdale, NJ: Erlbaum.

Mandler, G. (forthcoming) "Memory: Conscious and Unconscious." In P. R. Solomon, G. R. Goethals, C. M. Kelley, and R. B. Stephens (eds.), *Memory—An Interdisciplinary Approach.* New York: Springer.

Mandler, J. (1984) "Representation and Recall in Infancy." In M. Moscovitch (ed.), *Infant Memory: Its Relation to Normal and Pathological Memory in Humans and Other Animals.* New York: Plenum, pp. 75–101.

Marcel, A. J. (1980) "Conscious and Preconscious Recognition of Polysemous Words: Locating the Selective Effects of Prior Verbal Context." In R. Nickerson (ed.), *Attention and Performance,* VIII. Hillsdale, NJ: Erlbaum.

Marcel, A. J. (1983a) "Consciousness, Masking, and Word Recognition." *Cognitive Psychology* 15: 198–237.

Marcel, A. J. (1983b) "Conscious and Unconscious Perception: An Approach to the Relations between Phenomenal Experience and Perceptual Processes." *Cognitive Psychology* 15: 238–300.

Marin-Padilla, M. (1990) "The Pyramidal Cell and Its Local-Circuit Interneurones: A Hypothetical Unit of the Mammalian Cerebral Cortex." *Journal of Cognitive Neuroscience* 2: 180–194.

Markov, A. A. (1951) "The Theory of Algorithms." In Russian, *Trudy Mathematicheskogo Instituta imeni V. A. Steklova* 38: 176–189.

Marks, C. E. (1981) *Commissurotomy, Consciousness, and Unity of Mind.* Montgomery, VT: Bradford.

Marr, D. (1977) "Artificial Intelligence—A Personal View." *Artificial Intelligence* 9: 37–48.

Marr, D. (1982) *Vision: A Computational Investigation into the Human Representation and Processing of Visual Information.* San Francisco: Freeman.

Maull, N. (1977) "Unifying Science without Reduction." *Studies in History and Philosophy of Science* 8: 143–71.

Maunsell, J. H. R., and Newsome, W. T. (1987) "Visual Processing in Monkey Extrastriate Cortex." *Annual Review of Neuroscience* 10: 3416–3468.

Maurer, D., and Barrera, M. (1981) "Infants' Perception of Natural and Distorted Arrangements of a Schematic Face." *Child Development* 47: 523–527.

Maurer, D., and Lewis, T. L. (1979) "A Physiological Explanation of Infants' Early Visual Development." *Canadian Journal of Psychology* 33: 232–252.

Mayo, D. G. (forthcoming) *Error and the Growth of Experimental Knowledge.* Chicago: University of Chicago Press.

Mayo, D. G., and Gilinsky, N. L (1987) "Models of Group Selection." *Philosophy of Science* 54: 515–538.

Mayr, E. (1961) "Cause and Effect in Biology." *Science* 143: 1501–1506.

Mayr, E. (1982) *The Growth of Biological Thought.* Cambridge, MA: Harvard University Press.

McAuley, J. D., and Stampfli, J. (1993) "Analysis of the Effects of Noise on a Model for the Neural Mechanisms of Short-Term Active Memory." ms.

McCabe, B. J., and Horn, G. (1988) "Learning and Memory: Regional Changes in N-Methyl-D-Aspartate Receptors in the Chick Brain." *Proceedings of the National Academy of Science, USA* 85: 2849–2853.

McCabe, B. J., Cipolla-Neto, J., Horn, G., and Bateson, P. P. G. (1982) "Amnesic Effects of Bilateral Lesions Placed in the Hyperstriatum Ventrale of the Chick after Imprinting." *Experimental Brain Research* 48: 13–21.

McCall, R. B., Dennedy, C. B., and Dodds, C. (1977) "The Interfering Effect of Distracting Stimuli on the Infant's Memory." *Child Development* 48: 79–87.

McCallum, W. C., Farmer, S. F., and Pocock, P. K. (1984) "The Effects of Physical and Semantic Incongruities on Auditory Event-Related Potentials." *Electroencephalography and Clinical Neurophysiology* 62: 203–208.

McCarthy, G., and Donchin, E. (1981) "A Metric for Thought: A Comparison of P300 Latency and Reaction Time." *Science* 211: 77–80.

McCarthy, R. (1993) "Assemblying Routines and Addressing Representations: An Alternative Conceptualization of 'What' and 'Where' in the Human Brain." In N. Eilan, R. McCarthy, and B. Brewer (eds.), *Spatial Representation: Problems in Philosophy and Psychology*. Cambridge, MA: Basil Blackwell, pp. 373–399.

McClelland, J. L., Rumelhart, D. E., and the PDP Research Group (1986) *Parallel Distributed Processing: Explorations in Microcognition*, vol. 2. Cambridge, MA: MIT Press.

McLaughlin, B. (1989) "Type Epiphenomenalism, Type Dualism, and the Causal Priority of the Mental." *Philosophical Perspectives* 3: 109–168.

Meltzoff, A. N. (1993) "Molyneux's Babies: Cross-Modal Perception, Imitation, and the Mind of the Preverbal Infant." In N. Eilan, R. McCarthy, and B. Brewer (eds.), *Spatial Representation: Problems in Philosophy and Psychology*. Cambridge, MA: Basil Blackwell, pp. 219–235.

Meltzoff, A. N., and Burton, R. W. (1979) "Intermodal Matching by Human Neonates." *Nature* 282: 403–404.

Meltzoff, A. N., and Moore, M. K. (1983) "Newborn Infants Imitate Adult Facial Gestures." *Child Development* 54: 702–709.

Meltzoff, A. N., and Moore, M. K. (1989) "Imitation in Newborn Infants: Exploring the Range of Gestures Imitated and the Underlying Mechanisms." *Developmental Psychology* 25: 954–962.

Menzies, P. (1988) "Against Causal Reduction." *Mind* 97: 551–574.

Meyer, D. H., Barlow, H. F., and Settlate, P. H. (1951) "A Survey of Delayed Response Performance by Normal and Brain-Damaged Monkeys." *Journal of Comparative Physiological Psychology* 44: 17–25.

Middleton, F. A., and Strick, P. L. (1994) "Anatomical Evidence for Cerebellar and Basal Ganglia Involvement in Higher Cognitive Function." *Science* 266: 458–461.

Milner, A. D., Perret, D. I., Johnston, R. S., Benson, P. J., Jordan, T. R., Heeley, D. W., Bettucci, D., Mortara, G., Mutani, R., Terazzi, E., and Davidson, D. L. W. (1991) "Perception and Action in Visual Agnosia." *Brain* 114: 405–428.

Milner, B., Corkin, S., and Teuber, H. L. (1968) "Further Analysis of the Hippocampal Amnesic Syndrome: 14-Year Follow-Up Study of H. M." *Neurophysiologia* 6: 215–234.

Mishkin, M. (1957) "Effects of Small Frontal Lesions on Delayed Alternation in Monkeys." *Journal of Comparative Physiological Psychology* 44: 17–25.

Mishkin, M. (1982) "A Memory System in the Monkey." *Philosophical Royal Society of London (Biology)* 298: 85–95.

Morgan, C. L. (1923) *Emergent Evolution.* London: Williams and Norgate.

Mormann, T. (1988) "Structuralist Reduction Concepts as Structure-Preserving Maps." *Synthese* 77: 215-250.

Morton, J. (1979) "Facilitation in Word Recognition: Experiments in Causing Change in the Logogen Models." In P. A. Kolers, M. E. Wrolstad, and H. Bouma (eds.), *Processing of Visible Language,* vol. 1. New York: Plenum, pp. 259–268.

Moscovitch, M. (1982) "Multiple Dissociations of Function in Amnesia." In L. S. Cermak (ed.), *Human Memory and Amnesia.* Hillsdale, NJ: Erlbaum, pp. 337–370.

Moscovitch, M. (ed.) (1984) *Infant Memory: Its Relation to Normal and Pathological Memory in Humans and Other Animals.* New York: Plenum.

Musen, G. (1989) "Implicit and Explicit Memory for Novel Visual Patterns." ms.

Musen, G., and Squire, L. R. (1991) "Intact Text-Specific Reading Skill in Amnesia." *Journal of Experimental Psychology: Learning, Memory, and Cognition* 16: 1068–1076.

Musen, G., and Treisman, A. (1990) "Implicit and Explicit Memory for Visual Patterns." *Journal of Experimental Psychology: Learning, Memory, and Cognition* 16: 127–137.

Nadel, L., Cooper, L. A., Culicover, P., and Harnish, R. M. (eds.) (1989) *Neural Connections, Mental Computations.* Cambridge, MA: MIT Press.

Nagel, E. (1949) "The Meaning of Reduction in the Natural Sciences." In R. Stauffer (ed.), *Science and Civilization.* Madison, WI: University of Wisconsin Press, pp. 97–135.

Nagel, E. (1961) *The Structure of Science.* New York: Harcourt, Brace, and World.

Nahm, F. N. (1989) "The Developmental Exuberancy of Corpus Callosal Projections as Possible Substrate for Neural Plasticity in the Visual System." unpublished ms.

Natsoulas, T. (1987) "Consciousness and Commissurotomy: I. Spheres and Streams of Consciousness." *The Journal of Mind and Behavior* 8: 435–468.

Neisser, U. (1967) *Cognitive Psychology.* New York: Appleton-Century-Croft.

Nelkin, N. (forthcoming) "Patterns. "

Neville, H. J., Pratarelli, M. E., and Forster, K. I. (1989) "Distinct Neural Systems for Lexical and Episodic Representations of Words." *Society of Neuroscience Abstracts* 15.

Newell, A., and Simon, H. A. (1972) *Human Problem Solving.* Englewood Cliffs, NJ: Prentice-Hall.

Newell, A., and Simon, H. A. (1976) "Computer Science as Empirical Inquiry: Symbols and Search." *Communications of the Association for Computing Machinery* 19: 113–126.

Newell, A., Shaw, J. C. and Simon, H. A. (1958) "Elements of a Theory of Human Problem Solving." *Psychological Review* 65: 151–166.

Nissen, M. J., and Bullemer, P. (1987) "Attentional Requirements of Learning: Evidence from Performance Measures." *Cognitive Psychology* 19: 1–32.

O'Reilly, R. C., and McClelland, J. L. (1992) "The Self-Organization of Spatially Invariant Representations." Technical Report PDP. CNS. 92. 5, Carnegie Mellon University.

Oatley, K. (1993) "Freud's Cognitive Psychology of Intention: The Case of Dora." In M. Davies and G. W. Humphreys (ed.), *Consciousness.* Cambridge, MA: Blackwell, pp. 90–104.

Oppenheim, P., and Putnam, H. (1958) "Unity of Science as a Working Hypothesis." In H. Feigl, M. Scriven, and G. Maxwell (eds.), *Concepts, Theories, and the Mind-Body Problem* (Minnesota Studies in the Philosophy of Science, vol. 2). Minneapolis: University of Minnesota Press, pp. 3–36.

Osherson, D. N., and Lasnik, H. (1990) *An Invitation to Cognitive Science,* vol. 1: *Language.* Cambridge, MA: MIT Press.

Osherson, D. N., and Smith, E. E. (1990) *An Invitation to Cognitive Science,* vol. 3: *Thinking.* Cambridge, MA: MIT Press.

Osherson, D. N., Kosslyn, S. M., and Hollerbach, J. M. (1990) *An Invitation to Cognitive Science,* vol. 2: *Visual Cognition and Action.* Cambridge, MA: MIT Press.

Otte, R. (1985) "Probabilistic Causality and Simpson's Paradox." *Philosophy of Science* 52: 110–115.

Owens, D. (1989) "Disjunctive Laws." *Analysis* 49: 197–202.

Owens, J. (1987) "In Defense of a Different Doppelganger." *The Philosophical Review* 96: 521–554.

Paiget, J. (1954) *The Construction of Reality in the Child.* New York: Basic.

Paller, K. A. (1990) "Recall and Stem-Completion Priming Have Different Electrophysiological Correlates and Are Modified Differentially by

Directed Forgetting." *Journal of Experimental Psychology: Learning, Memory, and Cognition* 16: 1021-1032.

Paller, K. A., and Kutas, M. (1992) "Brain Potentials During Memory Retrieval: Neurophysiological Indications of the Distinction Between Conscious Recollection and Priming." *Journal of Cognitive Neuroscience* 4: 375-391.

Papousek, H. (1969) "Experimental Studies of Appetitional Behavior in Human Newborns and Infants." In H. W. Stevenson, E. H. Hess, and H. L. Rheingold (eds.), *Early Behavior.* New York: Wiley.

Parasuraman, R., and Beatty, J. (1980) "Brain Events Underlying Detection and Recognition of Weak Sensory Signals." *Science* 210: 80–83.

Parkin, A. J. (1982) "Residual Learning Capacity in Organic Amnesics." *Cortex* 18: 417–440.

Passingham, R. (1975) "Delayed Matching after Selective Prefrontal Lesions in Monkeys (*Macaca mulatta*)" *Brain Research* 92: 89–102.

Pattee, H. H. (1969) "Physical Conditions for Primitive Functional Hierarchies." In L. L. Whyte, A. G. Wilson, and D. Wilson (eds.), *Hierarchical Structures.* New York: Elsevier, pp. 161–177.

Pattee, H. H. (ed.) (1973) *Hierarchy Theory.* New York: Braziller.

Patterson, C. (1980) "Cladistics." In J. M. Smith (ed.), *Evolution Now.* San Francisco: W. H. Freeman, pp. 10–120.

Pellionisz, A., and Llinas, R. (1985) "Tensor Network Theory of the Metaorganization of Functional Geometries in the Central Nervous System." *Neuroscience* 16: 245–273.

Penney, J. B., Jr., and Young, A. B. (1983) "Speculations on the Functional Anatomy of Basal Ganglia Disorders." In W. M. Cowen (ed.), *Annual Review of Neuroscience,* vol. 6., Pal Alto, CA: Annual Reviews, pp. 73–94.

Pereboom, D., and Kornblith, H. (1991) "The Metaphysics of Irreducibility." *Philosophical Studies* 61: 131–151.

Perenin, M. T., and Jeannerod, M. (1975) "Residual Vision in Cortically Blind Hemifields." *Neuropsychologia* 13: 1–7.

Pettigrew, J. D., and Konishi, M. (1976) "Neurons Selective for Orientation and Binocular Disparity in the Visual Wulst of the Barn Owl (*Tyto alba*)." *Science* 193: 675–678.

Pettit, P. (1994) *The Common Mind: An Essay on Psychology, Society, and Politics.* New York: Oxford University Press.

Piaget, J. (1954) *The Construction of Reality in the Child.* New York: Basic.

Picton, T. W., Campbell, K. B., Baribeau, B., and Proule, G. B. (1978) "The

Neurophysiology of Human Attention; A Tutorial Review." In J. Requin (ed.), *Attention and Performance* VII. Hillsdale, NJ: Erlbaum.

Posner, M. I. (1989) *Foundations of Cognitive Science.* Cambridge, MA: MIT Press.

Posner, M. I., and Snyder, C. (1975a) "Attention and Cognitive Control." In R. Solso (ed.), *Information Processing and Cognition: The Loyola Symposium.* Hillsdale, NJ: Erlbaum.

Posner, M. I., and Snyder, C. (1975b) "Facilitation and Inhibition in the Processing of Signals." In P. M. A. Rabbitt and S. Dornic (eds.), *Attention and Performance* V. New York: Academic.

Post, E. L. (1936) "Finite Combinatory Processes—Formulation I." *Journal of Symbolic Logic* 1: 103–105.

Post, E. L. (1943) "Formal Reductions of the General Combinatorial Decision Problem." *American Journal of Mathematics* 65: 197–215.

Pour-El, M., and Richards, I. (1981) "The Wave Equation with Computable Initial Data Such That Its Unique Solution Is Not Computable." *Advances in Mathematics* 39: 215.

Pribram, K. H., Mishkin, M., Rosvold, H. E., and Kaplan, S. J. (1952) "Effects on Delayed-Response Performance of Lesions of Dorso-Lateral and Ventro-Lateral Frontal Cortex of Baboons." *Journal of Comparative Physiological Psychology* 45: 565–575.

Ptito, A., Lepore, F., Ptito, M., and Lassonde, M. (1991) "Target Detection and Movement Discrimination in the Blind Field of Hemispherectomized Patients." *Brain* 114: 497.

Putnam, H. (1960) "Minds and Machines." In S. Hook (ed.), *Dimensions of Mind.* New York: New York University Press, pp. 138–164.

Putnam, H. (1967) "Psychological Predicates." In W. H. Captain and D. D. Merrill (eds.), *Art, Mind, and Religion.* Pittsburgh: Pittsburgh University Press, pp. 37–48.

Putnam, H. (1973) "Reductionism and the Nature of Psychology." *Cognition* 2: 131–146, reprinted in abridged form in J. Haugland (ed.), *Mind Design: Philosophy, Psychology, Artificial Intelligence.* (1983) Cambridge, MA: MIT Press, pp. 205–219.

Putnam, H. (1975) "The Mental Life of Some Machines." In his *Mind, Language, and Reality.* Cambridge: Cambridge University Press.

Pylyshyn, Z. (1980) "Computation and Cognition: Issues in the Foundation of Cognitive Science." *Behavioral and Brain Sciences* 3: 111–134.

Pylyshyn, Z. (1984) *Computation and Cognition.* Cambridge, MA: MIT Press.

Quine, W. V. O. (1964) "Ontological Reduction and the World of Numbers." *Journal of Philosophy* 61: 209–216.

Quine, W. V. O. (1969) "Natural Kinds." *Ontological Relativity and Other Essays*. New York: Columbia University Press.

Rabinowicz, T. (1979) "The Differential Maturation of the Human Cerebral Cortex." In F. Falkner, and J. M. Tanner (eds.), *Human Growth*, vol. 3: *Neurobiology and Nutrition*. New York: Plenum.

Railton, P. (1981) "Probability, Explanation, and Information." *Synthese* 48: 233–256.

Ramachandran, V. (1988) "Perceiving Shape from Shading." *Scientific American* 259: 76–83.

Reber, A. S. (1992) "The Cognitive Unconscious: An Evolutionary Perspective." *Consciousness and Cognition* 1: 93–133.

Reissland, N. (1989) "Neonatal Imitation in the First Hour of Life: Observations in Rural Nepal." *Developmental Psychology* 24: 464–469.

Richardson, R. C. (1979) "Functionalism and Reductionism." *Philosophy of Science* 46: 533–558.

Richardson, R. C. (1982) "How Not to Reduce a Functional Psychology." *Philosophy of Science* 49: 125–137.

Ritter, W., Simson, R., Vaughan, H. G., Jr., and Macht, M. (1982) "Manipulation of Event-Related Potential Manifestations of Information Processing Stages." *Science* 218: 909–911.

Rolfe, S. A., and Day, R. H. (1981) "Effects of the Similarity and Dissimilarity between Familiarization and Test Objects on Recognition Memory in Infants Following Unimodal and Bimodal Familiarization." *Child Development* 52: 1308–1312.

Rorty, R. (1965) "Mind-Body Identity, Privacy, and Categories." *Review of Metaphysics* 19: 24–54

Rose, S. A., Gottfried, A. W., and Bridger, W. H. (1978) "Cross-Modal Transfer in Infants: Relationship to Prematurity and Socioeconomic Background." *Developmental Psychology* 14: 643–652.

Rose, S. A., Gottfried, A. W., and Bridger, W. H. (1979) "Effects of Haptic Cues on Visual Recognition Memory in Fullterm and Preterm Infants." *Infant Behavior and Development* 2: 55–67.

Rosenberg, A. (1985) *The Structure of Biological Science*. Cambridge, MA: University of Cambridge Press.

Rosvold, H. E., Szwarcbart, M. K., Mirsky, A. F., and Mishkin, M. (1961) "The Effect of Frontal-Lobe Damage on Delayed-Response Performance in

Chimpanzees." *Journal of Comparative Physiological Psychology* 54: 368–374.

Rott, H. (1987) "Reduction: Some Criteria and Criticisms of the Structuralist Concept." *Erkenntnis* 27: 231-256.

Rugg, M. D. (1985) "The Effects of Semantic Priming and Word Repetition on Event-Related Potentials." *Psychopathology* 22: 642–647.

Rugg, M. D., and Doyle, M. C. (1992) in H. Heinze, T. Munte, and G. R. Mangun (eds.), *Cognitive Electrophysiology.* Cambridge, MA: Mirkhauser Boston.

Rumelhart, D., McClelland, R., and the PDP Research Group (1986) *Parallel Distributed Processing: Explorations in the Microstructure of Cognition.* Cambridge, MA: MIT Press.

Rybak, I. A., Podladchikova, L. N., and Shevtsova, N. A. (1993) "Physiological Model of Orientation Sensitivity in the Visual Cortex and Its Use for Image Processing." ms.

Salmon, W. (1971) *Statistical Explanation and Statistical Relevance.* Pittsburgh: University of Pittsburgh Press.

Scarborough, D. L., Cortese, C., and Scarborough, H. S. (1977) "Frequency and Repetition Effects in Lexical Memory." *Journal of Experimental Psychology: Human Perception and Cognition* 3: 1–17.

Scarborough, D. L., Cortese, C., and Scarborough, H. S. (1979) "Accessing Lexical Memory: The Transfer of the Word Repetition Effects in Lexical Memory." *Memory and Cognition* 7: 1–12.

Schachter, S. (1964) "The Interaction of Cognitive and Physiological Determinants of Emotional State." In L. Berkowitz (ed.), *Advances in Experimental Social Psychology,* vol. 1. New York: Academic, pp. 8 –49.

Schachter, S. (1965) "A Cognitive-Physiological View of Emotion." In O. Klineber and R. Christie (eds.), *Perspectives in Social Psychology.* New York: Holt, Rinehart, and Wilson, pp. 75–105.

Schachter, S., and Singer, J. (1962) "Cognitive, Social, and Physiological Determinents of Emotional State." *Psychological Review* 65: 121–28.

Schacter, D. L. (1985a) "Multiple Forms of Memory in Humans and Animals." In N. M. Weinberger, J. L. McGaugh, and G. Lynch (eds.), *Memory Systems of the Brain.* New York: Guilford, pp. 351–379.

Schacter, D. L. (1985b) "Priming of Old and New Knowledge in Amnesic Patients and Normal Subjects." *Annals of the New York Academy of Sciences* 444: 41–53.

Schacter, D. L. (1990) "Perceptual Representation Systems and Implicit Memory: Toward a Resolution of the Multiple Memory Systems Debate." *Annals of the New York Academy of Sciences* 608: 435–571.

Schacter, D. L., and Graf, P. (1986) "Preserved Learning in Amnesic Patients: Perspectives from Research on Direct Priming." *Journal of Clinical and Experimental Neuropsychology* 8: 727–743.

Schacter, D. L., and Graf, P. (1989) "Modality Specificity of Implicit Memory for New Associations." *Journal of Experimental Psychology: Learning, Memory, and Cognition* 15: 3–12.

Schacter, D. L., and McGlynn, S. M. (1989) "Implicit Memory: Effects of Elaboration Depend on Unitization." *American Journal of Psychology* 102: 151–181.

Schacter, D. L., and Moscovitch, M. (1984) "Infants, Amnesics, and Dissociable Memory Systems." In M. Moscovitch (ed.), *Infant Memory: Its Relation to Normal and Pathological Memory in Humans and Other Animals.* New York: Plenum, pp. 173–216.

Schacter, D. L., Cooper, L. A., and Delaney, S. (1990) "Implicit Memory for Unfamiliar Objects Depends on Access to Structural Descriptions." *Journal of Experimental Psychology: General* 119: 5–24.

Schacter, D. L., Cooper, L. A., Tharan, M., and Rubens, A. B. (1991) "Preserved Priming of Novel Objects in Patients with Memory Disorders." *Journal of Cognitive Neuroscience* 3: 117–130.

Schacter, D. L., McAndrews, M. P., and Moscovitch, M. (1988) "Access to Consciousness: Dissociations between Implicit and Explicit Knowledge in Neuropsychological Syndromes." In L. Weiskrantz (ed.), *Thought Without Language.* Oxford: Oxford University Press.

Schaffner, K. F. (1967) "Approaches to Reduction." *Philosophy of Science* 34: 137–147.

Schaffner, K. F. (1976) "Reduction in the Biomedical Sciences: Problems and Prospects." In R. S. Cohen, C. Hooker, A. Michalos, and J. van Evra (eds.), *PSA 1976.* Dordrecht: Reidel, pp. 613–632.

Schaffner, K. F. (1980) "Theory Structure in the Biomedical Sciences." *Journal of Medicine and Philosophy* 5: 57–97.

Schaffner, K. F. (1993) *Discovery and Explanation in Biology and Medicine.* Chicago: University of Chicago Press.

Schiffer, S. (1982) "Intention Based Semantics." *Notre Dame Journal of Formal Logic* 23:

Schiffer, S. (1989) *Remnants of Meaning.* Cambridge, MA: MIT Press.

Schneider, G. E. (1969) "Two Visual Systems." *Science* 163: 895–902.

Schneider, W., and Shiffrin, R. M. (1977) "Controlled and Automatic Human Information Processing: I. Detection, Search, and Attention." *Psychological Review* 84: 1–66.

Schwartz, E. L. (ed.) (1990) *Computational Neuroscience.* Cambridge, MA: MIT Press.

Seager, W. (1991) "Disjunctive Laws and Supervenience." *Analysis* 51: 93–98.

Searle, J. (1983) *Intentionality.* New York: Cambridge Press.

Searle, J. (1992) *The Rediscovery of Mind.* Cambridge, MA: MIT Press.

Segal, G., and Sober, E. (1991) "The Causal Efficacy of Content." *Philosophical Studies* 63: 1–30.

Segel, L. A. (1965) "The Nonlinear Interaction of a Finite Number of Disturbances to a Layer of Fluid Heated from Below." *Journal of Field Mechanics* 21: 359.

Sejnowski, T. J., and Churchland, P. S. (1988) "Brain and Cognition." In M. I. Posner (ed.), *Foundations of Cognitive Science.* Cambridge, MA: MIT Press, pp. 301–356.

Sereno, M. I. (1990) "Language and the Primate Brain." *CRL Newletter* 4.

Shagrir, O. (1991) "Computation." unpublished ms.

Shapere, D. (1974) "Scientific Theories and Their Domains." In F. Suppe (ed.), *The Structure of Scientific Theories.* 2d ed. Urbana, IL: University of Illinois Press (1977), pp. 518–565.

Shapiro, L. (1994) "Indication, Cognitive Science, and Lego Naturalism." ms.

Shepherd, G. M. (1979) *The Synaptic Organization of the Brain.* 2d ed. New York: Oxford University Press.

Shiffrin, R. M. (1975) "The Locus and Role of Attention in Memory." In P. M. A. Rabbitt and S. Dornic (eds.), *Attention and Performance* V. New York: Academic.

Shiffrin, R. M., and Geisler, W. (1973) "Visual Recognition in a Theory of Information Processing." In R. Solso (ed.), *Contemporary Issues in Cognitive Psychology: The Loyola Symposium.* Washington, DC: Winston.

Shiffrin, R. M., and Schneider, W. (1977) "Controlled and Automatic Human Information Processing: II. Perceptual Learning, Automatic Attending, and General Theory." *Psychological Review* 84: 127–190.

Shimamura, A. P. (1986) "Priming Effects in Amnesia: Evidence for a Dissociable Function." *Quarterly Journal of Experimental Psychology* 38A: 619–315.

Simon, H. A (1969) *The Sciences of the Artificial.* Cambridge, MA: MIT Press.

Sirosh, J., and Miikkulainen, R. (1992) "Self-Organization with Lateral Connections." Technical Report AI92–191, University of Texas, Austin.

Skillen, A. (1984) "Mind and Matter: A Problem That Refuses Dissolution." *Mind* 43: 514–526.

Smart, J. J. C. (1959) "Sensations and Brain Processes." *Philosophical Review* 68: 141–156.

Smart, J. J. C. (1963) *Philosophy and Scientific Realism.* London: Routledge and Kegan Paul.

Smart, J. J. C. (1971) "Reports of Immediate Experience." *Synthese* 22: 346–359.

Smart, J. J. C. (1980) "Sensations and Brain Processes." In C. V. Borst (ed.), *The Mind-Brain Identity Theory.* New York: St. Martin's, pp. 54–66.

Sneed, J. (1971) *The Logical Structure of Mathematical Physics.* Dordrecht: Reidel.

Sober, E. (1984) "Holism, Individualism, and the Units of Selection." In E. Sober (ed.), *Conceptual Issues in Evolutionary Biology.* Cambridge, MA: MIT Press, pp. 184–209.

Sober, E. (1990) "Putting the Function Back into Functionalism." In W. Lycan (ed.), *Mind and Cognition.* New York: Basil Blackwell, pp. 97–106.

Sober, E., and Lewontin, R. C. (1984) "Artifact, Cause, and Genic Selection." In E. Sober (ed.), *Conceptual Issues in Evolutionary Biology.* Cambridge, MA: MIT Press, pp. 210–231.

Sosa, E. (1984) "Mind-Body Interaction and Supervenient Causation." *Midwest Studies in Philosophy* 9: 271–281.

Sosa, E. (1993) "Davidson's Thinking Causes." In J. Heil and A. Mele (eds.), *Mental Causation.* Oxford: Clarendon Press, pp. 41–50.

Sperry, R. W. (1965) "Brain Bisection and Mechanisms of Consciousness." In J. C. Eccles (ed.), *Brain and Conscious Experience.* New York: Springer-Verlag, pp. 298–313.

Sperry, R. W. (1977) "Fore-Brain Commissurotomy and Conscious Awareness." *Journal of Medicine and Philosophy* 2: 101–126.

Sperry, R. W. (1985) "Consciousness, Personal Identity, and the Divided Brain." In D. F. Benson and E. Zaidel (eds.), *The Dual Brain.* New York: Guilford, pp. 11–26.

Squire, L. R. (1987) *Memory and the Brain.* New York: Oxford University Press.

Squire, L. R. (1992) "Declarative and Nondeclarative Memory: Multiple Brain Systems Supporting Learning and Memory." *Journal of Cognitive Neuroscience* 4: 232–243.

Squire, L. R., and Cohen, N. J. (1984) "Human Memory and Amnesia." In J. McGaugh, G. Lynch, and N. Weinberger (eds.), *Proceedings of the Conference on the Neurobiology of Learning and Memory.* New York: Guilford, pp. 3–64.

Squire, L. R., and Zola-Morgan, S. (1991) "The Medial Temporal Lobe Memory System." *Science* 253: 1380–1386.

St. James-Roberts, I. (1981) "A Reinterpretation of Hemispherectomy without Functional Plasticity of the Brain." *Brain and Language* 13: 31–53.

Stabler, Jr., E. P (1987) "Kripke on Functionalism and Automata." *Synthese* 70: 1–22.

Stegmüller, W. (1976) *The Structure and Dynamics of Theories.* Berlin: Springer-Verlag.

Stich, S. (1983) *From Folk Psychology to Cognitive Science: The Case against Belief.* Cambridge, MA: MIT Press.

Stich, S. P. (forthcoming) "Puritanical Naturalism." In K. Neander and I. Ravenscroft (eds.), *Prospects for Intentionality, Working Papers in Philosophy,* vol. 2. Research School of Social Science, Australian National University.

Stich, S. P., and Laurence, S. (forthcoming) "Intentionality and Naturalism." In K. Neander and I. Ravenscroft (eds.), *Prospects for Intentionality, Working Papers in Philosophy,* vol. 2. Research School of Social Science, Australian National University.

Stillings, N. A., Feinstein, M. H., Garfield, J. L., Rissland, E. L., Rosenbaum, D. A., Weisler, S. E., and Baker-Ward, L. (1987) *Cognitive Science: An Introduction.* Cambridge, MA: MIT Press.

Stoutland, F. (1980) "Oblique Causation and Reasons for Action." *Synthese* 43: 351–367.

Strongman, K. (1987) *The Psychology of Emotion.* 3d ed. New York: Wiley.

Suppe, F. (1974) *The Structure of Scientific Theories.* Urbana, IL: University of Illinois Press.

Suppe, F. (1989) *The Semantic Conception of Theories and Scientific Realism.* Chicago: University of Illinois Press.

Suppes, P. (1956) *Introduction to Logic.* Princeton, NJ: Van Nostrand.

Suppes, P. (1962) "Models of Data." In E. Nagel, P. Suppes and A. Tarski (eds.), *Philosophy of Science Today.* Stanford, CA: Stanford University Press, pp. 252–261.

Suppes, P. (1967) "What Is a Scientific Theory?" In S. Morgenbesser (ed.), *Philosophy of Science Today.* New York: Basic, pp. 55–67.

Swanson, L. W., Teyler, T. J., and Thompson, R. F. (1982) "Hippocampal Long-Term Potentiation: Mechanisms and Implications for Memory." *Neuroscience Research Program Bulletin* 20: 613–675.

Taylor, G., and Chabot, R. (1978) "Differential Backward Masking of Words and Letters by Masks of Varying Orthographic Structure." *Memory and Cognition* 6: 629–635.

Thompson, J. M., Baxter, L. R., and Schwartz, J. M. (1992) "Freud, Obsessive-Compulsive Disorder and Neurobiology." *Psychoanalysis and Contemporary Thought* 15: 483–505.

Thompson, K. S. (1986) "The Relationship Between Development and Evolution." In R. Dawkins and M. Ridley (eds.), *Oxford Surveys of Evolutionary Biology*. New York: Oxford University Press, pp. 220–230.

Thompson, P. (1983) "The Structure of Evolutionary Theory: A Semantic Approach." *Studies in the History and the Philosophy of Science* 14: 215–229.

Thompson, P. (1989) *The Structure of Biological Theories*. Albany: State University of New York Press.

Tipper, S. P. (1985) "The Negative Priming Effect: Inhibitory Priming by Ignored Objects." *Quarterly Journal of Experimental Psychology* 37A: 571–590.

Tischler, M. D., and Davis, M. (1983) "A Visual Pathway That Mediates Fear-Conditioned Enhancement of Acoustic Startle." *Brain Research* 276: 55–71.

Touretzky, D. S. (ed.) (1991a) *Advances in Neural Information Processing Systems* 1. San Mateo, CA: Morgan Kaufman.

Touretzky, D. S. (ed.) (1991b) *Advances in Neural Information Processing Systems* 2. San Mateo, CA: Morgan Kaufman.

Travis, J. (1994) "Glia: The Brain's Other Cells." *Science* 266: 970–972.

Treisman, A. (1986) "Features and Objects in Visual Processing." *Scientific American* 114b–125.

Treisman, A., and Gelade, G. (1980) "A Feature Integration Theory of Attention." *Cognitive Psychology* 12: 97–136.

Treisman, A., and Schmidt, H. (1982) "Illusory Conjunctions in the Perception of Objects." *Cognitive Psychology* 14: 107–141.

Tulving, E., Schacter, D. L., and Stark, H. A. (1982) "Priming Effects in Word-Fragment Completion Are Independent of Recognition Memory." *Journal of Experimental Psychology: Learning, Memory, and Cognition* 8: 336–342.

Turing, A. M. (1936) "On Computable Numbers, with an Application to the Entscheidungs problem." *Proceedings of the London Mathematics Society* (Series 2) 42: 230–265.

Turvey, M. (1974) "Constructive Theory, Perceptual Systems, and Tacit Knowledge." In W. Weld and D. Palermo (eds.), *Cognition and Symbolic Processes.* Hillsdale, NJ: Erlbaum.

van Fraassen, B. (1970) "On the Extension of Beth's Semantics of Physical Theories." *Philosophy of Science* 37: 325–339.

van Fraassen, B. (1980) *The Scientific Image.* Oxford: Oxford University Press.

van Fraassen, B. (1990) *Laws and Symmetry.* Oxford: Oxford University Press.

van Gulick, R. (1985) "Physicalism and the Subjectivity of the Mental." *Philosophical Topics* 13: 51–70.

van Gulick, R. (1992) "Nonreductive Materialism and Intertheoretic Constraint." In A. Beckerman, N. Flohr, and J. Kim (eds) *Emergence or Reductions? Essays on the Prospect of Nonreductive Physicalism.* Berlin: De Gruyer, pp. 157–179.

van Gulick, R. (1993) "Who's in Charge Here? And Who's Doing All the Work?" In J. Heil and A. Mele (eds.), *Mental Causation.* Oxford: Clarendon, pp. 233–256.

von Eckardt, B. (1993) *What is Cognitive Science?* Cambridge, MA: MIT Press.

Warrington, E. K., and Weiskrantz, L. (1970) "Amnesic Syndrome: Consolidation or Retrieval?" *Nature* 228: 629–630.

Warrington, E. K., and Weiskrantz, L. (1974) "The Effect of Prior Learning on Subsequent Retention in Amnesic Patients." *Neuropsychologia* 12: 419–428.

Weiskrantz, L. (1984) "On Issues and Theories of the Human Amnesic Syndrome." In N. Weinberger, J. McGaugh, and G. Lynch (eds.), *Memory Systems of the Brain: Animal and Human Cognitive Processes.* New York: Guilford, pp. 380–415.

Weiskrantz, L. (1988) "Some Contributions of Neuropsychology of Vision and Memory to the Problem of Consciousness." In A. Marcel and E. Bisiach (eds.), *Consciousness in Contemporary Science.* Oxford: Clarendon, pp. 183–199.

Weiskrantz, L. (1992) "Unconscious Vision: The Strange Phenomenon of Blindsight." *Science* 32: 22.

Weiskrantz, L., and Warrington, E. K. (1979) "Conditioning in Amnesic Patients." *Neuropsychologia* 17: 187–194.

Weiskrantz, L., Warrington, E. K., and Saunders, M. (1974) "Visual Capacity in the Hemianopic Field Following a Restricted Occipital Ablation." *Brain* 97: 709–728.

Williams, G. C. (1966) *Adaptation and Natural Selection.* Princeton, NJ: Princeton University Press.

Williams, G. C. (1985) "A Defense of Reductionism in Evolutionary Biology." In R. Dawkins and M. Ridley (eds.), *Oxford Surveys of Evolutionary Biology.* New York: Oxford University Press, pp. 1–27.

Williams, G. C. (1992) *Natural Selection: Domains, Levels, and Challenges.* New York: Oxford University Press.

Wilson, C. J., and Groves, P. M. (1980) "Fine Structure and Synaptic Connections of the Common Spiney Neuron of the Rat Neostriatum: A Study Employing Intracellular Injection of Horseradish Peroxidase." *Journal of Comparative Neurology* 194: 599–615.

Wilson, C. J., Groves, P. M., Kitty, S. T., and Linder, J. C (1983) "Three-dimensional Structure of Dendritic Spines in the Rat Neostriatum." *Journal of Neuroscience* 3: 383–398.

Wimsatt, W. C. (1976) "Reductionism, Levels of Organization, and the Mind-Body Problem." In G. Globus, G. Maxwell, and I. Savodnik (eds.), *Consciousness and the Brain: A Scientific and Philosophical Inquiry.* New York: Plenum, pp. 205–267.

Wimsatt, W. C. (1984a) "Reductionist Research Strategies and Their Biases in the Units of Selection Controversy." In E. Sober (ed.), *Conceptual Issues and Their Biases in the Units of Selection Controversy.* Cambridge, MA: MIT Press, pp. 142–183.

Wimsatt, W. C. (1984b) "Reductive Explanation: A Functional Account." In E. Sober (ed.), *Conceptual Issues in Evolutionary Biology.* Cambridge, MA: MIT Press, pp. 477–508.

Wimsatt, W. C. (1993) "The Ontology of Complex Systems: Levels of Organization, Perspectives, and Causal Thickets." Unpublished ms.

Winfree, A. T., and Strogatz, S. H. (1983) "Singular Filaments Organize Chemical Waves in Three Dimensions." *Physica* 8D: 35.

Wood, C. C. (1975) "Auditory and Phonetic Levels of Processing in Speech Perception; Neurophysiological and Information-Processing Analyses." *Journal of Experimental Psychology: Human Perception and Performance* 104: 3–20.

Wood, R., Ebert, V., and Kinsbourne, M. (1982) "The Episodic-Semantic Memory Distinction in Memory and Amnesia: Clinical and Experimental Observations." In L. S. Cermak (ed.), *Human Memory and Amnesia.* Hillsdale, NJ: Erlbaum.

Woodger, J. H. (1952) *Biology and Language.* Cambridge: Cambridge University Press.

Wright, L. (1974) "Functions." *Philosophical Review* 82: 139–168.

Wundt, W. (1873) *Grundriss der Psychologie.* Leipzig: W. Englemann.

Yablo, S. (1992) "Mental Causation" *Philosophical Review* 101: 245–280.

Yakovlev, P. I., and Lecours, A. R. (1967) "The Myelogenetic Cycles of Regional Maturation of the Brain." In A. Minokowski (ed.), *Regional Development of the Brain in Early Life.* Philadelphia: Davis.

Yorke, J. A., and Li, T-Y. (1975) "Period Three Implies Chaos." *American Mathematical Monthly* 82: 985–992.

Zeki, S. M., and Shipp, S. (1988) "The Functional Logic of Cortical Connections." *Nature* 335: 311–317.

Zipser, D. (1991) "Recurrent Network Model of the Neural Mechanism of Short-Term Active Memory," *Neural Computation* 3: 178-192.

Zola-Morgan, S., and Squire, L. R. (1984) "Preserved Learning in Monkeys with Medial Temporal Lesions: Sparing of Motor and Cognitive Skills." *Journal of Neuroscience* 4: 1072–1085.

Zucker, K.J. (1982) *The Development of Search for Mother During Brief Separation.* Ph.D. Thesis. University of Toronto.

INDEX

A

AB error, 108, 112
abstraction, 21
action potential, 48, 81
addivity, 59
adults, 99, 106, 109–111, 114, 117–118, 120
aggregations, 37
agnosia, 112–114, 128–129
Alzheimer's disease, 144
amnesics, 111–114, 118, 123, 128, 134, 138, 171, 196n23
amygdala, 123–125
anatomy, 46
anomalous monism, 20
anthropology, 8, 61, 141
antirealism, 30
approximations, 65–66, 69
Aristotle, 44–45, 54
arousal, 7, 92–93
artifact: problem of, 25, 58
artificial intelligence, 6, 8
atomism, 38
attention, 7, 21, 107–108, 115, 132, 147, 175–180
Audi, R., 18–19, 185n35

B

Barrett, S., 153
basal ganglia, 7, 46, 56
Bechtel, W., 96
behavior, 21, 35, 118, 123, 125, 131, 144, 151, 193n16; connection to mind, 19; explanation of, 73; and frontal cortex, 38–39; and lesion studies, 121; motor, 7–8, 48, 56; and neuroscience, 143; and split brain patients, 189n22, 189n23; versus meaningful movements, 31

behaviorism, 14, 21, 72
beliefs, 13
bias, 59–60, 118, 188n3, 197–198n46
binding, 176, 178
biology, 6-7, 33, 57, 184n22, 189n14; and emotion, 93; evolutionary, 58, 73. *See also* natural selection
birth, 109–110, 126, 149
blindsight, 113–114, 128
Block, N., 75-76
Bogan, J., 186n43
brain, 1, 6-7, 17, 38, 53–54; causal closure, 74; causality 38; chick, 122; development of, 126–127; evoked response potentials, 149; Freud, 27; function of, 38; functionalism, 64; glia cells, 188n3; hemispheres, 40–41, 189n22–24; hierarchies in, 34, 36, 41, 60; levels of analysis, 9, 170–171; levels of organization, 19, 33–34; models of, 125; motor control, 7–8; multiple instantiation, 182–183n14, 183n18; networks in, 35; organization of, 7; place in cognitive science, 9; recordings of, 34–35, 154–165, 166–169; relation to mind, 15; split, 189n22, 189n23; theories of, 55. *See also* lesion patients, neurons
bridge principles, 87, 90–94, 106, 193n11
bridge science, 10, 143, 146, 150, 169–170, 173; and evoked response potentials, 143, 146
Burton, R., 109

C

Cajal, S., 34
Carey, S., 110
Cartwright, N., 191n17
CAT scans, 55
caudate nuclei, 46, 48

causal closure, 13, 14, 17, 31, 74, 184n24
causal etiology, 11, 14, 40, 55, 111, 125,
    135–136, 149
causation, 9, 17–19, 24, 111, 130, 185n35;
    and explanation, 18–19, 58, 190n36;
    generalizations of, 183n18; individual-
    ism and, 37; and laws, 20, 191n17;
    mechanisms of, 138; mental, 16, 19–
    20, 25, 27, 30, 31; models, 24; necessary
    and sufficient conditions, 39; neuro-
    scientific, 55; overdetermination of,
    184–185n33; patterns, 20; powers of,
    15, 17–18; probabilistic, 24; relations,
    3–5; role, 72; and symmetry, 26; tran-
    sitivity, 38, 57; types of, 54
cerebellum, 7
cerebral cortex, 46, 48
ceteris paribus clauses, 20, 22, 66
chaos, 17
chicks, 121–123, 130–131
Church, A., 65, 191n5
Church-Turing thesis, 64–65, 69, 191n14
Churchland, P. M., 30
Churchland, P. S., 30, 82, 94, 96
codependency, 4
coevolution of science, 96, 102, 106
cognition 1, 4–6, 63–64
cognitive dissonance, 182n7
cognitive interpretation, 92–95
cognitive science, 1–2, 5, 32–33, 60, 63,
    141; causal etiology, 136; computer
    metaphor, 79; disciplines in, 8, 10; and
    evoked response potentials, 172; expla-
    nations in, 61; functionalism, 72–74,
    85; hierarchies in, 34; and identity the-
    ories, 143; as an interdisciplinary sci-
    ence, 83, 126, 143–144; laws, 22; and
    memory research, 107; and neuro-
    science, 6; reduction, 106; and seman-
    tic view of theories, 175; textbooks, 6;
    theories in, 6, 11, 133, 135, 137–139
cognitivism, 14
complexity, 39
computability, 72
computational satisfaction, 69-71
computationalism, 4–6, 8–9, 63–64, 69-
    71, 73, 127, 134, 169; and cognitive

psychology, 79; counterfactuals, 66–
    67; and evoked response potentials,
    148; and explanation, 71, 83; and
    Freud, 185n37; and functionalism, 64,
    72; and glia cells, 188n3; irrelevant fac-
    tors, 68; levels of analysis, 84; and
    memory, 111; neuroscience and, 6,
    125; and a pragmatics of explanation,
    68–69; and relevant factors, 70; and
    teleology, 72-73; and Turing, 191n14
computations, 63–64, 94
computer metaphor, 79–80
computer science, 8, 72
computer simulation, 4–5, 6, 100–101,
    194–195n34
computers, 9, 72-73
conditioning, 99, 107–108, 112, 123–124,
    131, 144, 193n16, 196n26
connectionism. See distributed processing
consciousness, 40–41, 92–94, 107, 116,
    144–145, 151, 153, 165, 176, 189n22,
    189n23
consolidation, 132
content, 93–94
context: of cognizer, 36, 92; conditioning
    108, 111; of explanation, 88, 96; and
    explanatory extension, 103; and func-
    tion/structure distinction, 82–83; and
    memory, 116, 131–132; of science, 2,
    6–8, 10, 27–28, 67–68, 71, 95, 120, 143,
    173, 179–170, 187n65
contrast class, 10, 28, 68, 71, 88, 95–96,
    143, 171, 173, 178
corpus callosa, 189n22, 189n23
cost-benefit analysis, 186n55
counterfactuals, 66–68
covering laws, 55. See also D-N models
Crick, F., 178–179, 204n13
Culp, S., 194n20
culture, 6
Cummins, R., 63, 191n15

                    D

D-N model, 61, 141. See also covering laws
Dallas, M., 116, 197n36
Damasio, A., 113
data sets, 21, 24, 186n43

data: gathering, 10. *See also* matching to sample tasks, perceptual identification tasks, word completion tasks

Davidson, D., 20

deduction, 134

dendrites, 122

Dennett, D., 29–30, 80, 142, 144–147, 151, 165, 169, 172, 186n51

dependence, 16

Descartes, R., 54

development, 3, 6, 11, 111, 121, 126

Diamond, A., 110

disciplines, 10, 104, 129–131, 135, 138–139, 173, 175

distributed processing, 5, 35, 52–53, 48, 59–60, 100–101, 107, 122, 126, 176

Dretske, F., 31, 54

dualism: property, 16

dynamical systems, 45

dysmorphopsia, 113–114, 128

Dziurawiec, S., 110

E

EEG, 146, 148–149

Eldredge, H., 41

electric fish, 49–54, 59–60

electrical field theory, 147, 171

eliminative materialism, 16, 30–31, 37

Ellis, H., 110

emergentism, 37–38, 47, 189n30

emotion, 7, 90–92, 182n7, 193n16; experience of, 92–94; theories of, 93–95

engineering, 8

entorhinal cortex, 123–124

environment. *See* context

epiphenomenalism, 14, 18, 22–24, 74, 80

epistemology, 29, 31

equilibrium, 76-77

evidence, 10

evoked potential, 148–150

evoked response potentials, 150, 153, 165, 166, 170, 200n8, 201n20, 201n22, 201n23, 202n25, 203n26, 203n27; and bridge sciences, 170; differences waves, 151–152, 201n23, 202–203n26; and explanatory extension, 169; models, 171; N1, 202n26; N250, 153; N375,

201–202n23; N400, 151–153, 161, 171, 201n21, 202n24; and neuroscience, 147–150, 153; ;P2, 202n26; P3, 153–154, 161, 165, 171–172, 201n22, 202n24; priming, 151–164; and psychology, 146–147; research in, 171–172

expectation, 92

experiments, 5. *See also* matching to sample tasks, perceptual identification tasks, word completion tasks

explananda, 55–56, 61, 86, 133–135, 150

explanans, 55, 135, 180

explanation, 15–16, 20, 23, 29; and artifacts, 25, 58; and bias, 60; causal, 16, 54, 187n59, 190n36; computational, 71, 83, 125; and context, 88, 95; framework, 143; and functionalism, 63, 65, 72-74, 78, 83; and the function/structure distinction, 80; hierarchy, 129; irrelevant factors, 68; levels of, 31; levels of analysis, 106; levels of organization, 53–54; mechanism, 61; of memory 134; mental, 18; morphological, 78–80, 83, 103, 106; in neuroscience, 48, 53, 124–125; and patterns, 9, 53; physical system, 71; and properties, 25; in psychology, 30–31, 91, 180; reductive, 90; systemic, 78–80, 106, 120, 125. *See also* pragmatics of explanation, theories.

explanatory extension, 10, 83, 86, 91, 95–96, 100–102, 111, 143–144, 149, 178–179, 194n21; in cognitive science, 104; and evoked response potentials, 169

eye, 16–17

F

facial recognition, 109–110, 126, 130, 119–120

feature-integration hypothesis, 61, 68, 175–178, 204n9, 204n10. *See also* Treisman, A.

feed-forward pathways, 40

feedback, 40, 129

field. *See* discipline

flowchart, 72

Fodor, J., 19–20, 86, 89, 91, 104, 185n33

folk psychology, 20
forebrain, 7
formal systems, 2, 4–6
Forster, K., 61, 170
Freud, S., 3, 19, 22, 24, 26–27, 185n37
frontal cortex, 7, 38–39, 98–100, 124, 142, 153
function/structure distinction, 79–81, 83–84, 90, 106, 125, 169–171; and a pragmatics of explanation, 82; relative, 81–82
functional analysis, 85, 71, 75, 91, 134–135, 142–143, 150, 171; and explanation, 79; and ionic flow, 81; multilevel, 83
functionalism, 3–4, 9, 36, 63, 94, 120, 138, 149; and causal closure, 74; and cognitive psychology, 79; and computationalism 64; constraints on, 102–103; definition of, 71-72; and explanation, 75, 78, 83; and explanatory extension, 97; and frontal cortex, 99; higher levels, 86; and meaning analysis, 92, 94–95; and memory, 111; and Nernst equation, 77; and neuroscience, 125; and physical systems, 66–67; and reductionism, 88–90; and theories, 75
functions, 48, 61–64, 71; computable, 65

G

galvanic skin response, 113
gene, 17
general principles, 11, 130, 133, 135, 137–139, 142, 172–173
generalization, 22–26, 40–41, 91, 118, 183n18; and neuroscience, 57
glia cells, 188n3
globus palladus, 46–47
goals, 39
Gödel, K., 65
Godfrey-Smith, P., 59
Goldman-Rakic, P., 98–99, 107
Golgi, C., 34
Goodman, N., 23, 31
Grene, M., 42–45, 53, 58
gymnotid fish, 49–54, 59–60

H

H.M., 112, 128. See also amnesics
habituation, 108–109, 130
Harnad, S., 144–145
Haugeland, J., 78-79
Heilingenberg, W., 49, 53, 59
Heindel, W., 144
hemispherectomies, 40–41
hierarchies, 9, 16, 18, 41, 96, 189n30; aggregational, 42, 45, 189n30 ; in brain, 29, 46; and computationalism, 73; constitutive, 42, 45–47, 134, 189n30; control, 42, 44–46, 48–49, 53, 60, 120, 129; embedded, 42, 45, 134, 189n30; exclusive, 41–42, 45; and explanation, 129; inclusive, 42, 45; of models, 172; of neurons, 35–36
hippocampus, 7, 123–125, 128, 132–134, 142
holism, 36–37
homunculi, 73
Hubel, D., 39, 101
Hull, D., 60
Humphries, P., 183–184n19
Huntington's disease, 55–56, 144
Hutchins, E., 61
hypothesis, 4–5
hysteria, 33, 19, 24, 26–28, 185n37

I

identity theories, 72-73, 80, 143
IMHV, 121–122
implementation, 16
imprinting, 121–122, 124, 189n30
individual differences, 40–41, 155, 70
individualism, 36–38
infant, 106–109, 114, 118, 121, 126–127, 130, 138, 182n7, 196n23; evoked potentials, 149; facial recognition, 110, 119–120; memory, 111–112; recall, 97–100
information processing, 1–2, 8–9, 80, 149; infant, 109–111; and levels of analysis, 84
information, 44–45, 142, 149, 153, 165
innate, 109–110, 118, 120, 121, 198n52

input, 3–5

instantiation, 4–5, 13–14, 24, 81–82, 89, 102, 182–183n14, 183n18, 186n48, 187n59; multiple, 2, 4–5, 13–14, 32, 121

intentionality, 73

interdisciplinary, 10–11, 28, 31, 75, 103, 106, 132–133, 173, 195n4; cognitive science, 85, 126, 138, 143–144, 170; evidence, 106; evoked response potentials, 146–147; functionalism, 84; general principles, 119; hierarchy, 129; level of analysis, 83; memory research, 196n17; models, 131; semantic view of theories, 175, 180; theories, 2, 8–9, 114, 118, 120; two part theories, 133–136, 142, 172–173; versus multidisciplinary, 103

interpretation, 69, 103, 117–118

intralaminer nucleus, 46, 47

ionic flow, 75-76, 78-79, 81, 133, 184n22

J

Jackson, F., 187n58, 187n59

Jacoby, L., 116, 197n36

jamming avoidance response, 49–54, 59–60

Johnson, M., 110, 198n53

K

Kant, I., 54

Kim, J., 16, 23, 183n18

Kinsbourne, M., 142, 144–147, 151, 165, 169, 172

Kitcher, P. S., 86, 96–97, 143, 194n20

Kitcher, P. W., 181n14

Klagge, J., 187n66

L

language, 6, 40–41, 152–153, 182n7, 189n23, 201n21, 202n24

lateral geniculate nucleus, 126–128, 148

Latour, B., 61

law and semantic 136

laws, 14–16, 19–20, 184n32, 191n17; basic, 21, 23; in biology, 33; causal, 24; and data, 23; natural, 70; physical, 66–67; and physical systems, 22; psychological, 20, 23, 102; scope of, 22

learning, 109–110, 121–124, 131, 198n52

Lehky, S., 101–101, 195n34

LePore, E., 15, 20, 186n48, 187n58

lesion patients, 38–39, 114, 118, 121, 123, 128, 130, 138, 170, 200n6. *See also* agnosia, amnesics, blindsight, dysmorphopsia, prosopagnosia

levels of aggregation, 133–134, 150

levels of analysis, 5, 8–10, 17, 31, 33–34, 38, 58, 111, 90, 133, 141–142, 184n22; and brain, 170–171; and cognitive science, 138; in disciplines, 129; and evoked response potentials, 149; and explanation, 106; in frontal cortex, 39; and function/structure distinction, 82; interdisciplinary, 120–121; multilevel, 83, 185; parallels among, 85–87

levels of organization, 5, 8–10, 15–19, 25–26, 29, 31, 33–34, 60, 115, 146; in brain, 38, 39, 75; and causal etiology, 40, 57; and explanation, 53–54, 59; and functionalism, 61; hierarchy, 48; higher, 102–104, 129; and information, 59; interdisciplinary, 120–121; lower, 102–104; and mechanism, 55; middle, 35; and the pragmatics of explanation, 186–187n55; and reduction, 58–59, 96; relations among, 45; relevant, 35, 41; and Wimsatt, W., 96

limbic system, 7, 142, 193n16

linguistics, 8, 21, 141

Loewer, B., 14, 20, 186n48, 187n58

long-term potentiation, 123–124, 133

long-term store, 107

Lycan, W., 82

M

magnocellular pathway, 128

Mandler, G., 90–95

Mandler, J., 98

Marcel, A., 117, 145, 197n43

Markov, A., 191n5

matching to sample tasks, 39, 99, 123, 129–130

materialism, 8, 14–16, 23, 73, 183n14, 183n18, 185n35

Mayr, E., 42, 45, 54, 96

McCarthy, R., 114, 127–128

meaning analysis, 92, 94–95

mechanism, 16, 20, 102, 142–143; causal 61, 130, 134, 138, 171; and evoked response potentials, 171; and mental states, 73-74; and reductionism, 87; visual processing, 40

Meltzoff, A., 109

memory, 6, 11, 39, 97–98, 106–107, 114–115, 119–120, 126, 130, 142, 145–146, 151, 182n7; definitions, 129; declarative, 98, 142; and delayed response tasks, 39; disorders, 112–114, 128; episodic, 7, 115, 118, 123, 131–132; explanation of, 134–135; explicit, 61, 113–114, 116–119, 132, 144–145, 149; and habituation, 108; implicit, 61, 116, 119–120, 138, 153; imprinting, 121–122; and interdisciplinary studies, 129; priming, 203n28; procedural, 98, 131; repression, 19, 22, 24–25 ; "SEE," 114, 118, 122–125, 127–129, 132–133, 138, 142, 144–145, 153–154, 149, 165, 169, 171; "STE," 118, 131–132, 138, 142, 145, 149, 153–154, 165, 169, 171; subliminal, 145; theories of, 61; visual, 132. See also amnesics, infants, monkeys, rats

mental: and behaviorism, 72; causation, 29–31; as distinct from physical, 32; functionalism, 72, 86, 88–89; and holism, 37; levels of analysis, 31; and philosophy of mind, 73; and physical interaction, 13; properties, 16, 19; representation, 72; states, 4–5, 9, 13–15, 24, 118; theories of, 22. See also epiphenomenalism, mind

metaphysics, 29, 31

methodological solipsism. See individualism

methodology, 38

middle level of description, 91, 103–104, 130–131, 138

mimicry, 109

mind, 3–4, 6-7, 9, 17; categories of, 6; and Freud, 27; and functionalism 64, 73, 80; and the function/structure distinction, 79–80; and information processing, 1; and level of organization, 33; multiple instantiation, 182–183n14, 183n18; physical, 18; relation to brain, 15. See also instantiation, mental

modality; 109, 111 113, 118, 142; and priming, 115–116

model-theoretic account of theories. See semantic view

models, 11, 22–24, 125, 130–131, 136, 169, 187n55, 187n68, 199n75, 204n4; animal, 114, 133, 142; in cognitive science, 129; computational, 74; of data, 197–198n46; and evoked response potentials, 171; and data, 172–173; and general principles, 135, 137–139; fit among, 28; incompatible, 30; and mental causation, 30; of neuroscience, 180; and semantic view, 136–137; and theories, 134, 136

monkey, 123, 125, 128, 130–131; and facial recognition, 126–127; and frontal cortex, 99

Morton, J., 110, 198n52

Moscovitch, M., 112, 138

motor cortex, 7–8, 48

MRI, 55, 148

multi-disciplinary approaches, 10, 103, 106, 119. See also interdisciplinary

multiple instantiation. See instantiation

Musen, G., 154

mylination, 126

N

Nadel, L., 132

Nagel, E., 86, 193n6, 193n11

natural kind, 11, 18, 87, 89, 136, 183n18, 184n32

natural selection, 21, 73. See also biology, evolutionary

Necker cubes, 117

Neisser, U., 2

neocortex, 47–48, 132, 142

neostriatum, 46–48

Nernst equation, 76-78
network. *See* distributed processing
neurons, 26, 34–35, 47, 53–54, 121; and attention, 178–180, 204n13; complex, 39, 100–101; connections among, 38; and delayed response tasks, 39, 99; development, 105, 107, 126–127; and evoked response potentials, 147–150, 171; functional analysis of, 85; and information, 94; ionic flow, 75-77; levels of organization, 57–58; long term potentiation, 124; and patterns of behavior, 40; and priming, 165; and reductionism 59; simple, 39, 100–101; spiney, 47–48; synapses, 179; and vision, 195n34. *See also* brain
neuroscience, 1, 5–6, 10, 21, 26, 47–48, 55, 138, 141; and arousal, 93; and attention, 178–180; and behavior, 143; and bridge sciences, 170; cause, 55, 190n36; and computationalism, 195n34; and content, 94; development, 126; and emotion, 93–95; explanations, 53, 55–56, 61, 124–125; and explanatory extension, 96–97, 102; and functionalism, 93; hierarchies, 34; interdisciplinary, 75, 129; and individualism, 38; levels of analysis, 82; and memory, 121, 129, 131, 135, 146; models in, 129; relation to psychology, 28–29, 83, 85–86, 97, 101–104, 106, 146–147, 149–150, 169, 170, 172; and split brain patients, 189n22, 189n23; and vision, 39–40
Neville, H., 153, 170, 202n24
Newell, A., 2
Newton, I., 54
NMDA receptors, 124, 133

O

observations, 22
occipital lobes, 128
operational definitions, 119, 149, 171
output, 3–4

P

pain, 26

parallel processing. *See* distributed processing.
parallelism, 96, 103
paraphippocampal cortex, 123–124
parietal lobe, 124, 142, 153
Pattee, H., 44
pattern matching, 94, 132, 147
patterns, 17–18, 20, 23, 26, 29, 31, 154–155; and explanation, 53; and information, 58; higher level, 40, 45; of neurons, 53, 57, 59–60
Patterson, C., 42–44
perception, 95, 100, 102, 117. *See also* vision
percepts, 40
perceptual identification task, 114–115, 138, 171, 197n36
perirhinal cortex, 123–124
PET scans, 55, 148
Pettit, P., 187n58, 187n59
philosophy of mind, 1, 6, 8, 36, 73, 97, 102; and functionalism, 74, 83; and reductionism 86–87, 106
physical system, 9–10, 21–24, 26, 125, 136, 138, 172, 191n7, 171n14; approximations, 69; and computationalism 64–66; and explanation, 71; and functionalism, 73; internal processing, 70; and interpretation 66–67, 69; and models, 133
physical: distinct from mental, 32
Piaget, J., 97–98, 108
plasticity, 40–41
Post, E., 191n5
pragmatics of explanation, 9–10, 27–31, 64, 67, 96, 169–170, 173, 186–187n55; and explanatory extension, 103; and functionalism, 74; and function/structure distinction, 82; and irrelevant factors, 68; and Nernst equation, 77-78; and physical systems, 70-71
preferences, 108
prefrontal cortex. *See* frontal cortex
primates. *See* monkeys
priming, 116, 151, 197n36, 200n6, 201n20, 201n22, 201n23, 202n25, 203n26, 203n27; implicit, 112, 114–115, 128, 144, 150, 154–169; explicit,

priming *(continued)*
114–115, 128; masked, 116, 154–155, 162–170; semantic, 151–165; subliminal, 116, 144, 150; using novel visual stimuli, 154–165, 203n28
principal sulcus, 99
program, 3
properties, 15–16, 18; abstraction, 21; causally relevant, 16
prosopagnosia, 113
psychiatry, 8
psychology, 1–2, 8, 10, 14, 26, 120, 141, 184n22; and arousal, 93; cognitive, 97–98, 118; computer simulation, 101; context, 178; developmental, 118; and emotion, 95; and evoked response potentials, 149–150, 153, 200n8; experiments, 129, 144; explanation, 180; and explanatory extension, 96–97, 102; and functionalism, 83; and function/structure distinction, 79–80; and individualism, 38; interdisciplinary, 75; laws, 22–23; levels of analysis, 81; and memory research, 111, 131, 135; methodology, 91; operational definitions in, 171; and priming, 115; problems with 145–146, 165; and semantic view of theories, 175; relation to neuroscience, 28–29, 85–97, 101–104, 106, 142–143, 146–147, 149–150, 169, 170, 172; theories, 61, 138. *See also* matching to sample tasks, perceptual identification tasks, word completion tasks
putamen, 46, 48
Putnam, H., 2–3, 73-74, 80, 86, 95–96, 189n30
Pylyshyn, Z., 80

R

Ramachandran, V., 100, 102, 195n34
Ramsey definition, 76
rats, 124–125, 134
realism, 30
reasoning, 6
recall, 2, 97–98, 106–107, 114–115, 123, 132, 138
receptive field, 100–101, 148

recognition, 97, 106–107, 112, 114–116, 121, 147, 153, 169, 197n36
recursion, 65, 191n5
reduction, 10, 14, 17, 27, 37, 39, 44–45, 58, 61, 73, 79, 85–86, 91, 95–96, 102, 139, 143, 150, 169, 172, 183n18, 189n20, 193n6; in cognitive science, 86, 104; domain specific, 90; examples of, 87–90; and explanation, 95; failure of, 96; and functionalism, 88–90; and function/structure distinction, 104; of theories, 87–88; and theory of emotions, 92–95
regularity. *See* patterns
representation, 37, 98, 101, 109, 115–116, 131, 144, 177; and priming, 115–116
research paradigm, 8–9
resting potentials, 75-78, 81
reticular activating system, 7, 178–179
retina, 100, 125–127, 176
retinal ganglion, 100, 128
retrieval, 97–99, 107, 118
Richardson, R., 193n6, 193n11
Rosenberg, J., 194n19
Rugg, M., 153
Rybak, I., 170

S

Schacter, D., 112, 114, 138, 144, 154–155
Schacter, S., 193–194n17
Schaffner, K., 87, 106, 133–137, 199n75, 199n76
schemas, 92–93, 109, 117, 132, 177
Schneider, W., 61, 107, 177–178
Schwarz, G., 63
science, 9–10, 87
screening-off relation, 25–26, 58, 186n54, 186n55
Sejnowski, T., 101–101, 195n34
semantic view of theories, 21–22, 24, 96, 135–136, 175, 197–198n46, 199n76
semantics, 6
serial processing, 107
Shagrir, O., 190n3
shape-from-shading, 100–101
Shiffrin, R., 61, 107, 177–178
short term store, 3

Simon, H., 2
Singer, J., 193–194n17
skepticism, 30
skills, 112, 123, 131, 144
smell, 124
Sober, E., 19, 37, 184n26, 188n9
society, 105
sociology, 8, 61, 141, 198n52
species, 17
spreading activation, 115
Squire, L., 123, 125, 128
Stabler, E., 66–68
Stark, H., 114
state space, 10, 70, 90–91, 169, 171
Stich, S., 30
Stillings, N., 8
stimulus-response circuit, 107–108, 112, 116, 118, 121–122, 126–128. *See also* habituation, visuo-motor pathway
subcortical pathways, 126–129, 142, 149, 189n24
substantia nigra, 46–47
subthalamic nuclei, 46–47
superior colliculus, 126–127
supervenience, 13, 15, 18–19, 23, 32, 194n19
Suppe, F., 21–22, 136–137, 185n451
Suppes, P., 172
symbol manipulation, 2, 8
symbols, 6
synchronization, 48
syntax, 6

T

technology, 172–173
teleology, 72-73
temporal lobe, 123–124, 128, 132–133
thalamus, 7, 47, 55–56, 178–179, 204n13
theories, 10, 11, 15, 20, 22, 55, 67, 105, 144, 184n32, 196n23; biological, 33, 134; building, 9, 11, 60, 169; constraints on, 68; false, 30; functional, 125; and models, 136; neuroscience,

60; overlapping interlevel, 133–137, 199n75; relevant factors, 68; and semantic view, 136; and state space, 70; underdetermination of, 90, 103, 145
Thompson, K., 44
Treisman, A., 21, 68, 154, 175–176, 178–180, 186n42, 204n10
truth, 30, 187n67, 187n68
Tulving, E,. 114
Turing machine, 2, 65, 69, 72
Turing, A., 65
type/token distinction, 3–4, 24, 40, 60

V

van Gulick, R., 14, 185n39
vision, 6, 39–40, 100–101, 103, 126–129, 132, 175–178, 180, 194n33, 195n34, 198n61; infant, 109, 149
visual cortex, 39, 128, 170
visuo-motor pathways, 107–108, 114, 118, 121–122, 124, 126–129, 138, 144. *See also* habituation, stimulus-response circuits
vocabulary, 118, 130, 135, 137, 172–173
von Eckhart, B., 181n14
von Neumann, R., 6

W

Weisel, T., 39, 101
"what" pathway, 127, 170
"where" pathway, 127, 170
Williams, G., 58
Wimsatt, W., 96, 186n55, 188n15
Woodward, R., 186n43
word completion tasks, 114, 112
Wundt, W., 91

Y

Yablo, S., 31, 187n58, 187n59

Z

Zipser, D., 170
Zola-Morgan, S., 123, 125, 128